THE HUMAN SIDE OF INNOVATION

THE HUMAN SIDE OF INNOVATION

THE POWER OF PEOPLE IN LOVE WITH PEOPLE

MAURO PORCINI

Chief Design Officer of PepsiCo

FOREWORDS BY RAMON LAGUARTA AND INDRA NOOYI

BK®

Berrett–Koehler Publishers, Inc.

Berrett-Koehler Publishers, Inc.
1333 Broadway, Suite 1000
Oakland, CA 94612-1921
Tel: (510) 817-2277
Fax: (510) 817-2278
www.bkconnection.com

ORDERING INFORMATION

Quantity sales. Special discounts are available on quantity purchases by corporations, associations, and others. For details, contact the "Special Sales Department" at the Berrett-Koehler address above.

Individual sales. Berrett-Koehler publications are available through most bookstores. They can also be ordered directly from Berrett-Koehler: Tel: (800) 929-2929; Fax: (802) 864-7626; www.bkconnection.com.

Orders for college textbook / course adoption use. Please contact Berrett-Koehler: Tel: (800) 929-2929; Fax: (802) 864-7626.

Distributed to the U.S. trade and internationally by Penguin Random House Publisher Services.

Berrett-Koehler and the BK logo are registered trademarks of Berrett-Koehler Publishers, Inc.

Printed in Canada

Berrett-Koehler books are printed on long-lasting acid-free paper. When it is available, we choose paper that has been manufactured by environmentally responsible processes. These may include using trees grown in sustainable forests, incorporating recycled paper, minimizing chlorine in bleaching, or recycling the energy produced at the paper mill.

Library of Congress Cataloging-in-Publication Data
Names: Porcini, Mauro, author.
Title: The human side of innovation: the power of people in love with people / Mauro Porcini.
Description: First edition. | Oakland, CA: Berrett-Koehler Publishers, [2023] | Includes bibliographical references and index.
Identifiers: LCCN 2022014860 (print) | LCCN 2022014861 (ebook) | ISBN 9781523002887 (hardcover) | ISBN 9781523002894 (pdf) | ISBN 9781523002900 (epub) | ISBN 9781523002917
Subjects: LCSH: New products. | Design, Industrial. | Design—Human factors. | Human engineering.
Classification: LCC HF5415.153 .P67 2022 (print) | LCC HF5415.153 (ebook) | DDC 658.5/752—dc23/eng/20220608
LC record available at https://lccn.loc.gov/2022014860
LC ebook record available at https://lccn.loc.gov/2022014861

First Edition
28 27 26 25 24 23 22   10 9 8 7 6 5 4 3 2 1

Book production, text, and cover design: Debbie Berne
Author photo by Dave Puente

To Beatrice,
to Carlotta,
to Stefano,
to Mom and Dad,
and to those still to come . . .

Contents

Foreword *by Ramon Laguarta*

When I became CEO of PepsiCo in 2018, one of my first initiatives was to organize a two-day meeting every month for our top executives to co-create with me the vision and mission of the company. On the first day of our first meeting, during one of the breaks, I approached our chief design officer, Mauro Porcini. I told him that I had a special assignment for him. I needed him to be one of those individuals on the leadership team who think differently. I asked him to bring design thinking into the mix—to question our assumptions. I asked him and his teams around the world to bring a disruptor's mindset to a company that wanted to shake things up.

By that time, Mauro had been leading our design function since its formation in 2012. For the first six years of its existence, the design function had been operating with a start-up mindset, as a creative group of pioneers churning out high-quality work. Now, I wanted PepsiCo to take things to the next level and become a fully design-driven company, a company aiming to be the most human-centered and innovative organization in the world. That meant design needed to graduate to a scale-up mindset. And it meant Mauro and his team needed a seat at every table, and they needed to be among the loudest voices at those tables.

This elevation of a human-centered approach to innovation was directly tied to the changes we were seeing in society—changes that have only accelerated over the past few years. People are demanding what they want, when they want it, at a price they can afford. They want products that are better for themselves and the planet. And they want to feel a personal connection to their favorite brands. In other words, the future of brand building and product innovation, along with the future of organizational culture, is *human*.

In this book, Mauro explains the steps that any company should take to apply this approach at scale. Let me give you two examples mentioned in these pages that come from our PepsiCo world.

The first is a product innovation example: SodaStream Professional. This is our custom beverage fountain that lets people customize their own water experience—from flavors and functional ingredients to temperature, carbonation, and more—adopting reusable bottles and a QR code to limit single-use plastic and save the individual's personal preferences. SodaStream Professional is a critical tool for building out our ecosystem of customized beverage options, while also helping to meet the needs of people who are looking to lead healthier, more sustainable lives. This is what human-centricity is all about: an approach to innovation that creates value for individuals and for society.

The second example is related to culture. When I approached Mauro on the first day of our monthly meeting, I wasn't asking him to design a specific product or experience. I was asking him to help transform our culture by voicing his opinions fearlessly, acting as an owner, and focusing and getting work done fast. And that's exactly what he has done—and what he talks about in this book. This approach was part of his instinct and his way of thinking and acting. I gave him an opportunity and a platform to unlock his potential. Today, we are a company infused with design-led thinking across our entire portfolio of products. Through this culture, we create new reservoirs of value for the end users—the human beings—who engage with our company.

These two examples only scratch the surface of Mauro's insights, gained over two decades of working in corporations and agencies. In this book, he goes into depth about the mindset and strategies he has used to champion a more people-focused approach to innovation. It is a fascinating study of what it takes to drive change at the team and organizational levels. And it offers a blueprint for anyone who aspires to build companies and brands while growing as a leader—and as a human being.

Ramon Laguarta, Chairman and CEO of PepsiCo

Foreword *by Indra Nooyi*

I have always loved the language of design—the artistry, the creativity, the ingenuity, the attention to detail. Design is one of the few universal languages capable of evoking a whole range of feelings without a single word. Good design is also good business. Design can help us find new, more powerful ways of making enterprises more dynamic, of engaging people and partners and firing their imaginations. A design-driven company is, by definition, human-centered and innovative.

When I was CEO of PepsiCo, I was determined to make design an integral part of our company's future. That's why, in 2012, we created our first ever corporate design team. We knew that to be successful, design needed to be central to how we ran our business. It needed a voice in the decision-making process. And it needed a leader who could command respect in every space he entered, from boardroom to fashion house. In other words, it needed Mauro Porcini.

The first time I met Mauro, I knew he was a complete original—one of one. And his influence on PepsiCo has been singular. I like to think of PepsiCo's history as unfolding in two stages: Before Mauro and After Mauro. Before Mauro, we didn't understand why great design mattered, much less how to integrate it into what we do. Now, people across the company are lining up to talk to Mauro and his team about designing everything, from concept to execution: from unique Pepsi limited-edition collections, celebrating different world cultures; to more sustainable beverage dispensers, avoiding single-use plastic; to innovative food solutions, redefining the way people snack.

In this book, Mauro uses the language of design to help his readers understand the human side of innovation. Page by page, he peels back the layers of interpersonal connection and excavates the substance of what moves us, what excites us, what inspires us—when it comes to both brands and the people who build them.

For Mauro, leadership is the secret sauce that transforms design from a concept to a creation. Those who have it all—who combine vision and execution, innovation and productivity, kindness, respect, and optimism—are deemed "unicorns." While some might argue that unicorns are born, not made, Mauro takes a different approach. He believes there is a unicorn in all of us if we nurture three key talents.

The first is embracing your entrepreneurial spirit. In many ways, this is about cultivating a mindset that is "both/and" rather than "either/or." It means honing your analytical abilities while also sharpening your intuition; taking big risks, while also being appropriately cautious. Entrepreneurial spirit combines the savvy of an MBA holder with the skills of a chief technical officer and the creativity of an artist.

The second is leading with empathy. To drive human-centric innovation, you have to be what Mauro calls a "person in love with people." Take the time to get to know your colleagues. Treat them with kindness, sincerity, and respect. Earn a reputation as trustworthy. And don't take yourself too seriously. Knowing when to have fun, occasionally at your own expense, can be the difference between a team that is on edge and a team that is on track.

The third is enabling others to succeed. There is no higher compliment than "This person makes everyone around them better." And when it comes to human-centric innovation, everyone needs to be at their best. As a leader, it's your job to lift others up by being curious, confident, and decisive and to create space for your colleagues to push boundaries, even if it makes you uncomfortable.

Ultimately, what Mauro is saying is that you don't have to be a CEO or a chief design officer to make these talents a part of your life, to adopt a human-centered approach to innovation and leadership. Anyone can do this. And this book can be your guide. I hope you'll get started today.

Indra Nooyi, former Chairman and CEO of PepsiCo (2006–2018)

There simply is no innovation without risk.

INNOVATION IS AN ACT OF LOVE

Innovation is an act of love—or at least it should be. Always. It is a gesture of empathy, respect, generosity, of one human being's devotion to another. This is the innovation that I hope for. This is the innovation that I want for my children and their children, for the society of today and of tomorrow. This is the very best innovation: meaningful, useful, beautiful, and sustainable innovation, the kind that continues to improve the status quo, now and for always. This is the innovation that the new world we are living in requires. Not only because it is the right thing to do, ethically speaking—this should be the first and final word in the matter, though it often isn't. But also because, at last, in our global, technological, and digital society, ethical goals are increasingly aligning with business goals for both enterprises and individuals. Innovation as an act of love is today (also) becoming good business!

It has not always been this way, of course. We are surrounded by thousands of products, brands, and services that represent the outcomes of a very different kind of logic. Yet today, matters are changing. There is no alternative. This is a real historical turning point, one that needs to be understood, celebrated, and accelerated. Mediocre, poorly thought-out innovation, without any humanity—selfish innovation dictated only by the economic interests of the individual enterprise, at the expense of users and the society the enterprise serves—is beginning to struggle to keep up, and there is no turning back. The old world's traditional barriers to entry are gradually crumbling away in the face of a global, hyperconnected, accelerated universe. The kind of innovation that wins out today is genuine and authentic, and it aims to create personal and social value first and financial and economic value afterward, as a consequence.

But this kind of true, deep, long-lasting innovation is not easy to do. It does not just arise from processes, data, and tools; it doesn't pop up spontaneously from artificial intelligence, financial analyses, and economic plans. This kind of innovation flourishes naturally in the mind of a certain breed of human beings: the visionaries, the dreamers—real visionaries and dreamers who sincerely believe in their visions and dreams. This kind of innovation burns like an unstoppable flame ignited in their hearts; it breathes through their skin and explodes in their actions. This kind of innovation comes from the guts and brains of individuals who are able to understand other people's needs and dreams, all while looking at matters with a different and unique perspective, finding solutions that no one has ever thought of or acted on before. This kind of innovation is generated, essentially, by people who are inspired by a deep love for humanity and a constant desire to generate real value for those around them and for society as a whole. They are *people in love with people*: that's what I like to call them.

These people in love are the ideal *innovators*—whatever other title they might have. In the business world they can be CEOs or scientists, designers or marketers, lawyers or singers, caregivers or sales reps, governors or writers—and they may play many other roles as well. The people that these innovators love are similarly categorized in a vast range of ways, according to any given cultural context: sometimes they are end users, at other times they are consumers; sometimes they are clients, at other times they are the target audience. I like to call them what they truly are, each and every time: *human beings*.

Innovation Should Start from Our Personal Lives

Then there is all the innovation that does not occur within a professional scenario. Over the course of our lives, each of us, in one way or another, is constantly called upon to innovate. Some of us decide to accept the invitation; others don't. For some people, there is no choice: innovation becomes an obligation, imposed upon them by circumstance. Some do it often; others very rarely. We innovate for ourselves when we decide to take on a new job, to throw ourselves into an unexpected project, to move to a new city, to become part of a different community, to learn to play an instrument, or to get out of a difficult relationship. In all of these cases—and in an infinity of other situations—we take on a double role: we become both innovator and target audience, both the lover and the loved. We innovate within our private lives as an act of love toward ourselves, willingly or otherwise. People who don't know how to love themselves, who aren't able to innovate for themselves, are rarely able to love others—and it follows that they are rarely able to innovate for someone else. Private and professional lives, when it comes to the innovation mindset, are intimately connected.

This is the story I want to tell you in this book—the story of a world that is radically changing and is forcing us to innovate as never before, both in our personal and professional lives, with a new, humanistic focus on people. I want to tell you the story of these people, of the ones who innovate and the ones we innovate for. I want to take your hand and have you walk alongside me on a very personal journey through the human side of innovation. It won't be a story about processes and tools. And it won't even be a story made up of case studies and projects. It will be a personal story instead, told by a human being with a warm, beating heart. The story of a kind of innovation entirely focused on people and experienced, imagined, and sweated away at by people. I will, of course, mention processes and tools, and I will cite some case studies and projects, but I will do so only to provide some chromatic accents, some tones and details, to make the story more three-dimensional. I will begin with the description of a society that is changing, and I will then dive into the sea of some of the many projects I have dealt with in my professional life. I will share these stories in a way that is entirely personal, intertwined with intimate and private experiences, weaving between logic and emotion.

You Can Do It, Too!

But this first section of the journey is only a preparatory stage, getting us ready with the facts for the story that I really want to tell you—the story that I love the most. This is the story of the *innovators*, those human beings on the constant hunt for new ideas, for the most meaningful, valuable, and relevant ideas. They seek to improve the condition of other people, society, and the planet—and ideally, in the process, to improve their own lives, too. This is a story about all those people on the hunt for the best version of themselves, for their own happiness and the happiness of everyone around them. It is a story about those human beings who see their lives as a journey in which there is space for growth and improvement for everyone: for each one of us and each one of you, whatever your own natural talent and background might be. This journey involves a kind of growth nurtured by education, awareness, sacrifice, and passion, in which a collective effort to achieve personal excellence creates excellence for the whole community: a democratic excellence, spreading on a mass level, from which everyone benefits, both the rich and the poor, the strong and the meek; an idea of excellence that is both human and humanist.

As such, this cannot be anything other than a story told through the eyes, heart, brain, and gut of a particular human being: Mauro the designer, the romantic, and the poet; Mauro the pragmatic executive of a multinational corporation; Mauro the dreaming teenager and the wise man. Each one of these characters weaves a tale that is at once very personal and also, in some way, absolutely universal. Biography encounters practice and brings theory together, painting a picture that is anchored in daily activity but reaches outward into those principles that have the ambition and the desire to be universal, general, and shared by all. I try to take a curious glance at all the different Mauros who appear between the lines of this book. I harness them into the logic of the story I want to share with you, but I also leave them free to express themselves in their own way within this container, with all of their passion, their differences, their poetry: a poetry that keeps me warm and that warms me up.

Innovation in the Blood

I was born in the 1970s in Gallarate, a small town in the north of Italy, nestled between the Alps and Milan, suspended between the spellbinding lakes and mountains of Lombardy on one side and the frantic, intense life of Italy's economic capital on the other.

When I was growing up, I had no idea what innovation was. I didn't even know that it had anything to do with any single form of work. When I was young, I just wanted to be an artist—or maybe a writer. I loved writing. I loved drawing. Both came to me quite easily. I ended up, however, becoming a designer, pretty much by accident.

I came from a middle-class Italian family, one of those many families that make countless sacrifices to send their children to university—a public university, to be clear, not a private one. Mine was one of those families that didn't have a way of supporting their children after university either, when they would need to look for their own path and follow their own dreams. In other words, when I finished studying, I had to go out into the world and get a job—right away. And in Italy, getting a job was far from taken for granted, whatever grades you had or school you went to. The job market was extremely difficult to break into. This is why, ever since I was young, my dreams were always injected with a healthy pragmatism. The uncertainty of my own path ahead was limited by the certain variable that once I left the university, I needed to find a fixed salary.

My parents were convinced that the chances of finding a steady job as an artist or a writer were not particularly good in our country back then. And the idea that I could go and search for my fortune abroad was out of the question for a family that had never left Italy, except perhaps to hop across the border into nearby Switzerland for a Sunday walk.

In the end I decided to listen to my parents' advice, trusting their wisdom, and so I opted to study architecture at the university Politecnico of Milan. It was a discipline that could give me some real job opportunities, while also being the area of study that was the closest to the world of art that I loved. It was also the discipline that my dad had studied, and my dad was a constant source of inspiration for me—a man who was an architect by profession but an artist in his heart and daily life.

A few weeks before the entrance exam, however, something happened that transformed all of my plans—one of those "sliding door" moments in life. It was a hot afternoon in the summer of 1994, a day I remember as though it were yesterday, when I got a call on the cordless Panasonic phone at home. It was Giovanni Martinengo, a friend from high school, who was calling me about a new degree course, the first of its kind in Italy. Called *industrial design*, it had been launched at Politecnico university the previous year. Giovanni was considering taking the entrance exam. I had never heard of this discipline until that moment—a new and interesting path defined by two words that back then sounded magical to my ears. The term "design" spoke to my dreams and my obsession with art and creativity. The word "industrial" resonated with pragmatism and business.

It wasn't entirely clear to me what kind of job the course would prepare me for: the world of design was completely new to me. But those two simple words—"industrial" and "design"—seemed to be the perfect bridge between my need to dream and my need to get real, between art and commerce, between passion and labor. And so I decided to throw my lot in with this course of study. Martinengo never took the exam, and he actually became an engineer. I took the exam, with results placing me first among thousands of candidates. Thus it was that I began along the road that would soon take me into the most beautiful profession in the world: a profession called *design*.

The Attraction of the Unknown and the Different

This choice, this leap into the void, crystallizes a lot of what has characterized my own professional and personal path over the past forty years. If I hadn't had the courage to dive into a discipline that was, essentially, entirely unknown to me, I would never have discovered this new world, made of creativity that has an impact on all of society, a world that I have fallen completely in love with.

This has been one of the main and recurring themes of my life: I have always been fascinated by the unknown. I have sought new worlds with the utmost curiosity, and somehow I have had the courage to dive in. I found my comfort zone within this feeling of discomfort. And this holds true not only for my professional path: the exploration of new situations and different cultures has always drawn me in—whether through physical voyages, enabled by airplanes and hotels, or virtual ones, enabled by the internet and fantasies; whether through intimate journeys, composed of precious conversations with friends and strangers, or public ones, based on the curious and intrigued observation of those who surround me.

I have always felt this tension within myself. I grew up in an Italian suburb, in the midst of an extraordinary, triumphant natural environment. Since my early years, I was surrounded by nature, I immersed myself in it, and it made a deep impression on me—and it has never left me. But the city lights always attracted me nevertheless. I lived all my life suspended between the two worlds, surrounded by jungles of trees and flowers on one side and mesmerized by very different jungles of asphalt and buildings on the other. Milan and Rome were the first metropolises that I learned to call my own. They are mere villages, perhaps, on an international scale, but mysterious, boundless cities measured by my standards as a young man from the outskirts of town. I loved the design of these cities' urban fabrics, their unresolved mixtures of ancient and modern, their tensions between sacred and profane, constant conversations between earth and sky. Art and architecture already meant for me the tangible sign of the human capacity to dream, to imagine, to plan, and to do.

But the deepest nature of my curiosity for the stimulating city transcended a mere exploration of somewhere that was simply "different." What fascinated me the most about the metropolitan forest of a city such as Rome or Milan was not so much what I saw and encountered, but rather the *potential* of what I might see and encounter. I was attracted by the possible, the diverse—by everything I didn't know, everything that might happen there. The big city meant the reification of something that I could discover, something that I couldn't devour in a single moment or ever fully understand: a mystery to be apprehended little by little, in a journey that would resonate in a nearly infinite way, tasting one bite, one experience at a time in a journey without any clear goal but with a very clear direction—the direction of exploration.

There are people who run away from the unknown, from the diverse; they fear it, they fight it. I have always been fascinated by it. And so it was that, ever since I was a boy, I have always been on the hunt for potential, in order to transform it into action. I look for it within myself, in others, in places, in events, in experiences—everywhere.

One evening, while we were dining in one of our favorite restaurants in New York, my dear friend Denis Dekovic, back then the head of design for Adidas, described me with an image full of poetry: "Mauro, you're like a straw bale that is ready to catch fire—you're always looking for that spark that can set it alight!" I imagined myself as straw: light, suspended in the air, on the lookout for that spark in new worlds, new cultures, in the uncertainty of the possible, in the darkness of the unexplored. This sacred fire is the initial flame of innovation. The attraction for the unknown and the love of diversity are its fundamental ingredients. The curious exploration of the world and an obsessive fascination for what's possible are its main drivers.

Innovation in the Eyes of a Child

All of this is part of my DNA. It has defined my life as something I have experienced every day, from my earliest years. My mother tells me that I came into the world with my eyes wide open, without crying, looking around me with curiosity, as if to ask where I was, fully enjoying the magic of that moment. Obviously, my mother was projecting her own emotions onto me, with her own interpretation of my first moment of life. But this image has remained with me and has intrigued me ever since, because it is exactly with that curious child's gaze that I have continued to explore the world.

There is another story that my mom loves to share. She never misses an opportunity to tell people about our first summer in Borghetto, a small seaside town in Liguria. I was two years old, and she couldn't keep me under the beach umbrella, not even for a moment. I was always driving her crazy, running away to explore every inch of the shore, speaking with anyone who passed by, with all of my infantile noises and gestures. That hunger for exploration and discovery started early on and never stopped. It has accompanied me for my whole existence and will only come to an end when life itself leaves my body, because exploration, discovery, and life have always been a single, inseparable substance that feeds my body. And they always will be.

This book is about precisely this: innovation and life. It discusses this topic, for the most part, through the filters and tales of my professional life, but the sensitive reader will find reflections and ideas that go radically beyond the professional dimension, with roots that dig down into the personal world of each and every one of us. Being able to innovate in the world of business means thinking and acting as innovators. And that begins with our own private lives. The two worlds are completely, intimately bound up with each other. You can't switch off your innovation mindset when you get home from the office. If you think you can, well, then probably you're not an innovator.

Creating Value for People

My five years of design at the university Politecnico of Milan were extremely illuminating. They made me discover a fascinating discipline that no one had ever mentioned to me before. Perhaps this is one of the reasons that I have decided to talk about it so much in the past twenty years, especially outside of the world of design, in every kind of situation and on every kind of platform. I wanted to expose as many people as possible to this incredible universe full of creativity and optimism, packed with joy and style, saturated with meaning and value, all of which I had discovered by accident through a phone call that I hadn't been expecting.

No one had ever told me about a school that teaches you how to be an innovator—or, to put it more exactly, not (only) a designer but an innovator! Innovation is what designers do and what you are taught to do in design school. You learn how to observe people, how to understand their needs and desires, and how to then invent meaningful solutions that respond to those desires and needs. These solutions can take the form of products, brands, spaces, services, or experiences. And then you learn that these solutions need to be technically realizable and also need to be able to be commercialized. In other words, you learn how to make something *desirable*, *technically feasible*, and *economically viable*. Well, these three dimensions are quite simply the key pillars of any innovation process. They frame the three fundamental ingredients of any successful innovation, which can be summarized using three relevant keywords: "human being," "technology," and "business." Designers innovate through a constant balancing of these three dimensions.

On top of all of this, designers do something else as well, which makes their approach more important in today's world than it has ever been before. They try to create value for people, for society, for the whole planet. Designers are driven by a sincere desire to create solutions that impact people's lives in a meaningful way. People value before business value: that's the kind of value designers are after. That's priority number one, two, and three for them!

If business leaders are assigned mediocre products to manage, they can still become stars in their field and have a wonderful career path if they find a way to grow their company and obtain financial success despite the mediocrity of those products. Designers who produce mediocre products are merely professionals who are as mediocre as their products, whatever economic success their sales might lead to.

And so let's ask the question: Who does our society need? Design thinkers in love with the excellence of their products, who create solutions that add value to people's lives, or business wizards, capable of drowning the world in mediocrity, without regrets, drawing vast riches into their own companies? Obviously, I'm making generalizations. I have met many business leaders in my time who are positively obsessed about the quality of their products, as well as designers who have aimed more at economic returns than at the exceptional character of their own projects. But on a cultural level, the truth is that the typical mindset of the design community—the design-driven mindset, the one that design school teaches you—is an approach entirely focused on the creation of meaningful value for society as a whole. That's usually what designers care about. And that's what design school teaches you to care about and expects you to care about.

"Design-driven," in other words, is a synonym for "human-centered." It's a human-centered way of thinking. Our world needs more people who think and act like designers. We call these people *design thinkers*, whether or not they are designers in the strict sense of the term. Yes, you—whether you are a marketer, scientist, musician, or politician— can be, and should be, a design thinker, too!

Therefore, let's be clear: this book is not a design book as such. Nor is it a book about designers. It's a book about innovation and innovators. But the world of design has had a fundamental role in my journey; it has transformed my natural and personal instinct for innovation into a profession, a real and recognized one. It has given this instinct a definition and, above all, a purpose, one that is greater and more important than I am.

I am sure that many other people have arrived at this vision of purposeful innovation by traveling down different paths. This book, nevertheless, is full of my own biographical experiences, which provide color and form to the book's messages—and this means that design, the vital element of my existence, will be a recurring filter, whether hidden between the lines or explicitly discussed in the text.

The design-driven and human-centered approach to business has perhaps often been considered superfluous by many organizations until recently, as this approach wasn't always necessary to win in the market. But today, in our new modern society, this mindset represents a primary competitive advantage: it is vital, essential, and unavoidable for any enterprise. The world is changing under the inexorable winds of globalization, new technologies, and digital platforms, and in this new and democratic competitive landscape, any form of mediocrity in products and brands can no longer be easily defended. A more humanistic business vision becomes indispensable: either you create extraordinary products and brands for the people you serve, or someone else will do it for you—and take your place.

To create extraordinary products and brands, you need an extraordinary breed of leaders. These individuals put the creation of value for other people at the center. Able to decipher and understand the dreams and needs of those people, these leaders know how to translate this understanding into extraordinary solutions, convince companies and investors to bet everything on those ideas, and inspire armies of other people in the direction of the leaders' own dreams and toward the creation of meaningful value for society and for business. These leaders are, yet again, *people in love with people*. You need to find them, to inspire them, to coach them, to retain them—to "create" them sometimes, uncovering their potential, unleashing their hidden talent. These people could be any of you, any of us. I will talk extensively about these individuals in the pages of this book.

CHAPTER 1

MAPPING THE NEW WORLD

My passion for exploration and my attraction to the unknown have always been important drivers in my life. They have been imprinted into my DNA and have been constantly stimulated by context and experiences. Over the years, however, this way of interpreting the world around me has taken on an even greater relevance, becoming even more precious and indispensable. The reason for this is that our world is evolving at a pace that is more accelerated than ever. With a capacity for adaptation that is entirely unique to the human species, we can see every day how today's great novelties become tomorrow's routine. What we are now often taking for granted were yesterday's dreams. We have all borne witness to this, whether more or less consciously: we are living through this metamorphosis in the way we buy things, communicate, eat, travel, and work.

The Metamorphosis of the World

At only a few years of age, our children—"digital natives"—learn how to use a tablet with the same natural spontaneity as they pick flowers or drink milk. During the COVID-19 crisis, millions of people, in every corner of the planet, became remote workers and virtual shoppers from one day to the next, when the day before, perhaps, they had no idea how to access a digital meeting or buy something online. In the era before social media, many industries had a very different face from the one we are used to today. Global city transport didn't have to deal with Uber, and the hospitality sector didn't have to face up to Airbnb. We are immersed in a world made up of incredible services, experiences, and products, from music streaming to digital photography, from electric cars to mobile phones, from social media to digital payments, from e-gaming to transportation apps. From the universe to the metaverse, we are all caught in a constant motion between the digital and the analog, the virtual and the real, the online and the off-line.

New ideas and new products are flooding the market: entering, evolving, disappearing or growing, and making their impact. Everything changes, at an unexpected rate of acceleration. And the only unchangeable constant is precisely this change itself. Transition is no longer a temporary state: it has become the norm. And whereas young people of years gone by dreamed of a stable job, perhaps in a renowned and prestigious company, in this evolving world, today's youth dream of founding their own renowned and prestigious company. Or, at least, they aspire to establish a company that is renowned and prestigious enough to be acquired by another one, ideally a multinational corporation. We live in the era of the start-ups: big companies and global brands no longer compete against one another in a predictable and defined context.

The Democratization of Innovation

Our children will study this current era of profound change in schoolbooks. They will read about how this unique cocktail—equal parts globalization, digitalization, artificial intelligence, advanced technologies, and natural phenomena—threw new layers of color over the contemporary palette, provoking deep shifts in the portrait of the global society that we have all become used to.

This shift has impacted everything we do. And it has changed how every business displays itself, evolves, flourishes, or fails. If the world has experienced other revolutions in the past (such as the cognitive, agricultural, and industrial revolutions) and other crises (from world wars to historic pandemics), then the anomaly of the current situation is the extreme speed of the transition and its global nature.

We are bombarded by change every day, and we take it for granted, because at this point it's just part of our lives. Some of these changes are obvious and visible. Others are less extreme. They are introduced to us day after day, in the most diverse range of situations, or we discover them on our own, during our own explorations of life's many paths. New products and brands that are beautiful, intelligent, useful, poetic, and entertaining enter our lives daily, gently, today more than ever.

I have met thousands of such products over the years, like anyone else in this world. And many of these small and brilliant innovations have become part of my routine, adding some kind of value to my life. Sometimes it was a touch of additional comfort; sometimes it was a new form of convenience, style, security, practical utility, or sensual pleasure, according to the given object or service.

Some years ago, for example, I was walking through the streets of SoHo in Manhattan, not far from our PepsiCo Design Center, when at a certain point, without even realizing it, I found myself in front of the Museum of Modern Art (MoMA) Design Store. I saw it and walked in, as I often do. I love this place; it has its own flavor of discovery and entertainment, of lightness and depth. Every object has been found, screened, and selected by people who possess a very particular sensitivity, passion, and admiration for art, design, and human intellect—something that seems to match somehow with my own way of thinking and feeling. Or at least this is what the sophisticated collection of objects makes me think of, reflecting the credibility of the institution, a place that is admired and respected by the entire creative community worldwide.

That afternoon, my attention was captured by an object on the opposite wall of the entrance, stacked up together with the others to create an interesting visual impact that could not and would not allow itself to go unobserved. I drew closer, and on first glance, I believed I was looking at nothing more than a book with a strange cover, made of a material that seemed similar to walnut. These books were left deliberately on the shelves, so that anyone might touch them and look through them. So I did. I took one of those books, and I tried to leaf through it. And something very surprising happened. The pages opened up, and a warm light emanated out toward my face. It wasn't a book; it was a lamp! And it was called Lumio. Opening up the pages little by little, you could reveal a subtle, timid light, barely switched on. But the more you opened the book, the more light came out. You could expand the book all the way until the back cover touched the front; a magnet inserted into the structure of the lamp allowed the covers to be connected, creating a beam of light that would radiate 360 degrees. The lamp was wireless but could be recharged using an orange USB cable made of a material that looked like a small rope and could be mistaken for a bookmark. As a casual passerby, I was fascinated by the magic and beauty of the object; as a designer I was struck by how clever and intuitive it was.

Max Gunawan, the creative based in San Francisco who came up with the product, had managed to translate the mechanical and functional act of regulating the light intensity and direction of a lamp into a natural, warm, and human gesture, that of opening a book. I immediately bought two. Two "copies" of the same lamp! The wordplay alone intrigued me. I put one on my nightstand in my Manhattan apartment and another on a small table full of books in the living room of my house in the Hamptons, camouflaged among the dozens of tomes, ready to astonish my guests as only that object would be able to. Over the following years, I have bought others for friends and family. The lamp has been the perfect birthday gift. It has been an object of conversation for anyone visiting my home, a catalyst for comments and wonder. I have celebrated its features with countless people, and I continue to do so. If I were ever to leave my job as a designer, I could certainly become an excellent sales rep for Max.

Max's Lumio is a perfect example of a simple, friendly product that makes its way into our homes in a gentle manner, adding a touch of poetry, style, and practicality into our daily lives. It remains a humble object; unlike products such as the mobile phone, radio, or television when they were invented, this lamp does not change your life. If, however, we start thinking about thousands of other products like the Lumio lamp, in a vast range of categories, then we can begin to understand how these useful and semi-anonymous solutions have an incredible collective power to raise the level of the emotional, aesthetic, and functional quality of our day-to-day experiences. I can think of dozens and dozens of objects of this kind that, in recent years, have come into my daily life, never to leave me again.

In a similarly casual way, but in quite different circumstances, I came across another product—a much better known one. I'm speaking about the virtual reality (VR) headset Oculus. One of my first interactions with this futuristic object happened some years back, for professional reasons, when we bought some models (in the Rift version) for our PepsiCo Design Center in New York. We were using them to design; to test out concepts with end users; and to share projects with clients, business partners, and even the media. I was already fascinated back then with the product's potential, and over the years we have continued to use it in a consistent way, with great satisfaction. But my more intimate, daily use knowledge of Oculus is a more recent affair.

Just before drafting this book, a close friend shared with me a different version of these headsets: Oculus Quest. Stefan Sagmeister—a designer, an artist, and a thinker who has little need of further introduction—had arrived at my home in the Hamptons one Friday afternoon to pass a chill weekend together. On Saturday morning, while the majority of the guests were still in their rooms in gentle slumber, I looked out into the garden and saw him there with a visor over his eyes and two controllers in his hands, sweating profusely in the summer heat, running around like a madman, waving his arms and legs and his whole body, as if beating back invisible flies.

A few minutes later, I understood that Stefan had not gone crazy—thank God! He was simply working out in virtual reality, using an app called Supernatural that was projecting him into an incredible world, from enchanted scenes of the Blue Lagoon in Iceland to the peaks of Machu Picchu in Peru, from the waters of Raja Ampat in Indonesia to the terraces of Yuanyang in China. In those magical lands, he had to beat back spheres of energy rushing toward him, using two light sabers reminiscent of *Star Wars*, ducking and diving through radiant triangles, moving at the speed of light to face the different portals that would open up on his flanks from time to time. All of this movement was burning an average of 350 calories every fifteen minutes. What a great way to keep yourself fit on a daily basis with an activity that was also enjoyable. The gym of the future? Maybe. Or maybe not—but it certainly looked very fun.

I tried it out immediately, along with the architect Michel Rojkind, another enthusiastic friend who was sharing that beautiful weekend with us, and within a few minutes we were both rushing to buy it online. Over the following months, I discovered a whole range of other applications, from boxing to tennis, that transformed Oculus Quest into a daily routine for physical exercise, taking the place of other traditional workouts that had always bored me in one way or another. In this way, Oculus has become another one of those useful, functional, and pleasurable products, able to generate a form of positive impact in my life.

I could carry on with a whole series of other examples, but Lumio and Oculus should be more than sufficient to give an idea of what I'm talking about. Let's pause for a moment to consider their real meaning. What do a lamp and a virtual reality headset have in common, aside from having been dreamed up, designed, and produced with a combination of functionality and style, creating useful, enjoyable innovation that adds value to my life every day? What makes these products special in this story that I'm telling you, aside from having names that, put together, have a sound and flavor reminiscent of fables, almost like the nicknames of the dwarfs in a modern Snow White story? Lumio and Oculus! Their common denominator, aside from my personal experiences and the fairy tale they remind me of, is in their origins, in that metaphorical womb that gave them the possibility of latching on when they were merely embryonic ideas in the busy imagination of visionary innovators, after which they found ways of growing, strengthening themselves, and coming into the world.

These products would never have existed without the internet; nor would they have existed if someone hadn't invented the concept of crowdfunding. These objects were both born through an investment campaign on Kickstarter, a digital platform for collectively financing creative projects. Kickstarter was launched in July 2009 and over the years has helped raise billions of dollars to finance hundreds of thousands of

Everything changes, at an unexpected rate of acceleration. And the only unchangeable constant is precisely this change itself.

projects. Lumio alone raised $580,000 in only thirty-one days following its launch. Oculus raised much more and has become one of the platform's greatest successes. Palmer Freeman Luckey was only seventeen when he created his first prototype in 2010, in the garage of his parents' house. The project was launched on Kickstarter two years later, in 2012, to clamorous success, raising around $2.5 million in a short space of time from more than ten thousand investors. In March 2014, when Oculus was still in its development stage, Facebook acquired it for $2 billion in cash and stock. Palmer was catapulted into the twenty-second place on the *Forbes* global list of the richest entrepreneurs under the age of forty, and Oculus became the benchmark in the world of virtual reality.

Kickstarter and the idea of crowdfunding have an important meaning in the current social and economic scenario. They are a clear and visible demonstration of the fact that it is easier than ever to access the capital necessary to develop a good idea and put it on the market, entering in competition, directly or indirectly, with existing products and services created over the years by consolidated brands and companies. My beloved Lumio and Oculus would never have existed without Kickstarter, which is the case with thousands of other objects, services, and software products launched on the platform since its creation and loved by individuals for the value these solutions have added to their lives. And that isn't even to mention all the products that have been created outside of this platform, competing with those launched on Kickstarter itself, triggering an unavoidable process of collective progress and evolution, in an almost Darwinian way. The best solution survives and prevails. The best solution then produces others, exponentially, whether to support that solution or to compete with it, creating an expansive ecosystem in which new "best solutions" continually come to light and, over time, win out.

Kickstarter is just one example, proof of a much broader transformation. The global market, new manufacturing technologies, and digital platforms have made it possible for a vast number of dreamers and entrepreneurs to create their own new businesses, sometimes with extraordinary results. This shift has generated a proliferation of investment funds on the hunt for ideas, products, and enterprises to invest in, exponentially amplifying the level of financing allocated to the world of innovation, year after year.

Four Key Drivers That Are Changing the World

We are living in an era distinguished by a new and very clear opportunity, something that has never happened before: if you have a good idea today, in comparison with only a few years ago, it is much simpler to take it to market. The four fundamental drivers of this change can be summarized as follows:

> *Access to capital:* Financial resources are more accessible than ever, thanks to crowdfunding, the proliferation of investment funds, start-up culture, and the digitalized and globalized world.

> *Increased efficiency and potential of manufacturing platforms:* Manufacturing is becoming more and more efficient, reaching unheard-of levels of efficiency; costs are lowering and productivity is increasing, driven above all by new technologies and global competition. And the quality level is rising exponentially as well.

> *E-commerce as sales platform:* In the majority of consumer categories, you can now sell directly to the end user by utilizing e-commerce platforms, eventually bypassing traditional distribution.

> *Digital media as a communication platform:* It's now possible to create a communication ecosystem that is efficient and impactful by leveraging the new digital channels and eventually bypassing traditional platforms—television, radio, and print.

In these four areas, until a few years ago, the established companies of the world were building their barriers to entry, constructed of scale of production, distribution, and communication. Today these barriers are crumbling away, eroded as never before by the winds of globalization, digitalization, and technology. Entrepreneurs with an innovative idea can potentially find investors in a relatively simple way, creating their own products at costs that are, on average, more competitive with respect to the past. These entrepreneurs can then leverage digital channels to both sell those products and communicate about them, directly reaching millions of people across the planet.

In this context, the most formidable barrier to entry that you can imagine and build to shield yourself from competition is no longer constructed by the brute force of money and scale. The greatest barrier you can have is one and only one: *the relevance of your product for the end user*—that is, your ability to create solutions, brands, spaces, services, and experiences that satisfy people's needs and wants, and indeed the needs and wants of all society, in the most extraordinary way possible. For the first time ever, the creation of real *value for people* is beginning to align itself more and more with the creation of *value for business*, and this holds true for a vast range of products and industries. It is finally happening!

Looking at the broader picture in this way, we can begin to grasp the unique character of our historical moment and the epochal dimensions of the seismic shift taking place, entirely unprecedented in the world of global business. All of this is possible for the first time in the history of humanity.

Incremental Innovation Is No Longer Enough

Over recent years, this evolving scenario has created new dynamics and expectations. Large companies—especially in the consumer world—are going through a moment of general strategic crisis, trying to understand how to generate a culture of innovation that, in many cases, they haven't practiced for decades and that they are now attempting to comprehend and then put in motion in an accelerated and meaningful way. What many of these enterprises used to call innovation often describes little more than the incremental evolution of their products: marginal changes to the same formulas, incremental functional modifications, minimal formal restyling.

In some industries, such as the automotive industry or consumer electronics, the majority of innovation has historically been marked by the linear progress of technology—less weight, longer life, more comfort, higher resolution, wider dimensions, smaller size, extended autonomy. Not much more happened in the way of innovation unless an anomalous and unexpected force entered the market and changed all the rules of the game: from Motorola's invention of the cell phone, to the constant disruptive innovations of Apple in Steve Jobs's years there, all the way to Elon Musk's Tesla, an electric vehicle at scale, to name a few. But these are exceptions. For most of the product categories we interact with on a daily basis, innovation continues to be incremental. And when big companies succeed in producing breakthrough innovations, they often come about through mergers and acquisitions, investments in external enterprises, joint ventures, or acquisition of patents.

This incremental approach to innovation is easy to explain: radical change is risky. And radical change at the scale of a multinational corporation can be *extremely* risky. In contrast, lack of change is efficient and profitable when the pressure of competition is contained. And the bigger the scale, the higher the efficiency and the profitability of this lack of change.

Although there are always exceptions to the rule, this was the practice for decades in many modern industries and especially in the consumer business. But the situation today is different. For the first time in their history, large multinational corporations have to compete with a plethora of new entrants who, leveraging the opportunities offered by the new scenario, are finding ways to create innovative products that stand out— and to bring them to market.

The formula for these enterprises is clear and as simple to understand as it is complicated to imitate: putting people at the center of everything, independent entrepreneurs in every corner of the globe—often young people in their parents' garages or new graduates in studio flats—analyze every product and industry, trying to figure out every frustration, desire, dream, and need that has not been resolved or dealt with by the available market solutions. Once these gaps have been identified, new products, services, brands, and experiences are imagined that can resolve the problems identified.

The big difference from the past, however, is that today these ideas can actually be realized and launched with far greater ease. With the historical barriers to entry of the traditional companies worn away by globalization, digitalization, and technology, the new entrants can leap over those barriers with more agility, arriving directly at the end user with meaningful proposals, while combining functionality and aesthetics, rationality and emotions. The different structure, low fixed costs, flexible culture, different financial expectations, and different legal pressures on these entities mean that they can avoid many of the rigid limitations imposed on—or self-imposed by—the large corporations. If you work in a business-to-consumer industry and your sector has still not been impacted by this revolution, it is simply a matter of time. You cannot avoid this risk—or, if you will, this opportunity (it depends on your point of view).

The situation, yet again, leaves us with only one choice: to create extraordinary solutions for the end user, without compromising. If you don't create something special for them, if you don't realize authentic, unique, and relevant solutions for their needs and wants, someone else will come onto the scene sooner or later and do so in your place. And then you will find yourself in the uncomfortable position of chasing behind them—if you're lucky. If you're less fortunate, then you will lose your market, as has happened in recent years to brands such as Kodak, Blockbuster, Toys "R" Us, and Sears, to name but a few.

Today's companies need to focus their efforts more than ever on the production of *meaning*, creating an ecosystem of products that *make sense* to people and provide them with that meaning in every moment of interaction with the brand. We are entering a new phase of human history in which there is no choice but to generate excellence from every standpoint, from the product to the brand, from the service to the experience, from storytelling to arriving at that full network of enablers and amplifiers that support the very existence of a product (logistics, production, business modeling). There is no longer any room to protect solutions that aren't human-centered—in other words, solutions that do not satisfy the needs and desires of users, articulated or otherwise.

The Age of Excellence

We are entering a new modern renaissance, fueled by the reborn, human-istic necessity of putting people at the center of everything. Technology is an enabling asset, the brand and distribution are the amplifiers, but the excellence of the product, put at the service of human beings, is the fun-damental variable for success. It will no longer be possible to win in the marketplace simply with the brute power of impermeable technological patents, inaccessible large-scale distribution networks, or multibillion communication budgets that others cannot match.

Paradoxically, in the era of technology's utmost triumph, we are also living through the utmost celebration of the person. In the era of e-com-merce, social media, 3D printing, and start-ups, we are living through the democratization of innovation, to the individual's ultimate advan-tage. In this hypertechnological, hyperconnected, digital world, there will be increasingly less space for mediocrity, step by step. Companies that know how to adapt to this model will survive, prosper, and win out. Those that do not adapt will be destined to a gradual but unavoidable extinction. The most positive consequence of the whole situation is that it will have an incredibly beneficial impact on the society of the future. The best products, the best brands, the best services, the best experi-ences will prevail. The human being will enjoy this. We are entering the "age of excellence."

CHAPTER 2

DREAM HUNTING

In the strenuous effort to interpret the developing economic and social situation, large and small companies alike are gradually understanding that their innovation processes need to be rethought in order to, finally, put the human being at the center of everything. Some enterprises call this approach human-centered; others call it people-centered or consumer-centric. The goal is always the same: to design something for a real person. This is all fine and proper—but the exact choice of wording is important. The choice of words, actually, is often also an interesting indicator of the culture behind an organization, a person, or a professional community.

Don't Call Them Consumers! They're Human Beings

I don't like the word "consumer" as it is used in the business world today. It's a term that I find alienating, to the point of being disrespectful to our human nature. My particular distaste for the word stems from two main reasons.

First of all, calling human beings "consumers" runs the risk of depriving them of their humanity, by viewing them merely as business entities to whom you are selling a product, in order to make them consume it for profit. Would you ever call your daughter, your son, your wife, your husband, or your parents *consumers*? I wouldn't. Isn't it an ugly word? Isn't it reductive? The image of my daughter as a little consuming being disturbs me. The word flattens us out onto a single dimension, the dimension of beings who do nothing with their lives but buy and consume. I don't want to be seen as a consumer. I would very much like to be seen as a being who lives, enjoys, suffers, dreams, invents, communicates, travels, and creates. We are *human beings,* not *consuming beings.*

The second reason that I have developed such a piqued intolerance for the term is that we are living in a society in which available resources are increasingly scarce, the act of *consuming* these resources needs to be limited and responsible, and the intelligent use and reuse of these resources ought to be our daily mantra. Pigeonholing the human being as a consumer (of these resources) sends a message diametrically opposed to the aims of every innovator, entrepreneur, designer, researcher, and marketer in the world. "User" is a far more dignified term, because it focuses on a person in the act of utilizing a product or service and finding some benefit in it.

An innovator who sees people as *consumers* prioritizes every possible and imaginable tool to sell them something and make them consume it. In contrast, an innovator who sees people as *users* focuses on the creation of positive functional and emotional value. Finally, the innovator who sees people simply as *human beings* will make their happiness the priority, and everything will gravitate around that single goal.

Consumer-centricity is about understanding people in order to sell them something. Human-centricity is about understanding people to build real value in their lives. The first approach sees a good product as one of several levers to generate business growth. The latter sees a good product primarily as a driver to improve people's lives.

I want to design for human beings. These human beings will acquire, consume, and utilize. But these will be dimensions, consequences, results—not the keywords by which to reduce or define these humans. Above all, I want to create solutions that aim at bringing human beings joy, that entertain them, provide security, simplify their lives, connect them, help them relax, make them happy.

There are other terms that have a similar function. I have always been fascinated, for example, by how the US retailer Target calls its clients "guests." For many these people are simply consumers; for the Minneapolis-based chain, they are sacred guests, welcomed into one's home and treated with care, attention, empathy, and respect. In this book, I have tried to avoid the term "consumer" as much as possible; on the rare occasions I use it, it's always in a strictly business context. Over the course of my life, I have always tried to limit my use of the word, relegating it to those situations in which I needed a particular audience to intuitively comprehend my messages, without risking any potential misunderstanding. In these cases, unfortunately, I have had to use the term, and I will do so in the future. But on all other occasions, the person for whom we design and innovate is and will remain, solely and simply, a human being.

At the Crossroads of Desirability, Technical Feasibility, and Economic Viability

In this new business scenario, where everything is becoming progressively more centered on the creation of value for people, the past few years have been extremely fertile ground for the growth of a particular professional community, whose members have always put human beings at the center of all their activities. Not consumers—human beings! This is a community that has lived for a long time on the margins of the business cosmos, in a kind of protected and isolated Eden; a community that has only recently begun to step outside of its own territory, tentatively navigating and adventuring out into new celestial orbits of this unexplored universe; a community composed of humanistic, multifaceted innovators; a community that has been often misunderstood and confused. This is the *design* community, and it draws on a process called "design thinking."

Some people will wonder what design has to do with the world of innovation. Anyone who asks this question has no idea what design really is. This is, nevertheless, a very frequent question.

As used in common parlance, "design" has come to be associated with two concepts: beauty and luxury. A designer object, a designer dress, and a designer car are all manufactured with high aesthetic content, and they often come at a high cost. The aesthetic dimension in particular is absolute; it's the priority, without compromise, to the point that often one doesn't even expect real functionality from a designer product. In other words, functionality becomes merely an optional value, something that's just "nice to have."

But designers in reality are much more than simple stylists—with all due respect and admiration for stylists, of course. Designers are professionals educated in the art and discipline of innovation.

Design processes always begin with an intuition by individuals who are observing reality, analyzing it, thinking it through, trying to grasp it, dreaming it. These individuals and their thoughts are a kind of ignition; everything expands out from the primary idea, which acts like an enzyme that brings down the necessary temperature to then trigger a reaction, becoming the catalyst for a project. But what do these individuals observe, analyze, and dream? What's the object of their intuition? What's the focus of their research? The reply is as simple as it is vast and difficult to contain—because the object of their investigation is reality in its totality; it can essentially be anything. In order to decipher this effort, without abandoning it to the laws of mere accident, we can summarize some of the main types of research within three distinct and fundamental dimensions:

1. The sphere of the person, with all their needs and wants
2. The sphere of science and technology
3. The sphere of business

Along with thousands of other students during my years at the university of Politecnico of Milan, I was educated precisely in these three fundamental dimensions:

Desirability: the dimension of the human being. We studied cultural anthropology, ethnography, semiotics, and a series of disciplines connected to the human sciences.

Technical feasibility: the dimension of science and technology. We studied physics, mathematics, material science, digital technologies. Every project had to be considered in terms of its feasibility and the technologies of its production.

Economic viability: the business dimension. We studied marketing, branding, and economics.

In the design curriculum, these three dimensions are then set alongside a series of technical courses to prepare us to actually design, from ideation to development and launch. We are taught hand-drawing, digital design, 3D modeling, prototyping, photography, color theory, and more. When we design, every solution has to be defined, balanced, and evaluated according to the three spheres: it has to be *desirable* (desirability), *feasible* (technical feasibility), and *able to be commercialized* (economic viability). You can see, fairly intuitively, that through structuring their thought and work in this manner, designers are essentially trained to become innovators: holistic, multidisciplinary innovators who are able to deal with any kind of problem, in every product category, in essentially any industry.

Striking a Balance Between Empathy, Strategy, and Prototyping

The intuition of an innovator can take off in any field within these three areas. The point of departure for an innovative project could be, for example, the casual observation of how a child plays with classmates in a schoolyard, or an epoch-defining scientific discovery by a researcher in a university lab, or a conversation with a client who opens up new business opportunities that were unexplored up until that moment.

One of the greatest challenges, at this point, is to connect all three dimensions in a flexible and efficient manner, maintaining an authentic focus on the end user. It's not easy at all. In the world of big companies, what makes this balancing act still more difficult is the entrance of factors such as scale, corporate culture, and financial strategies. These kinds of structures thus require professionals who understand all three dimensions and have the correct tools to put them into conversation with one another within the innovation process.

It is here that the much-vaunted "design thinking" comes into play. It is a process that alternates between investigation, creation, and validation, organizing them in a series of divergent and convergent phases (the famous "double diamond"). This process is enabled by three fundamental vectors: *empathy*, *strategy*, and *prototyping*.

Empathy

Empathy is nothing more than the capacity to understand the person you are innovating for in an authentic and profound way. It represents the phase in which the designer gets into the mind and spirit of that person, reading the person's emotional signals, taking on the person's subjective perspective, analyzing motivations, observing behavior and reactions in an objective and rational way, without being influenced by the designer's own personal bias.

When a designer manages to get into the head of the user and takes on the user's perspective, the designer can then understand the user's needs, desires, ambitions and fears, and thus design the ideal solution that takes all of these particular variables into account. In brief, in the process of design and innovation, empathy is the ability to understand what is *relevant to the user*.

Strategy

Once a user's need has been grasped, it is then necessary to understand whether the potential solution for that need makes any sense from a business point of view. The second vector of design thinking—strategy—has precisely this goal: to understand whether the idea is *relevant for the company* (whether an existing company or a new one) and, if it is not relevant, what needs to be done to make it so. Four different, complementary dimensions need to be borne in mind during this phase:

1. Do we have a *business model* that is up to sustaining this idea?
2. Do we have the right *technologies and manufacturing processes* to support the idea?
3. Do we have an appropriate *company culture* for managing this idea?
4. Are there any *external factors* that might negatively impact on the idea, either now or in the future?

Don't be afraid to dream big—you should always dream! If you don't have a dream, you'll never be able to make it come true!

Dream and then act!

Trying to understand these four areas in a deep way, right from the start, is fundamental for avoiding the most classic mistakes made by organizations dealing for the first time with real innovation projects. Many inexperienced managers fall in love with a winning "consumer proposition" (that is, an idea that makes sense for the people whom the managers want to serve). And so they begin in a rush, flying along on the wings of their enthusiasm, without taking into consideration all the other variables from the beginning, only to realize later, midway through the process, that the company cannot actually invest in the necessary manufacturing plant or technology, for example, or that the creation of a new sales channel is too ambitious a project and unjustified by the potential ROI (return on investment) of the new product, or that the funds simply aren't there to launch and manage a new brand in the portfolio.

Inexpert leaders, in most cases, fail to ask the right questions at the beginning of the project journey. They end up managing a *product* development process without knowing that in reality they were dealing with a project that should have been much broader in scope, impacting the company's *culture* and *organization*, as well as its *portfolio* and *manufacturing strategy*.

You have to know from the start which variables need to be considered, so as to then find the right questions and appropriate answers, in this order, phase by phase throughout the process. On this journey, the quality of the question is fundamental: far too often, people generate a whole set of correct answers for a whole set of wrong questions. And too often, people forget to question the validity of their questions, finding comfort instead in the correctness of their answers. The ability to evaluate and understand which dimensions need to be explored, and what are the correct questions to ask, is an essential criterion for practicing innovation in the right way.

Prototyping

In the innovation journey, prototyping is the catalyst desperately needed to support empathy and strategy. Its role is to make every idea, every solution, every business model, every technology unlock, more understandable, more tangible, and more shareable, through the entire development process and in every project phase.

Many people erroneously believe that a prototype is simply the concrete realization of an idea, created in order to share the idea's characteristics with an audience—whether colleagues, clients, or investors—and eventually to test the idea out. For example, you produce a prototype to present the project for a new lamp to a client, or to test a plane on a flight, or to showcase a new vehicle at a motor show. This is certainly a correct definition, but it's only part of the story. It captures one aspect of the value generated by prototyping. Before being put to these uses, the prototype is a catalyst for thinking.

From doodling on Post-it notes to the first functioning model of a car, the prototype is an example of the aesthetic and functional characteristics of a product—or a brand, a space, an experience, or a service—created with the aim of generating reactions, interactions, thoughts, and reflections. These reflections may be born from a dialogue and may be shared with others on a team or may simply arise spontaneously in an innovator's mind, evolving in that mind, animating that mind. The prototype can be an intimate and private experience as much as a public and collaborative activity.

The Superpowers of Prototyping

Prototyping has five distinct superpowers, which occur in every kind of process. I have consistently and strategically used the following superpowers over the past twenty-five years of my life to drive my ideas forward.

The Power of Alignment

Prototyping is about aligning all the interlocutors with one another, without constrictions on time and space, around a single interpretation of an idea—people in the same room with you, but also individuals in other parts of the world or in different layers of the organization, seeing the idea that same day or after weeks or months.

For example, if during a meeting I say the word "knife," every person in the room will visualize in their mind a different kind of knife. If I sketch a knife, though, we will all be aligned around that specific interpretation of a knife. The same goes for any idea you may try to share and drive in an organization.

The Power of Internal Co-creation
Prototyping is about enabling people with different backgrounds—technology, business, design, finance, manufacturing, and so on—to work together in synchrony on the development of an idea. Each expert works on the same prototype. The modification of the initial concept by one expert has an impact on all the other experts. By having all the experts work together on the same prototype, each of them can react to, manage, and adapt the evolving concept and the overall strategy, in real time, with an extreme agility and flexibility.

In the analogy of the knife, a marketer in the room may think that the brand that I just sketched on the knife is not visible enough. An ergonomist may think that the handle is not comfortable enough. Many people may think that I have designed a bad knife. But this is the power of design thinking in action: through that sketch I am enabling a dialogue among people with different backgrounds. That prototype activates an agile form of co-creation. Each person participates; they all have a role in making that knife better, in perfect synergy and with great speed.

The Power of External Co-creation
Prototyping can then be used to activate a dialogue with potential clients and users, allowing you to co-create with them.

Share the knife with your clients and users!

The Power of the Shiny Object
Prototyping is about exciting our target audience, including sponsors and investors. People fall in love with ideas that are tangible, that look real—and that are therefore perceived as realizable.

Make that knife meaningful and appealing. And make people dream and support you.

The Power of Confidence
Through these multiple iterative validations, the concept is progressively fine-tuned and gets better and better. The prototype helps you see things

that you can't otherwise see. The result is the generation, within the organization, of a widespread faith in the value of the idea.

Share that knife, evolve that knife, and build confidence about that knife in the entire company.

Prototype as soon as possible, even if you still don't have all the answers, precisely because you still don't have all the answers! The prototype amalgamates empathy and strategy. With a prototype, you validate your project hypotheses with efficiency, agility, and accuracy, in all three dimensions of innovation: the human being, technology, and business—or, in other terms, desirability, technical feasibility, and economic viability. This works in your professional life and in your private life, too.

The Principles of Meaningful Design

Once the needs and desires of the individuals we want to innovate for have been understood and a relevant business strategy has been defined, we are ready to prototype, creating the ideal solutions to satisfy these needs and desires. The innovator's talent, experience, sensitivity, and vision are fundamental variables for generating the best products, brands, spaces, services, and experiences. But some years ago, I realized that just having faith in innovators was not enough, especially in my complex world of multinational corporations. I needed a series of guidelines that I could refer to with my teams, a series of universal principles that could guide us and inspire us, mapping the road, constantly providing us with powerful filters to interpret and validate the meaning and value of each idea, and bringing us together around a single vision.

It was in this way, in the mid-2000s, that I drew up a list of principles derived from the experience of thousands of projects launched to market. I made this list for my teams, but I also made it for myself, to keep in my pocket, a treasured compass that could direct me on my innovation journey.

I call these the principles of meaningful design. They are a series of postulates to keep in mind every time we conceive and design something new, in order to consistently produce solutions to people's needs and wants that are meaningful to them.

The first two principles on this list are the *fundamental principles*, the ones that serve as the foundation for every innovation project and connect together all other principles. The following seven are the *enabling principles*, the essential principles to follow if we want to generate solutions that are aligned with the goals of the fundamental principles. The final three principles are the *clarifying principles*, the principles that aim at clearing up some very important aspects of design and innovation that are often misunderstood or undervalued, and which—if applied correctly—exponentially increase the impact of our solutions.

The Fundamental Principles

Human: Useful, Emotional, and Semiotic

The first principle of meaningful design, the human—and humanist—principle, lives at the intersection of utility, emotion, and semiotics. It is a synthetic principle that embraces everything and everyone, claiming the substantial necessity and value of designing solutions (whether product, brand, space, service, or experience) that can strike a perfect balance between a person's needs and desires.

Each and every one of our projects should resolve a specific *functional* need, generate an *emotional* connection with the user, and have a *semiotic* value—that is, it should manage to tell a story, with a communication flow that moves out from the user and into the surrounding world.

The stories that we can tell the world through brands and products come in all shapes and sizes. They can be narratives about economic and material status ("I'm rich") or mental, intellectual, or spiritual status ("I'm creative"). Or these stories can identify us with a particular community, such as a professional, religious, ethnic, political, or social group ("I'm an artist," "I'm an Orthodox Jew," "I'm a Catholic priest," "I'm Indian," "I'm a Masai warrior," "I'm an athlete," "I'm a rapper," "I'm an environmentalist").

Users might be aware of the semiotic value of the solutions they are using, or they can be unaware of that value. For instance, I may wear a jacket that I particularly like and am very proud of, but through that jacket, inadvertently, I may be screaming to the world that I have really bad taste in fashion. I may drive a car with custom colors and a unique aftermarket design, aiming to project my economic status and style, while ending up sharing only my lack of elegance and sophistication. Whatever the level of awareness, the solution communicates a story—like it or not. Through the products and brands that we experience, use, wear, eat, or drive, we communicate a story, 24/7, to the world around us. Always.

I call this first principle "human" because in its three aspects—utility, emotion, semiotics—it covers, directly and in a holistic way, all human needs.

Innovative: New, Unique, Distinct, and Extraordinary

The second principle of meaningful design specifies the innovative nature of the solution.

Meaningful design is new: It breaks the continuum of the known and expected, introducing at least one element of novelty, a variable that has never been adopted before in that specific context.

Meaningful design is unique: It is the only existing example of this new approach. There are no similar approaches. This unique nature might be an aspect already integral to the novelty of the solution, but I am highlighting it to further stress how much the solution must also be perceived as such. The solution must be, in other words, *obviously unique.* Sometimes I have come across products that were effectively new but were not obviously unique; in other words, in some way they recalled other, preexisting—albeit different—solutions. And for this reason, the products were not appreciated by people as new.

Meaningful design is distinct: If the first and second variables are present, then—by definition—the well-designed solution will also be different from all other existing solutions and thus distinct from all the competitors. In this case, again, the characteristic deserves to be considered explicitly—instead of being thought of as implicit in the concepts of the novel and the unique—because "distinction" from the competition is a key goal of any business strategy and thus an important dimension in any design process. Furthermore, verifying this distinctiveness can be a useful and simple test to evaluate the unique nature of your idea.

Meaningful design is extraordinary: According to the etymological meaning of the word, the "extraordinary" is distinct from the ordinary; it is an exception from the usual practices, special in relation to the normal way of things. Yet again, this characteristic is an integral aspect of the first variables, but it is worth treating separately because the extraordinary nature of a solution introduces the perspective of the human being into the definition of a solution's newness, uniqueness, and distinction. The solution is not just novel, the only kind in the world and distinct from the competition; the solution is also not ordinary—it is exceptional and special to the eyes and in the experience of the person who makes use of it. While the variable of distinction is a business variable, the extraordinary nature of a solution is a humanist one.

The Enabling Principles

Aesthetically Sustainable
The third principle of meaningful design is that it is beautiful, harmonious, pleasing to the senses, without any redundancy.

Functionally Sustainable
The fourth principle specifies that meaningful design is practical, efficient, convenient, and ergonomic.

Emotionally Sustainable
The fifth principle is that meaningful design is attractive and engaging.

Intellectually Sustainable
The sixth principle is that meaningful design is accessible, intuitive, and user-friendly.

Socially Sustainable
The seventh principle of meaningful design is that it is respectful, ethical, honest, and trustworthy.

Environmentally Sustainable
The eighth principle is that meaningful design is eco-friendly.

Financially Sustainable

The ninth principle specifies that meaningful design is valuable to the business and economically accessible to the user.

The Clarifying Principles

Relative

The tenth principle of meaningful design is that the solution depends entirely on the needs and desires of the person. There is no such thing as "good design" in absolute terms; "good design" is *absolutely relative*.

Poetic and Expressive

The eleventh principle of meaningful design specifies that the solution is permeated by a designer's perspective and sensitivity. The solution is not the mere output of a process, however valid that process might be. Using the same process, different designers will generate different outputs. Respect and embrace this truth, and get the best designer you can find for your project.

Storytellable

The twelfth and final principle of meaningful design is that the solution must have a story to share. Or, in other words, this solution must be storytellable. And this story must be an integral part of the product's DNA.

Over the past fifteen years of innovation and design, since the creation of this list, I have always had these twelve principles in my mind, my heart, and my pocket, as a kind of project compass. They are principles to hold by, to aspire to, in order to design with the human being at the center of everything. They are principles to never forget. Having this list printed out on a piece of paper or imprinted on your brain can help you constantly remember how to generate meaningful value for people— because it takes only a moment to forget some of these key qualities of meaningful design when we are overcome by the flurry of daily activities or the chaos of project trade-offs in the everyday struggle between desirability, technical feasibility, and economic viability.

A List for Everyone, Not Just the Designers

This is a list of principles relevant for anyone working in the world of innovation, no matter your background: design, marketing, research and development, consumer insights, sales, manufacturing, supply chain, commercialization, finance, legal, human resources, and every other function, from the CEO down to the junior employee, from the multinational to the start-up. Everyone plays an important role in this multidisciplinary journey to generate progress for the company and for society as a whole.

This list of principles has been forged with the human being at the center of everything: the human being who dreams, creates, produces, and the human being for whom those dreams, creations, and products are destined. These are humanist principles, not business principles—because innovation is first and foremost a humanist act, despite how frequently it is misunderstood as simply a lever for business.

The magical aspect of all of this is that if these principles are followed—putting human beings in their rightful place, in an authentic way, consistently over time—in the end, everyone reaps the fruits. Companies reach their economic goals, serving their clients and users in the best possible way. And our society as a whole enters into a new phase of progressive excellence, creating concrete value for each and every individual.

Those who do not reap any benefit from this new scenario will be those organizations and people who continue to think that you can find success with inauthentic brands or mediocre products based solely on scale—of manufacturing, distribution, and marketing. In the globalized and technological world in which we are living, that era has long gone, thankfully. Excellence will win out, and those who do not adapt to this destiny will disappear. And they won't be missed.

GOOD ANSWERS TO THE WRONG QUESTIONS

In my years at PepsiCo, we have applied this approach to design-driven and human-centered innovation in countless projects, and today this way of thinking and creating has become an integral part of the organization's DNA.

Design-Driven Product Innovation at PepsiCo

I joined the food and beverage multinational corporation PepsiCo in July 2012. At that time, the company was engaged in a project of high strategic relevance. It was refining a new and innovative soda fountain, of the kind that you find in restaurants, fast-food chains, hotels, and food stores. In a society that was witnessing an ever-increasing proliferation of products and choices enabled by new technologies, even these machines needed to develop alongside their surrounding world in order to remain up-to-date.

A cross-functional team (marketing and R&D) was working back then on a concept that invested entirely in a proprietary version of a recently developed technology called microdosing, which was also used by our direct competitor. A soda fountain is traditionally fueled through containers of concentrated syrup, which are stacked up in the back of the store and are generally known as "bag-in-box." Each syrup is then mixed with soda water to make the different drinks that we all know. The micro-dosing technology allowed you to get rid of those bags-in-box, replacing them with much smaller capsules, which had the primary advantage of reducing the space required to set up a soda fountain in a restaurant.

When I began my first conversations with PepsiCo—still in the interview phase—I quickly realized that the company was not satisfied with the concept that it was developing. This was true to the extent that, as soon as I accepted the offer to join the organization, Indra Nooyi, then CEO, along with Brad Jakeman, then president of PepsiCo's Global Beverage Group, immediately asked me to intervene in that project, with the clear goal of correcting its trajectory. The urgency was such that Brad began to get me on board before I even stepped foot in the company.

I remember it as though it was yesterday. It was a hot morning in June. I had just left 3M, but there were still a couple of weeks to go before the date planned as my first official day with PepsiCo. Brad had gotten together all the key people in the research and development, marketing, and food service teams, and we all flew out to Chicago, where he had planned a meeting to discuss the project and review the first prototypes. It was a real baptism of fire. Even before my formal start date, I was cat-apulted straight into one of the company's most complex and urgent innovation projects. *And I loved it!* It represented precisely the reason that I had decided to leave one of the most innovative enterprises in the world, 3M, to join PepsiCo.

In that meeting, I very quickly understood what had caused Brad and Indra to be less than satisfied. The dispenser I was presented with on that day was more expensive than the competition, without presenting any real functional advantage; the machine wasn't particularly beautiful, and it was also tricky to use. According to the fundamental principles of meaningful design, that product was neither *human* nor *innovative*. I still hadn't set foot in the company, yet I immediately had to understand how to turn that project in the direction that the company's leadership wanted, connecting all the different functions involved as well as the external partners. I immediately had to put my credibility on the line with a project that had extremely high visibility.

What I carried with me on that day was my enthusiasm, my experience, my creativity, and all my design tools and principles—the same tools I had been using for years, consisting of empathy, strategy, and prototyping. The project's challenge, like that of all preceding projects, was how to create a product that could be very desirable, technically feasible, and economically viable.

In those first weeks, I was completely alone, I didn't have a team of designers with me, and I was isolated in my uniqueness and diversity. As you can imagine, that was not the only project that I had to manage either. I was called on to create an entire design function within a multinational corporation that back then had a turnover of more than $60 billion. I thus decided to get in touch with a designer whom I highly respected and with whom I had worked on a number of projects in my previous role at 3M.

His name was Martin Broen. He was more or less my age, and he was living in Italy, though he was originally from Argentina. He had a smile constantly beaming across his face, optimism and resilience in his heart, and a passion for innovation branded by fire on his DNA. In those years, he was running his own agency in Milan. I called Martin and explained the project to him, but I also shared with him the much broader dream that had taken me to PepsiCo. I had been asked to transform the role that design had in the company, but my real desire was to go even beyond that goal: what I really wanted to do was to show the entire business world a new way of doing innovation! That project for a smart soda fountain would simply be the first of many others and would become part of a cultural, strategic, and organizational metaproject of much broader dimensions. I ended that conversation with Martin with a request: "If you believe in this vision, if you want to help me create a new, human-centered and design-driven approach to innovation, at PepsiCo and in the world, close your agency and come join me. Let's dream together." Martin, a dreamer like me, didn't need to be asked twice. He immediately recognized the opportunity, dropped everything, left Milan, and moved to New York to join our organization. He became vice president of industrial design and innovation on my new team. I had my first "partner in crime" at PepsiCo who belonged to my world of design.

During my first weeks in the company, there was someone on the research and development team whom I noticed immediately: a gentle man with an intelligent, attentive, keen gaze. His name was Steven Lim, but everyone called him Slim. He was an engineer who had been assigned the project I was working on. I understood very quickly that Slim could become another excellent ally. I found out soon afterward that he came from the automotive industry, and all through his career he had had a personal passion for design. I began to interact with him, and I immediately realized that he was speaking my language. He didn't just get it; he appreciated it, loved it, and was looking for it. I had found another partner, this time in an internal team. Years later, Slim left the R&D group to officially join the design team, and today he's head of all projects for equipment and structural packaging in our organization. He's also a trustworthy adviser to whom I turn whenever I want to verify the technical characteristics of a car that I am considering purchasing!

Together with Martin and Slim, I began to study everything that the team had developed up until then: data, research, concepts, prototypes. I immediately realized that the project had been entirely focused on two factors: technology and the competition. The fact that the competition had created an innovative project utilizing a recently developed technology had, right from the start, become a stubborn principle in the brief: the team's ambition was to create a product that might be better than the one already on the market, taking for granted, however, that we had to use the same recently developed technology, considered by many as a key competitive advantage in the industry.

We Should Question the Brief

Maybe those who considered that newer technology to be a competitive advantage were right—or maybe they weren't. I decided that I needed to develop my own point of view, with fresh eyes, without prejudice. I wanted to avoid the risk of accepting theories and hypotheses generated by other people based on facts and information that I hadn't directly analyzed and evaluated. The best thing to do was to go back to the drawing board—at least in my own head, because an actual clean slate would have been impossible to propose at that time. And so, in parallel with my official activities, I began with what should always be the first step of any project: trying to understand the real needs and concrete desires of the people for whom we were trying to innovate. I asked the team to share with me all of the insights they had about end users and customers. To my surprise, the reply that I received was that there wasn't much data available, and a formal study had never been undertaken. The team had focused entirely on creating a machine that was superior to the competition's, using a proprietary version of a similar technology.

At this point, we didn't have time to embark on a whole new study, and so, with Martin, we decided to draft up a list of hypotheses, identifying the potential needs of our target. We produced this list through a healthy mix of simple intuitions and a very large number of conversations with end users. We began with customers, the people working for the restaurants and hotels who were supposed to buy the machine. Using the enabling principles of meaningful design as a sort of compass, we soon realized that a whole series of important variables had been overlooked until then, consciously or otherwise.

First of all, we understood that it wouldn't be possible to make a single soda fountain that would satisfy all of the potential clients, given the sheer diversity of their needs. We found out, for example, that a fundamental variable was the machine's price. The concept we were working with, like the competition's product, was positioned in a high price range. Some clients were ready to pay very high figures for more complex and complete functionality, while others were interested in only some of those features and were happy to lose some others in exchange for a lower price. If those clients didn't have access to a version with a more accessible price, then they would opt for a more traditional offer.

The other essential criterion of choice was how much space the product occupied: both our prototype and the competition's had sizable dimensions, comparable to an industrial refrigerator, and were models that had to touch the ground and could not be positioned over an existing counter. In many restaurants, though, the only available space for the equipment was on top of that counter.

The other advantage people were looking for was a touch screen to allow them to select their own preferred drink. This wasn't just an aesthetic feature with an emotional appeal. The screen was a user interface with an important functional value. Its role was to give access to dozens upon dozens of flavors and brand combinations, something that wasn't possible with the interface of a traditional soda fountain. Changing the dimensions of the touch screen would have allowed us to provide different levels of potential engagement and functionality, as well as different price tiers.

We also found out that eliminating the bag-in-box, viewed as one of the main advantages of microdosing, wasn't particularly relevant for a great many of the restaurant managers, inasmuch as they already had a space set aside for the syrup containers and had no particular reason to change matters. We were told, however, that microdosing could allow for the mixing of concentrates and soda water with other flavors that could then be added to the drink to personalize it. This meant opening up the potential for hundreds of different mixes. Personalizing the drink was clearly an advantage for the end user, so it appeared that microdosing was necessary. We found out afterward, however, that this wasn't entirely true.

Martin and I began to sketch out a series of machines with different features that could respond to the different levels of customers' and users' needs. The cross-functional team was waiting for us to contribute to the project with a better machine that evolved from the existing prototype; we decided to redesign the brief itself.

As we had already seen, one of the biggest problems in innovation— in every industry and product category—is that flocks of designers, marketers, engineers, and scientists often invest vast financial, intellectual, and emotional resources, over months and months of research, processing, experimentation, and prototyping, in projects that respond perfectly to an entirely wrong set of questions. True, concrete, authentic, successful innovation, on the other hand, begins by asking yourself what the right questions are and translating them into a proper brief. In this project, the very first step to take, before anything else, was to rethink the initial question: What did our users really want? And that's what we tried to do.

The quality of the question is fundamental: far too often, people generate a whole set of correct answers for a whole set of wrong questions. And too often, people forget to question the validity of their questions, finding comfort instead in the correctness of their answers.

Arrogance Isn't Just Annoying—It's Dangerous

From a cultural point of view, however, for the team to digest this rethinking right away would have been far from simple. I was the last one in, the youngest person in the group, I dressed in a strange way, I had a strange accent, and above all I was a designer: I wasn't a business leader, an engineer, or a scientist. I was a creative. I was *culturally diverse*. And diversity is not always accepted by the system, above all when, in addition to being aesthetically different, you also behave in a different way, a way that doesn't conform. Many of my colleagues in those first weeks of collaboration probably were wondering, "What can this young guy from Italy know about a project like this? He doesn't even have any experience in food and beverage!" They just had no idea how much I loved to eat and drink; it's imprinted in our Italian DNA!

Jokes aside, they were partly right, of course. I knew innovation. I knew its tools, its processes, and its principles; I knew how to think, to reflect, to feel as an innovator—but I didn't know the industry, the customers, the company. I had the experience of hundreds of projects, but nothing from the world of food and beverage and nothing at PepsiCo. So I needed to have a little caution as I moved ahead; there was clearly a steep learning curve that I needed to take into account to avoid losing my footing or making naive generalizations. And no doubt I had much to learn from many of the leaders at the time, who had decades of experience in that industry.

Over the years, I have seen so many managers join companies in an impetuous, pedantic way, arrogantly believing that they already had all the answers in their possession, imposing top-down commands and approaches, even before they decoded the organization's culture, processes, problems, and opportunities. These are matters that need to be understood not superficially but on a very deep level, with all of the nuances and invisible changes in tone that make a difference. I have always wanted to avoid this error—not only because it's not in my nature, but because most of the time it's also a fatal mistake. I had to carefully mix respect and determination, facts and intuition, integration and change, humility and confidence, listening and doing. And so, while we were working on the initial brief—trying to absorb everything that we could about the company, the industry, the project, the end user, the distribution channel, the business model, the key technologies—Martin and I started to work in parallel on our alternative brief. We had to move very rapidly; there wasn't much time to lose.

Decisions That Can Change the Game

A meeting in mid-December 2012 represented the first official turning point in the right direction. A few months earlier, Indra Nooyi, unsatisfied with how the project was unfolding, had made three key decisions in an attempt to modify the endemic conditions necessary for an important change of tack.

The first decision had been to introduce an element of cultural disturbance, which acted as an ignition for a project shake-up. This element took the form of two people: Brad Jakeman, who had been brought in from the business world a year earlier, and myself, from the world of design and innovation. It was Brad who had found me in Minnesota, wanted me at PepsiCo, and presented me to Indra in New York; we had a very well-tuned synergy. Brad and Mauro, with fresh points of view on marketing and design, were meant to shake up that project—and much more besides.

The second key decision was to create a task force at the top of the company to monitor the project regularly and directly, ensuring that everything was moving forward in the right way and assuming the responsibility to eliminate any potential obstacle in the process. Indra was part of this task force as CEO, along with the chief technical officer, Mehmood Khan; the CEO of the US beverage business, Al Carey; the president of the global beverage business, Brad; the president of the food service channel, Tom Bené; and the chief human resources officer, Cynthia Trudell. This was indeed not simply a product innovation project, but also, and above all, a project that directly impacted culture, organization, and processes.

The third decision had already been made almost a year earlier and was a very important one. Indra created a specific cross-functional team, with its own significant budget, protected from other business priorities:

no one could touch that investment or reprioritize any part of it over the course of the year.

In other words, the formula to intervene in the situation relied on three essential elements: new technical and cultural know-how; direct, top-down support; and dedicated resources—in terms of both personnel and budget.

At that meeting in December, Indra was at the head of a horseshoe table, and around the table were all the members of the task force's executive team. We talked about the project for around an hour, revising prototypes, discussing timelines, investments, and risks. It was a meeting like many others before it. But in the last ten minutes, something happened that changed the direction of the whole project forever. Before the meeting ended, I whipped out of my bag, with a distracted air of nonchalance, a couple of printed pages with renderings that presented a set of soda fountains lined up one against the other. With a mix of calculated naivete, calibrated respect, and the reckless courage of a newcomer, I shared with them the idea that Martin and I had developed.

What I presented was a portfolio of machines that began with a small fountain, with an iPad-like screen, to set on existing countertops, and continued all the way to a machine with all the functions, similar to the competition in terms of dimensions but with a much bigger screen, of more than thirty inches. A couple of units with intermediate features were in the middle of the portfolio.

The basic intuition that allowed us to make a fountain with very small dimensions was to remove the ice maker, which completely changed the form of the dispenser, resulting in a much less cumbersome machine that could be positioned on any surface. By working hand in hand with the R&D team we learned that to mix the soda in different flavors, microdosing wasn't strictly necessary: we could change the valves, getting a similar result while exploiting the existing bag-in-box technology. We could use the traditional tech and still give users the option of creating any mix they desired: starting from drinks such as Pepsi, Mountain Dew, 7Up, and just plain soda water, the user could then add dozens of different flavors (lemon, vanilla, peach, cherry, and many more), whether individually or together, creating thousands of distinct combinations.

The competition was offering a preestablished mixture—for example, vanilla cola or cherry cola—without the chance to mix the basic soda with different flavors directly through the interface, which is what our own machine would be able to do.

As I've already mentioned, our conversations with customers had shown us that the size of the bag-in-box didn't really represent a big problem for most restaurants, which had already allocated space to the equipment and didn't feel a particular need to free up that space. We could thus use the traditional technology, lowering the production costs, reducing the dimensions, and investing in other features we believed to be more relevant for the end user—such as larger screens with higher resolutions and more powerful processors, which would provide the opportunity to improve the UX (user experience) and UI (user interface).

The renderings that I shared in the meeting—which depicted the soda fountains as if they already existed—were essentially bidimensional prototypes. We knew that they were technically feasible (technical feasibility), responsive to the needs of our target users and customers (desirability), and ideal for our business model (economic viability), but an infinite number of details still had to be discussed and resolved. We had created the renderings in a rush, to drive forward and facilitate the necessary preliminary conversations with users and customers, with the R&D team and our technological partners, and with marketing and top management. These renderings had the role that all prototypes must have in this phase:

- They were *shiny objects* that I could point to in order to gain the task force's support.
- They enabled the possible *alignment* of the team around the strategy to be taken.
- They could begin to generate *confidence* in our group's ability to create something exceptional.
- They would then function to activate further, increasingly detailed conversations with the cross-functional working group and then with users and customers, beginning the process of *co-creation* with them.

And the prototypes were up to the challenge: the task force gave the OK to go ahead with the idea. In the R&D team, from Slim to Mehmood Khan, we found a set of fantastic partners who couldn't wait to own this effort with us, and the project thus took off on the wings of enthusiasm in a new direction.

In transitioning from designing one machine to designing a set of fountains, one of the main problems could have been the cost, of both development and production. One key idea to guarantee the project's feasibility, therefore, was to reach a reasonable cost by using a platform approach: each machine shared a series of components to guarantee a level of production efficiency that would make the development of a whole family of products economically possible.

The design of the digital interface was another very important strategic element. The interface had a dual role: on the one hand, it had to attract people at a distance, who might come across it in a movie theater, a shopping mall, a restaurant; on the other hand, we wanted to create the perfect experience for users in the moment that they selected and poured their own beverage. Large screens gave us an exceptional competitive advantage from this point of view. The talented Richard Bates—whom I had just hired as vice president of corporate brand design—headed up that side of the project. We created a very dynamic animated experience, able to catch the user's attention from a distance of several feet or more, but also extremely intuitive and friendly to use when it came to creating your mix and dispensing your drink.

As far as the product design was concerned, we decided to celebrate one element in all of the different models, creating a visual reference and a branding cue that would be as iconic as possible. This element was the screen. It was the portal that accessed the whole experience, the interface that connected you to your favorite drink, the entry point to beginning your personal and personalized journey. It was the overarching protagonist of our design.

These were smart machines that would also provide us a real-time snapshot of all the different soda mixes created by our users. This was extremely precious data that could be passed on to our strategy team as they worked to define the beverage portfolio of the future. The screen would also give us the opportunity to communicate with users in different ways: functional communication, for example, in recommending the best food on the menu to pair with the user's drink; emotional communication, such as sharing the mixes created by other people in the user's community; and entertaining communication, such as candid camera moments that could be captured by filming users' reactions when surprised by a celebrity appearing on the screen and talking to them—wonderful viral content that could then be shared online.

Over the span of just a few months of hard work involving every function of the company, the food service business team managed to put three models of fountains on the market. And then we developed others to follow up on these. Our biggest success was the fountain that had the smallest dimensions but still retained very advanced functional features, achieved at a cost that gave us the ability to position it at a much lower price point than that of the competition. We broke all sales expectations, consolidating our relationship with existing customers—who enjoyed seeing a PepsiCo that was investing in real innovation—and helping us to find new prestigious clients, as well as winning dozens upon dozens of design awards around the world. But above all, we demonstrated to the company that we could do innovation in a different way, leveraging a new and disruptive culture. This kind of innovation was less about competing with other companies and brands and more about creating the most extraordinary experience for the end user. It was an entirely human-centered (or design-driven) kind of innovation.

That project also had a collateral effect that was particularly appreciated by your author. Success meant I didn't lose my job only a few months after entering the company—which is no bad thing.

In the years that followed, we designed and launched a whole series of pieces of equipment, including coolers, fountains, vending machines, and dispensers, continually reinforcing the role of this approach to innovation. We were always trying to find a perfect balance of desirability, technical feasibility, and economic viability—in other words, among human beings, technology, and business.

The Next Level of Human-Centered Innovation

I'm particularly proud of one of the most recent products we have generated through this approach, the Alternative Hydration Platform, later rebaptized as SodaStream Professional. The product is a dispenser that distributes water while providing the possibility to personalize the flavor according to your own tastes and physical needs: you can regulate the level of carbonation (from flat to sparkling) and the temperature (from cold to ambient), and you can also add a range of different flavors, selecting the intensity (from light to strong), as well as a series of functional ingredients (including vitamin B complex and electrolytes).

Users are provided with a reusable aluminum bottle with a QR code that is identified through a digital reader, or they can download an app that allows a contactless interaction with the machine. In this way, they can save their preferences and bring them up when needed. Different forms of payment are available, including a subscription formula with a monthly fee, similar to services used in the music industry, for example.

What I specifically love about this new evolution of these machines is that it represents a further step toward an ecosystem of beverage solutions that are eco-friendly, healthy, and personalizable. SodaStream Professional is part of a whole set of similar projects, all focused on researching and launching to market a series of products, packaging, and materials that are more sustainable, more meaningful to people, and tailored to their needs and wants. And the latest technologies are a wonderful enabler of this vision.

Gatorade GX is another perfect example. It's a platform that, like SodaStream Professional, utilizes a reusable proprietary bottle. In this case, though, the core innovation is a smart patch that you apply to your skin, to monitor your perspiration and receive advice, through an app, on the best Gatorade formula for your specific physical needs. That formula is provided through a pod with a concentrate that you then blend with water in your own personalized bottle. It's a healthy product, customized for you, sustainable, and enabled by the latest technologies—from wearable devices to smart apps.

These are just a few examples of a much broader strategy at the core of Ramon Laguarta's vision since he took the CEO position at PepsiCo in 2018. Ramon has seen the human-centered approach to innovation as a fundamental driver for the organization's growth, and he has enabled our design department to play an essential role in this strategy. I have no idea whether these devices, in this exact configuration, will still be around in ten years' time, but I am certain that future products will have the same design philosophy: they will be increasingly smart, adaptable to our needs, designed to be as healthy as possible, and always respectful of the environment, within the limits of what technology and society allow designers, engineers, scientitsts, and entrepreneurs to do.

Human-Centered Design Versus Environment-Centered Design

This is what human-centricity is all about: an approach to innovation that creates value for people and for the world in which they live. The sterile polemic that contraposes human-centered design and environment-centered (or eco-centered) design starts from a wrong understanding of what innovation focused on people is about.

Let me clarify my perspective with an example: If you were designing a series of products, brands, and services for your children using a human-centered approach, would you create solutions that destroy the bed where they sleep, the room where they play, and the house where they live? You wouldn't. That wouldn't be human-centered design; it wouldn't create any value for your kids. So why would anybody think that human-centered design could generate any product that consciously destroys our environment and the other species living in it that are part of our ecosystem?

It's in human beings' interest to preserve and protect the "house" in which they live, their planet, with its inhabitants. That's what real human-centered design tries to do. Environment-centered design is a key component of human-centered design.

CHAPTER 4

USER-GENERATED CONTENT

The human-centered approach to innovation is not limited to the creation of new products. We can apply the same principles to the world of branding as well.

In their brand-building projects, marketers the world over have spent years following a specific and consolidated playbook: you define the brand positioning, create a message, think up a story, build a campaign around it, and then you *impose it* on the end user through traditional media channels, with television crowned as the indisputable ruler for reach and impact. This was a communication flow that went in one direction: a brand would speak to the audience without any chance for reply, frequently interrupting the rhythm of content that for the viewer was much more interesting (such as a movie or a show). There was no way to avoid that communication except by switching channels while waiting for it to end. To be clear, sometimes those communications were appreciated for their informative content or for their level of entertainment. There were even some eagerly awaited moments, as with *Carosello*, a ten-minute advertising slot of sponsored entertainment that appeared on TV daily before the evening news in my own beloved Italy in the 1960s and 1970s—and there still are some today, such as the hyper-produced ads for the US Super Bowl. But that wasn't the norm, and it certainly isn't today. I remember my anxiety as a child when watching

TV with my parents, when my dad kept changing the channel with irritation as soon as there was a *réclame* (which is what we called the ads back in the 1980s); I was always scared that he wouldn't zap back in time for the movie we were watching and that we would miss precious minutes of the show. In general, people resented the intrusion of publicity, but they had no choice except to endure it.

This was the case until new platforms began to emerge, first taking the form of very simple internet sites and then gradually taking the shape of what we have come to call social media and content on demand. In this way, the entire context has been completely overturned in the space of a very few years.

In today's digital world, brands are no longer the sole senders of product messaging that is then passively received. Sometimes brands are engaged in a two-way conversation with active interlocutors who are often informed, frequently critical, and certainly interested in sharing their own point of view. Most of the time, though, brands are not even involved in a dialogue but instead become the passive object of conversation in an exchange that takes place between people dispersed across the global forum of social media.

Sometimes this conversation takes on positive tones, when the brand is admired, shared, even celebrated for its vision and behaviors. At other times, though, the conversation is tinged with a negative tone, and the brand is criticized, attacked, and censured. These exchanges and dialogues on the virtual stages of the web have an incredible potential impact: if the argument becomes fiery and people with the right network decide to amplify it, in the span of a few hours these messages can take on the dimensions of an uncontrollable planetary media tsunami, for better or for worse, reaching hundreds of millions of human beings in the blink of an eye.

Every brand in the world has had to evolve over recent years from the privileged condition of being the only *actor* in a one-way conversation, perfectly planned and carefully designed up front, to becoming the *object* of an exchange of ideas that is completely free and unpredictable instead. They have had to shift from a comfortable, controllable context in which they could simply *buy the right* to speak to an audience by acquiring media space, to the new current situation in which they have to *earn the chance*, not so much to speak to someone, but rather to become the topic of a conversation between free and autonomous beings. If the brand's content isn't relevant, interesting, current, and meaningful for the target audience, then it simply won't be taken into consideration. It won't be appreciated, it won't be discussed, and it certainly won't be shared and amplified. That kind of content will fail to inspire other content. It will be sterile and, as such, will die.

Either a specific audience is understood on a deep level, in terms of what is intellectually and emotionally interesting to that audience, in a process of monitoring and reacting to how those interests change on a daily basis—or the content is progressively condemned to the trash can. For sure, media space can still be bought; you can still pay to be present, to shout, to make yourself heard, and this is certainly an important lever. But if the messages that you're shouting aren't relevant, that content simply becomes irritating noise to be blocked out or even fought against. And now, viewers have a greater ability to make themselves be respected than they did in the past.

This generates a strikingly obvious consequence for any business: if our brands are able to engage their users in a good way, to the point of inspiring users to generate positive content on the brands' behalf, then we possess an extraordinary asset. The other clear consequence is that users do not react solely to content brought to them through traditional communication platforms—whether TV, print, or digital. We can reach users wherever they are, through their daily experiences: when they acquire a product, when they use it, when they practice a sport, when they walk in the street, when they go to a concert, when they dine at a restaurant. If these experiences with our brands are relevant, unique, and meaningful, then there is a greater chance that users will be disposed to share these experiences, creating their own content and becoming spontaneous brand ambassadors. This is "user-generated content." Our role as brand leaders is to understand how to inspire it!

User-generated content is made by individuals who communicate, either directly or indirectly, with other individuals. One of the most powerful forms of such content is that generated spontaneously, as a reaction to an experience and without commercial ends. For this kind of communication to have an impact, it's important that the receiver trusts the sender and that the sender doesn't betray that trust. This means that content commissioned and paid for by brands always poses a certain risk, both for the brand and for the creator. Creators can assume different forms: they might be a renowned influencer, a close friend, or a trusted colleague. They become creators when they tell a story about something they have discovered, used, or appreciated personally. We are then the receivers. Every one of us is surrounded by people who share messages of this kind every single day. And each one of us, in turn, can be that dear friend, trusted colleague, or even far-off influencer for someone else.

By pure chance, while I was writing these words something happened that took me almost by surprise, leaving me speechless for its striking relevance to this topic. I had just finished typing the last words of the previous paragraph and was taking a coffee break; while I sipped my drink (it wasn't my typical espresso; it was an American coffee and thus sippable), I started to write one of my usual daily posts on my social media channels, without even thinking about it. These posts are a sort of public journal, through which I share my thoughts, reflections, and emotions, day after day. And then they are also a way to detach and relax; this is how I found myself writing something even when I was supposed to be taking a break from writing.

A few moments before, with my cup of coffee in my hand, I had been leafing through a digital photo album on my cell phone, and I came across a particular image, snapped a few days earlier by my wife, Carlotta, in our house in the Hamptons. It showed me seated on a couch next to a series of rag dolls representing different famous figures from the history of world culture, from literature to science, from art to religion, from politics to philosophy and more: from Frida Kahlo to Sigmund Freud, from Abraham Lincoln to Edgar Allan Poe, from Albert Einstein to Andy Warhol. The dolls are called the Little Thinkers and make a wonderful gift for any child, offering the magic of a toy mixed with a history lesson and a life story. Entertainment meets with education, and it's a joy for both the eyes and the mind. And from personal experience, I can assure you that anyone who has an inner child, whatever that person's outer age, will greatly appreciate the dolls, too.

It was Tony Chambers—back then editor in chief at the magazine *Wallpaper*—who first showed me these dolls, one evening some years ago in a pub in Singapore. We were enjoying a Japanese beer and some unidentified starters when he told me about his daughter, Olive, who, at only four years old, held long conversations during dinner parties about Picasso, Frank Lloyd Wright, and Shakespeare (whom she called Shakey!). Obviously she wasn't talking about the real historical figures; she was just sharing tales about her dolls. But thanks to those puppets, the small girl was learning about these timeless creators of culture and had begun to fall in love with them, considering them to be her "friends."

Inspired by my wife's photo, I decided to share the memory online. Thousands of people appreciated it; hundreds of them took the time to write positive comments; and, above all, dozens of people decided to tell me that they had immediately bought one of those dolls as soon as they had read the post. One person in particular wrote me something that caught my curiosity: he was thanking me because, while looking at the Little Thinkers website, he had found a unique watch, with a quadrant depicting the face of the artist Salvador Dalí. I went online to check it out, found the object, also liked it, and bought one for myself as well.

My spontaneous "share," inspired by the value that those beautiful dolls had for me and for my friend Tony before me, generated value for the brand, value for the tens of thousands of people who connect with me through social media, and finally new value also for myself, inspired as I was by the inspiration kindled in my own followers. Value, value, value, multiplied to an infinite degree!

When I went back to the computer to continue writing this book, I realized that, in an entirely unconscious way, I had just experienced exactly what I was trying to describe in these pages. I had shared something with the world that had inspired me and that I hoped would inspire thousands of other people. I had done so without any commercial goal, without any personal interest, through pure gratitude for the value that I was personally enjoying and the pure desire to put that value in the hands of many other people like myself. More or less knowingly, I had become a formidable brand ambassador for those dolls. The brand had created value for me, and I was creating value for others. And in this virtuous circle, I had also given value back to the brand itself.

And my experience is certainly not an anomaly. It's something that happens all the time, on different scales, every day, between all of us. Before social media, how many times did we find ourselves talking about a product we loved, recommending a brand that fascinated us, or criticizing an object that had let us down? Malcolm Gladwell has eloquently recounted this story in his book *The Tipping Point*.[1] In the past, we shared brand experiences like this one only through personal conversations, on the phone with relatives or at dinner with friends. Tony did the same thing with me at that pub in Singapore. Today, we also share our experiences in the virtual *piazza* of the social media world, and our conversations no longer have any boundaries of time or space.

Value is thus the prime mover for generating content. Value is what drives someone to invest time, creativity, and intellect in creating and sharing a message about a product or an experience. Every individual reacts in a positive way to an experience that is *meaningful* to that person—that adds some kind of value to the person's own life.

This value can be emotional or functional; it can be a gentle gesture that touches our soul in a totally unexpected way or a major event, with very profound effects, that visibly impacts society as a whole. And value can take on many different forms: from entertainment to security, from comfort to enjoyment, from sustainability to health, from convenience to style, in our own lives and in the lives of the people surrounding us. When we come into contact with a particularly functional object that makes a task exponentially easier; when we interact with a brand that is purposefully impacting our community in an extraordinary way; when we come across beautiful limited-edition packaging that was designed for an occasion important to us; when we enjoy a memorable experience during a concert by our favorite band; when we find an unexpectedly pleasing lotion, drink, or piece of furniture in a hotel room; when we are inspired by a show put on by a brand in a shopping mall; when we walk into a marvelous pop-up store in the city—in all of these moments and many more, a spring is activated inside of us. We are inspired and excited by the experiences that touch our hearts and minds; we discover them and make them our own, both intellectually and emotionally. When that happens, there is then a good chance that this special moment will drive

A trend is designed on a chart like a curve; a trend is a wave. The innovator—at least the good innovator—is a surfer of trends, the kind who gets the wave before anyone else!

us to take our phone from our pocket, snap a photo or record a video, and share that experience with the rest of the world—in a spontaneous, authentic, and meaningful way.

Discovering, Owning, Sharing

What I have just described is a three-phase process that I have summarized using a simple acronym, DOS—for *discovering, owning,* and *sharing.*

We *discover* something we have never experienced before that is relevant to us.

That experience—in the very moment in which we live it—becomes our own and only ours; we *own* that experience.

We are then ready to *share* it, with pride, passion, and joy—or sometimes with disdain, depending on the nature of the experience.

This is a journey full of extremely important implications for any business, an alchemist's recipe that has practical potential to transform every touchpoint of a brand into user-generated content. This is the huge novelty of the world we're living in today as entrepreneurs, business leaders, designers, and innovators. Every object, brand, space, service, and experience can be turned into potential content created by people—content that is real, spontaneous, and difficult to tame.

This is new and partly unexplored territory, for the most part still to be developed by many organizations big and small, from recently formed start-ups to consolidated multinational corporations. This is the realm of true innovation: innovation that, instead of being applied to the invention and creation of a new product, is applied to the world of branding; innovation in channels and platforms, in codes and languages, in meaning; innovation that creates value first for people and then, as a consequence, for business. This is human-centered innovation applied to the world of branding.

Empathy + Strategy + Prototyping Applied to the World of Branding

Yet again, just as in the world of product innovation, we need the proper tools for navigating the complexities of these lands awaiting discovery. And that's why the synergic use of *empathy, strategy,* and *prototyping,* typical of the design world, becomes a powerful approach to use in the realm of branding as well.

We need to understand our users with *empathy* to comprehend their needs and wants, desires and frustrations, curiosities and ideas, and to then respond with content that is passionate, informed, engaging, coherent, and ultimately relevant, across different channels, making use of nontraditional media such as packaging, interior design, licensing, and real-world experience, whether in a shop, a restaurant, a stadium, or a theater. That same user who was reached once upon a time by one-way, aggressive communication that traveled calmly, without interruption, along the highway of television, radio, and print media, now needs to be approached with relevant content on multiple platforms, made up of many roadways, alleys, and public squares, with *omni-channel,* 360-degree communication. Products, packaging, services, and environments, if designed in a meaningful way, will trigger an emotional and intellectual process that pushes users to share content with others. "Meaningfulness" is the keyword; the main starting point to reach that relevant meaning is the ability to listen to people every day with the heart and mind, leveraging all of the tools that technology can offer us, from data to artificial intelligence, and combining them with a strong dose of intuition and personal sensitivity.

Based on these insights, we can then build *strategies* and *prototypes,* in a repeatable process, similar to the one described earlier for a product but in this case applied to different elements: the elements of communication.

CHAPTER 5

THE MAGIC OF EXPERIENCES

At PepsiCo, in the past several years, we have experimented with energy and passion on a vast range of projects aimed at building and growing our brands with an experiential approach, outside of the traditional grounds of communication, transforming every touchpoint of those brands into potential content to share. This has been a journey made up of attempts—some in error, many successful—that we have strongly believed in and that we've learned from, product after product, experience after experience, one step at a time but on a scale that has grown bigger and bigger with each step.

I want to share with you a few brand innovation stories. I won't talk only about the results but also about the journey that generated them; the difficulties we had to overcome; and the approaches, strategies, and behaviors of the people who imagined, desired, and created these results.

Pepsi, Michael J. Fox, and *Back to the Future 2*

Beginning in my first months at PepsiCo, I tried to think about how to increasingly transform the packaging of our products into potential content for communication, and I never lost an opportunity to share this vision with the team that I was forming. One day, in February 2013,

Martin Broen came into my office and told me about an idea he'd had. The year 2015 would be the thirtieth anniversary of the release of the movie *Back to the Future 2*, and October 21 of that year was the exact date on which, in the movie, Marty McFly and Doc Brown flew into their future. PepsiCo had taken pride in the film's having featured one of the most famous product placements in the history of cinema. The actor Michael J. Fox walks into a bar and asks for a Pepsi, and magically a bottle of our cola appears before him, with a futuristic design, a redesigned logo, and a name never heard of before: "Pepsi Perfect." Martin's idea was to make Pepsi Perfect into a reality, designing it, producing it, and launching it in the very year that Marty and Doc Brown went back to the future in the movie. "It's sure to be a success!" We started work right away: empathy, strategy, prototyping in action. The movie was known and loved on a mass level; its audience was the perfect target for our brand. We could make a limited edition bottle to sell online. The price would be higher than that of a standard bottle, considering the high costs of production, but it would really be a collector's piece more than a product acquired to be consumed. In fact, the product wouldn't even need to be profitable, so long as it covered the costs of its design, production, and distribution. In other words, producing the product was purely a branding operation.

We began by sharing the idea with a range of colleagues in marketing and R&D, and then with friends and family, to start collecting feedback from end users that could offer a fresh take. We were gathering insights and ideas in the three spheres of innovation: desirability (Did people want the product?), technical feasibility (Could we produce it? How complex would it be to produce it?), and economic viability (Did the product make sense from a business point of view?). We didn't need to have a design, because the product already existed in the film; a quick Google search allowed us to share this first prototype with anybody. We found a general and widespread interest among the people we spoke to within the company, but no one demonstrated that extreme enthusiasm necessary to officially kick off the project. That didn't come as a surprise; the business team was made up of people who were constantly bombarded with new project proposals and related requests for funding. To convince them of the strength of any given idea was never an easy task.

Now that we were aware of the realities of the situation, the next step was to take the product—which until then had only been experienced in a bidimensional frame of a film—and make it into something concrete, tangible, and three-dimensional. We made a 3D prototype in resin, without any graphics, to try out the size, to understand its dimensions, and mostly to have an object in our hand, something we could show people and share. And, as we expected, the level of interest began to increase. The conversations were the same, but people's reactions began to be more excited; they felt involved, they were engaged, and their questions were more on point. Encouraged by these encounters, over the following months we kept improving the quality of the model, arriving at a mock-up similar to what ended up being the final product, and people's enthusiasm started to be increasingly evident and clear. The prototyping strategy was working.

But we knew that our idea would still come up against the annual marketing agenda, which had been strategically defined months before, with a whole series of activations already planned for the year. There was no place for an idea of this kind, which didn't fit into a plan for the summer, for Christmas, for back-to-school, or in those sponsored partnerships with, for example, the NFL and the Super Bowl or Live Nation and its musical events. But we kept on nevertheless, with endless passion, driving forward the idea with our prototypes in hand, putting them on the desks of all the key decision makers—the people with the authority and resources to activate the program.

This is how we continued until finally, in February 2015, an inspired marketer decided to give the idea a go, making use of a gap that happened to occur in the year's calendar. Anyone who knows anything about the complexity of planning and developing operations of this kind in a company of our size will immediately realize that the time span at our disposal was extremely narrow. And yet, despite all this, with a full cross-functional effort, carried along on the wings of our collective enthusiasm, we managed to pull it off.

On October 21, 2015, at 4:29 a.m., the company launched Pepsi Perfect on Amazon and on Walmart's online shopping platform. This was the exact date and time in which Marty McFly was meant to have arrived in the future, to which he had traveling from thirty years earlier. Long virtual queues of people had already lined up online, ready to jump on the product. We sold every item in the space of a few minutes. Pepsi announced on Twitter that morning: "As promised, our limited edition bottles of #PepsiPerfect went on sale this #bttf morning! It sold out faster than we can say 1.21 Gigawatts." "Bttf" was an acronym referring to the title of the movie, while "1.21 Gigawatts," for film buffs, was a reference to the electricity needed to fuel Doc Brown's time machine. We produced only a limited number of bottles. The thousands of fans who were left without the product expressed their disappointment in a such a loud way that we decided to start a second production run to satisfy at least a part of the pressing demand made by the most enthusiastic of them.

We developed the bottle in collaboration with Universal to ensure we stayed true to the original object. The secondary packaging—the collector's box that the bottle came in to protect it—reproduced the DeLorean time machine that carried the story's hero into the future, showing the hour, day, month, and year of the characters' arrival, which was the same hour, day, month, and year as the product's online launch. We then designed a series of fashion accessories to celebrate the project: caps, T-shirts, and jackets. Within a few weeks, we had sold a completely unexpected number of them, beating all expectations.

The product was distributed only in the United States, but it was discussed for months the whole world over, with millions upon millions of media impressions. The bottle found a way of reaching every corner of the globe, far outside of North America. The project was a further demonstration of the fact that we are living in a completely "glocal" world, where local operations organically become the object of global conversations, given that the internet has neither borders nor dividing walls. Even when one zone of the world tries to enforce these borders, by creating a program that on paper is supposed to remain local, people find a way of getting around those walls. Usually, this kind of universal dissemination happens when a program has global relevance, with content of international interest. And it can occur whether the reaction to the content is positive or negative overall.

Over the following months—and even for some years afterward—we found the collector's packaging on sale on digital platforms such as eBay, going for sums much higher than the original price and reaching peaks of $500 at times.

The project was the first in a series to demonstrate the potential of a "medium" that didn't fit into traditional categories of communication. The project did not involve a TV ad or digital content per se. The "medium" was an object. That bottle was both a communication channel, encapsulating a message created by Pepsi for its own users and influencers, and also communication content, as produced consequentially by the product's users and influencers when they then shared their experience with the whole world.

Pepsi and Beyoncé

The same approach can also be applied to the graphic design of a product's packaging, without changing its structure. My very first project in PepsiCo was of this kind. We had to celebrate a collaboration between Pepsi and Beyoncé on the occasion of the Super Bowl in New Orleans. We organized a photo shoot with one of the most famous fashion photographers in the world, Patrick Demarchelier, and starting from these pictures we generated a series of paintings of the American superstar. We used pop-art language, full of colors and energy, reminiscent of Andy Warhol, an artist I really love. The campaign was an implicit homage to Warhol's exceptional creativity and his unique celebration of the mixing of art and business. We used these images on cans and bottles, on secondary packaging, on billboards, online, and on a whole variety of different platforms. The campaign was a huge success, bouncing across world media, with content partly created by ourselves for the big media channels, but mostly generated by millions of people who reacted with appreciation for this artistic dialogue between Beyoncé and Pepsi. The images are still there on the walls of the PepsiCo headquarters in Purchase, just outside New York City.

This has always been our challenge: to define the artistic level of every design operation, in a portfolio with more than twenty brands with revenues of more than a billion dollars, dozens of other brands with revenues of hundreds of millions of dollars, and products consumed more than one billion times every single day, in more than two hundred countries around the world. The complexity lies entirely in the capacity to create products that are both culturally accessible to billions of people across the globe and, at the same time, sophisticated enough to be celebrated by a very refined public of trendsetters and influencers. This balancing act is more necessary than ever before if we want packaging to become content—that is, to be able both to attract target audiences and to be shared, discussed, and ideally decanted in an authentic way onto digital platforms with the greatest possible reach and impact.

The ability to rise to this challenge is not just "technical." You need a kind of talent that is able to generate the right design, with the right empathy and aesthetic sensibility, based on the correct business strategy. But that talent also needs to have all the gifts essential for driving forward "anomalous" ideas in a system that might try to reject them. The person must be able to protect those ideas from the grinding machines of processes and culture, from the constraints imposed by market standards and system inertia, from the obstacles of superficial consumer research, and even from the pushback of risk-averse business leaders.

An enterprise's ability to handle packaging—both its graphics and structure—first as a channel of communication and then as content can exponentially amplify the potential of the enterprise's communication strategy. Some categories have been historically more inclined to this approach—for example, in the world of chocolate, from Baci Perugina to Ferrero Rocher to Hershey's Kisses; in the world of champagne, from Veuve Clicquot to Moët & Chandon, Dom Pérignon, and many more; and in the domain of fragrances and perfumes, from Jean Paul Gaultier to Chanel to Reed Krakoff, just to name a few. These are categories of products that lend themselves to the ritual of gift giving, and thus their brand strategists exploited this approach first.

But what we've developed at PepsiCo over the years, in a systematic way, with hundreds of operations throughout the world, connects with another kind of opportunity. This strategy mixes impulse buying of an unexpected product—one that is visually innovative, aesthetically attractive, formally distinct from the competition, emotionally and intellectually meaningful—with the desire to share that discovery through social media. And the strategy does so in product categories that don't belong to the traditional gift-giving ritual. This is a fundamental aspect. Remember DOS? *Discovering, owning, and sharing.* We discover a chocolate, a bottle of champagne, a cola, a snack, in unique, engaging, beautiful, high-quality packaging, and the experience becomes ours and ours alone; we make it our own. And then we're ready to share our experience—with members of our families when they come home, with our friends when we show off the product, and with the whole world if we decide to speak about it in the virtual forum of the internet.

The Super Bowl

Product and packaging are the most important touchpoints for a brand; they are the gates to access both purchase and use, the points in time that Procter and Gamble wisely defined some years ago as the "first moment of truth" and the "second moment of truth"—the phase in which the user comes into contact with the product for the first time, even before buying it, and following this, the phase in which the user uses the product and benefits from it. Thanks to the world of social media, product and packaging are no longer simply objects of purchase and use but also become, in users' hands, the potential content of communication.

There is nevertheless a series of other touchpoints that have this same potential. One of those touchpoints, which has become increasingly important for us, is the platform of events. PepsiCo has historically always invested in two main categories of events: music and sport. Exemplary are the significant sponsorships of the NFL and the Super Bowl, the NBA and the All-Star Game, the UEFA Champions League, and Live Nation—one of the most important live entertainment organizations in the world. Investment is also made in the stadiums of many sports, whose beverage stands are generally divided between the two main competitors, PepsiCo and the Coca-Cola Company. In the past, presence at these events was mainly exercised through our brands, with logos placed across walls, billboards, restaurant menus, soda fountains, and coolers. And on the occasion of big shows like the Super Bowl, important budgets would be allocated for the TV ads and the halftime show, which count as some of the most viewed—and most expensive—media events in the world.

In 2013, I began to work on my first Super Bowl, which was to take place in New York in February 2014. I had just gotten a flavor of the scale of the event during the project with Beyoncé, but having joined the company only in July 2012, I still hadn't had the chance to have an impact on the design of an event that needed to be planned more than a year in advance. The New York Super Bowl was my first chance to collaborate with the US business team to try to make something truly different.

On that occasion we decided to introduce a design tool that the company had never utilized before on this type of project: mapping the user journey. This is a process that I fell in love with when I was attending university and that I have always used to design any kind of experience. I led this project with a small team headed up by one of my closest leaders, Leighsa King. Leighsa is an intelligent, empathic, and brilliant thinker, responsible for what we used to call "business design," which played an essential role in the success of our nascent capability at PepsiCo back then and in all the years afterward. We began the project by dividing our target audience into six groups: customers and VIP guests of various kinds; influencers; the media; fans; our own employees; and finally all those New Yorkers who had little interest in football but, like it or lump it, would be reached by the presence of an event of that scale and grandeur in their city—we could make it fun for them to enjoy or an annoyance for them to endure.

Although the Super Bowl usually takes place on a Sunday, the majority of the audience begins to come to the hosting city in the week running up to the event, to start the festivities in advance. Each of the six groups would experience those days in a different way and with a different flow. We defined the unique phases of those experiences in great detail.

For our PepsiCo guests, for example, everything would start with the arrival in the airport—for those who were coming from other locations.

Every moment after that would be carefully considered and defined: the transport to their lodgings, their stay in hotels, their visits to the city, evening entertainment, the journey to the stadium, the game itself, the post-game moments, being ferried back to the airport, and finally departure for home. We designed every element, from the uniform of the workers welcoming people in the airport to what the workers would write on the placards to identify themselves, from the decoration of the shuttle exterior to the drinks, snacks, and gadgets our guests would find inside.

In the city, we concentrated on two different moments: people's experiences in their hotel rooms and their experiences in the outside world during the days leading up to the final game. We identified a strategic area in the hotel and completely transformed it, creating an installation that we called PepCity, the city of PepsiCo. At PepCity, we wanted to entertain and inform, to amuse and support. For example, in that space, that year in New York, we first presented our big customers with our new intelligent soda fountain, Spire, while creating unique musical moments and culinary journeys to entertain them. Every detail—from the design of the chairs to the food—was planned to create an encounter with the brands and the products that could be both iconic and memorable.

The other dimension we concentrated on was the entertainment outside of the hotel. We created a tent structure in New York's Bryant Park and filled it with art, music, and food experiences, in a disruptive, exuberant, explosive way. We selected emerging artists, such as the very talented Marcela Gutierrez, who painted to the rhythm of rap, entertaining fans, clients, and passing New Yorkers; we brought together a dream team of celebrity chefs, including David Burke, Marc Forgione, and Michael Psilakis, who made dishes and cocktails inspired by our snacks and drinks; and in the evening we concluded with concerts by stars such as Austin Mahone, Prince Royce, and Ziggy Marley. The space hosted a sculpture of a vintage Pepsi-Cola sign, inspired by the famous landmark by the East River facing Manhattan, re-created by the artist Daniel Arsham in his typical style, all in white. The most refined art and design crossed over with the most popular food and music, aimed at celebrating sport in a way that was simultaneously easy and sophisticated, in a democratic event open to all.

This experiential approach made more sense than ever because it was exponentially amplified through social media. The image of Pepsi-Cola sculpted by Arsham, the first dish served up by Burke with Quaker Oats, Prince Royce's performance in the park—all this bounced across the web, with content generated for us by people of every kind and moved along on the wings of genuine interest and spontaneous enthusiasm.

The key to success for this kind of initiative is not just the definition of the user journey and the envisioning of ideal experiences. What makes the difference is the quality of the execution, in that usual, challenging, and complex balancing act between extreme sophistication and mass market appeal—between art and commerce, inspiration and fun.

The approach generated such positive results that the company decided to repeat it every year, perfecting it and adding new elements, new variables, new criteria, new forms of entertainment. The following Super Bowl we had memorable collaborations with stars at the level of Bruno Mars, Snoop Dogg, and Pink; and that's without even mentioning the performers in the halftime show, with whom we worked in a variety of ways, from Lady Gaga to Justin Timberlake, from Katy Perry to Beyoncé, from J.Lo and Shakira to Coldplay, Maroon 5, and The Weeknd, from Eminem and Dr. Dre to Kendrick Lamar, Mary J. Blige, and many others. Art, food, music, and sport all came together in a unique, unforgettable experience, which then became content in the hands of users and amplified itself in an exponential yet entirely natural way. Marketing and design worked hand in hand; it's not an obvious marriage, but it works perfectly. When we began to sponsor the UEFA Champions League over the following years, we brought this approach to that world as well. The first final was in my very own Milan, and I will always remember with great affection the beautiful concert in Piazza Duomo given by my good friend Benny Benassi.

Milan Design Week

These events, aside from representing communication moments for our company and brands, have been playing another important role for us over the years. They have also served as precious platforms to test innovative ideas.

We have frequently utilized Milan Design Week in this way. On the one hand, it works as a sophisticated window display of our brands for a public coming from every corner of the globe; around half a million people from 188 different countries flock to the city for a week. On the other hand, the event also functions as a workshop, where we can test out innovative ideas and establish a new conversation with partners, designers, influencers, customers, journalists, and end users. Essentially, we manage to transform a moment of communication into a fully fledged experimental laboratory—a laboratory that, by the way, is essentially free of cost, as it is built on the strong back of an existing platform in which we would have invested anyway.

We create installations that are experiments in all but name. They act as prototypes in the process of innovation and, as such, they unlock the whole set of benefits that we have previously discussed: alignment, co-creation, shiny objects, and confidence. Through them we collect feedback and insights. This feedback and these insights are priceless, as they help us to understand how desirable an idea is, to better define its feasibility and validate its economic viability. And they produce confidence within the company about the effective potential of a project, aligning the organization around the power of the concept.

In Milan, we have generated completely unexpected activations with our products. For example, the legendary Bublz, a multisensorial soda experience, then evolved into successful installations for customers such as Disneyland Shanghai and Hersheypark in Pennsylvania; our Tea House became a summer pop-up in Manhattan and a modular approach in communication for our tea business; the Kola House was later transformed into a restaurant and club in the Meatpacking District in New York; and Lay's Chiperie became the basis for events and installations from China to the United States.

In Milan we have also experimented with fashion, creating a partnership with *Vogue Italia* and the late Franca Sozzani, the magazine's passionate chief editor and a much-loved friend, designing a fashion collection inspired by the Pepsi brand, as well as launching a creative challenge for young talents worldwide. We have worked with Lapo Elkann, creating surprising and refined products inspired by the world of Pepsi, from eyewear to a Fiat 500 car, all in tune with the brand equity and vibe. And we did much, much more. These collaborations and collections were our early prototypes to inspire the company with a new and successful approach to our licensing strategy.

We've opened up dialogues and projects with stars across the creative world, with names such as Karim Rashid, Fabio Novembre, Marcelo Burlon, Stefano Giovannoni, Job Smeets from Studio Job, Patricia Urquiola, Paola Antonelli, Nicola Formichetti, Davide Oldani, and many more. I cite this long list of names because they are somehow unexpected: not, perhaps, the ones you usually associate with brands in the mass market. Once again, we were playing on the delicate and difficult blending between art and commerce, niche sophistication and mass appeal. For years, Milan Design Week has been a winning forum, representing a magical mix of communication, experimentation, and engagement with customers and users.

One of the key variables of success has always been the balance between the desire to dare, on the one hand (imagining installations and concepts that match up to one of the most important design events in the world), and on the other hand, the ability to create solutions that could be commercially relevant. Experiences were not generated for themselves; instead, we always obsessed over the business relevance of our ideas in the eyes of our customers. We wanted to inspire them by making them dream, sharing with them our ability to think big—but at the same time we wanted to demonstrate our pragmatism, which has the strength to transform those dreams into business value, both for them and for us together.

It's no coincidence that the key drivers of my design team's work in Milan were two global managers who were perfectly combining these two dimensions in their roles. On one side, there was Richard Bates, the experienced, sophisticated, intuitive, and gentle designer who for many years led our work for the food service business, the unit that owned PepsiCo's relationships with some of our biggest customers. On the other side, there was Matthieu Aquino, the first person I hired at 3M back in 2003—an intelligent, creative, astute, and headstrong leader, who then joined me at PepsiCo and, back then, was in charge of the experience design team.

By having those two roles oversee Milan Design Week, I was creating a healthy tension between experience and commerce, inspiration and business, dreaming and selling. Matthieu and Richard are two holistic design leaders who, during that part of their professional journey, were playing two specific and complementary roles. But they are also leaders who are perfectly capable of balancing the two dimensions on their own, to the extent that they swapped roles several times over the years, leading the two biggest units in our organization: the beverage business on one side and the food business on the other. And that's why that partnership worked so well, because the two leaders understood each other, and within that context, they knew how to interact with each other in perfect harmony.

And so we shared our vision with the top executives of some of the biggest chains of hotels, restaurants, and retail establishments in the world, immersing them in the reality of an innovative and visionary PepsiCo and then taking them out on a journey through the city in which every last detail was curated, to understand how other brands—in a vast range of categories, from automotive to furniture, from fashion to consumer electronics—create innovation for products, brands, services, and experiences during the Milan show. And our clients appreciated it. Our work in Milan was a way to strengthen our partnerships, create new ones, and nurture surprising and memorable dialogues. On our return from Milan, we followed up with meetings, brainstorming, new conversations, and new projects. Milan Design Week has been a central event for establishing and consolidating different relationships with important actors in our industry in unexpected ways—relationships that have then indirectly led to important contract renewals and hugely successful projects over the years.

Last but not least, this innovative approach contributed to repositioning PepsiCo in the eyes of the design and creative media. The late Marcus Fair, founder and chief editor at *Dezeen*, wrote in 2016, "Megabrands like Nike and PepsiCo have stolen the spotlight at this year's Milan Design

Week and are upstaging the traditional design brands." In the same article, he compared the two companies to Apple, which was also present at the Milan show that year. Only a few years earlier, PepsiCo would never even have been taken into consideration by the global design elite. Now it was being celebrated on a par with the sacred legends of design. The quantity of articles, spontaneous posts, and enthusiastic feedback that had sprung from social media across the world was generating new value for the company—a unique and different kind of value, unusual for a corporation in the CPG (consumer packaged goods) industry and, therefore, particularly precious, because it was also completely incremental. These events, products, and collaborations—all these touchpoints of the brand—became content in the global world of social media. A physical event seen by dozens of thousands of people was then exponentially amplified on the digital stage, reaching millions upon millions of other people. What this represents is innovation in how a mass market company communicates, a company that creates products to be sold at Carrefour and Walmart in the suburbs, in mom-and-pop stores in our neighborhoods, and in food trucks by our offices.

From Pepsi and Dsquared2 to Gatorade and Nike

The fashion collaborations in Milan have been early manifestations of a brand strategy that we started to work on years before, from 2014 onward, especially through our design team in Shanghai. From the very first day I joined PepsiCo, I have always appreciated the potential of our brands' merchandising and licensing in the world of fashion, apparel, and beyond. I see these pursuits as offering incredible opportunities to activate new connections and conversations with people all around the world.

You might not share your photos with your friends while drinking a Pepsi, because you might not consider it to be a particularly interesting moment—but you might proudly share your photo while wearing a "Pepsi by Dsquared2" hoodie that you just bought in a boutique store in your city. Gatorade might be your favorite sport drink, but it might not appear in any of your social media posts. And yet, you might perhaps share with the world the wonderful Gatorade edition of the Nike Air Jordan shoes that you just purchased online. Licensing is potential user-generated content waiting to happen. Licensing that is done well is positive exposure for your brand. And it's communication that pays for itself, as it also generates revenue. The ROI is crystal clear. That was our intuition and our strategy.

Back then, when we started to experiment in the world of licensing, Shanghai represented a magical and unexpected alchemy for us, a situation born out of an unusual mix of heterogeneous elements. China was—and still is today—the manufacturing engine of the fashion world, used behind the scenes by hundreds of luxury Western brands. The region's society was naturally predisposed to innovation and was comfortable with risk. The area's marketing culture therefore was naturally inclined toward innovation and risk, too, as a direct consequence. And the population was ready to experiment with brands and excited by novelty.

Now combine all of this with a very Italian design leader in love with the world of fashion. At the time PepsiCo's head of design in China was a young man with a Tuscan accent and Tuscany in the blood. His name was Gianmauro Vella, but everyone called him Gimmy. His style was cool, transgressive, sophisticated; you could easily spot him in Shanghai, with his visible earring and tattoos all over his body. He was a lover of social life and well connected to the creative community. I hired Gimmy as an intern at 3M in 2008, fresh out of the European Institute of Design, and in 2010, I asked him to move to Shanghai. When I joined PepsiCo and then decided to open the design center in China, I proposed that he come with us. It was the summer of 2014. With Gimmy, we immediately began to invest in licensing as a tool for supporting our brands in a new way. What PepsiCo China gave me—aside from Gimmy's aesthetic sensibility and cultural approach—was a unique agility, speed, and entrepreneurship that I have never witnessed at such levels in any other part of the world. I guess that my own Italy during the economic boom, or postwar America in the 1950s, might have had a comparable kind of energy and drive. Over time, Gimmy and I found a whole set of local marketers who understood us and wanted to go down the road of this new approach to brand building—people who had the will and desire to experiment.

Over the past few years, we have introduced a great number of fashion collections inspired by our brands, generating both revenues and enthusiasm, while also supporting the business teams in their own campaigns and promotions. Pepsi became the official sponsor of Shanghai Fashion Week and created an ecosystem of activations, products, and experiences that connected our fashion items with events, limited edition cans, online promotions, and digital content. China is a rich terrain for experimentation where we have pushed our user-generated content strategy to an extreme. The partnerships in fashion, limited edition packaging and products, and design-driven events are quantitatively on a par with what happens in the United States. But often, driven by local culture, China beats the United States in risk-taking and aesthetic innovation. China has been a space for prototyping, as well as a benchmark that I have used over the years to push many other countries to be more daring with design.

Our licensing and merchandising strategy today has grown a great deal, and since 2018 our design function has taken over the entire business responsibility, on top of art direction. To be clear: the company has trusted a bunch of designers with managing profits and incomes—and the business has grown exponentially! The credit goes to a series of business executives for believing in this idea and trusting the designers and to a series of creative leaders for delivering on the vision and exceeding expectations—two complementary forms of leadership, without which this initiative wouldn't be where it is today.

Matthieu Aquino manages the entire department from New York today, with a small team of experts. On top of this, over the past several years he first led the entire global beverage design team, with dozens of creative talents under him, and then the food design group, in full integration with the business leadership of these organizations, synching up our design vision with their commercial strategy. This has given us the opportunity to further accelerate the overall licensing strategy as both a revenue-generating platform and also, above all, a brand-building tool. Operations such as the collaborations between Pepsi and Puma, Fila and

Dsquared2, Cheetos and Forever 21, Ruffles and Nike, and Gatorade and Air Jordan are just some of the many examples of a new approach to branding, able to create enthusiasm and conversations, forming new and solid connections with our brands.

This is an extremely difficult platform to manage, requiring a holistic aesthetic sensibility and mastery of the world of fashion design, product, graphics, interiors, and digital, as well as a detailed understanding of business strategy. People such as Matthieu and Gimmy, who have grown up with me over the years and have matured as leaders through their journeys in both 3M and PepsiCo, have an entirely natural intuition, mixed with decades of experience, that cuts across worlds. They have been indispensable partners in repositioning licensing in the company as a branding tool. No process, business model, or strategy would have been sufficient if it weren't managed by the right people with the right characteristics—a topic we will discuss in more depth in the following pages.

Human-Centered Innovation Applied to Culture

What I have been sharing with you represents only the tiniest fraction of the long series of human-centered innovation projects, applied to brands and products, that we have driven forward over the years. This is a kind of innovation that perhaps not many people would expect in the food and beverage world. Before joining PepsiCo, I, too, failed to realize the infinite possibilities that this approach might offer to the company and indeed the entire industry.

When a recruiter called me in November 2011 at my home in Minneapolis, telling me that PepsiCo wanted to connect with me for the role of chief design officer of the corporation, I told her that I wasn't interested. I was the chief design officer of 3M; I was working on exciting innovation projects, leveraging more than fifty different technology platforms, covering more than sixty industries in almost every existing product category. What could I do at PepsiCo? Design pretty packaging for a set of their brands? That wasn't what inspired me. But the recruiter and PepsiCo's talent acquisition team were persistent (thank you, Sarah King, and thank you, Courtney Hagen!) and persuaded me to reflect and have a chat with Brad Jakeman and afterward with Indra Nooyi. That activated a journey of discovery that brought me to fully understand the infinite opportunities that an intelligent approach to design-driven innovation could generate in this industry.

With that awareness in my heart and a book in my hands, I went to my first meeting with Indra and Brad in New York. The book had a page flagged with a red Post-it. The book was Walter Isaacson's biography of Steve Jobs, and the Post-it on page 154 signaled the description of a conversation that had taken place in an unidentified place between two people who had made world business history: "Steve's head dropped as he stared at his feet. After a weighty, uncomfortable pause, he issued a challenge that would haunt me for days. 'Do you want to spend the rest of your life selling sugared water, or do you want a chance to change the world?'"[2] Steve was talking to John Sculley, then president of Pepsi-Cola, trying to convince him to leave PepsiCo and become the CEO of Apple.

I took this phrase and pointed it out to Brad while we were in the car, outside of the PepsiCo lab in Valhalla, and then I showed it to Indra when we met in her office in Purchase. I told them, "I want to join you to prove to Steve Jobs—may he rest in peace, the great Steve!—that PepsiCo is much more than sugared water and that we, too, can change the world in our own way." Redefining the art of brand building, inventing the company's future portfolio, composed of drinks and snacks that a multitude of people throughout the world put into their bodies every single day, dealing with the vast problems of sustainability and of health and wellness, and figuring out the enabling role of new technologies in all of this—these were the challenges that excited me. Maybe we wouldn't invent an iPhone, but surely we could have the chance to make a positive impact on the lives of billions of people. I joined PepsiCo in 2012 with that dream. Ten years earlier I had joined 3M with another ambitious dream: to use design to evolve the innovation culture of one of the biggest innovation companies in the world, generating positive global impact. I will never stop my dreaming; it's stronger than I am.

Over the following years, I found a whole range of wonderful coconspirators, partners, and sponsors at PepsiCo. Ramon Laguarta, the

Everything that surrounds us, and that hasn't been created by Mother Nature, has been imagined, thought up, designed, and built by a human being, by a designer, an innovator, an entrepreneur. Every single thing.

CEO who took over from Indra in 2018, continued to believe in this human-centered and design-driven approach to innovation. Under his leadership, the design team amplified its relevance. It has tripled in size and has increased its level of integration into the company's DNA as never before, doubling down its impact in several areas, including our efforts in purposeful innovation and sustainability.

While I was writing these words on my laptop, a notification flashed on my phone—for real. It was a message from Ramon, with a sketch that he drew on a piece of paper for a project that we're working on together. This is what we mean by a "prototype." A sketch made by our CEO to share a potential approach for a sustainability strategy that we discussed last week is by all means a prototype. Ramon is not a designer, and yet he understands very well the power of prototyping. He is not afraid to roll up his sleeves and sketch an idea. He is not afraid to share that sketch with people who make sketching and designing their job and business, because he understands that a prototype, in all of its forms, activates conversations; advances ideas; allows for co-creation, alignment, and excitement; and generates confidence.

Since the first day that he took the company's reins, Ramon has made sustainability and human-centricity the fundamental pillars of his mission as leader of the second-largest food and beverage company in the world. And he lives this mission in his heart and soul, in the big strategic decisions and in the daily conversations, in the actions and facts, in the words and numbers—including through these kinds of sketches and prototypes.

What has made all the difference in my journey are the dreams of leaders such as Ramon, Indra, and so many others I have met over the years. They would be too many to mention, but know that I remember you all, each one of you, with my heart full of gratitude and respect. Multinational companies might seem to some, from the outside, like enormous machines made up of countless processes and human cogs— but in truth they are simply communities of people with visions and aspirations, emotions and fears. They are collectives of individuals who think, hope, experiment, love, suffer, enjoy, try, fail, and aspire to be successful, regardless of their level and title. This is how you change the world: with the strength of ideas and actions; with the strength of people. With *people in love with people.*

I have spent more than two decades working for big corporations, on a journey characterized by thousands of projects spread across hundreds of product categories and dozens of different industries. Over this time, I have gradually realized that my largest and most important project wasn't going to be connected to any particular object, brand, service, or experience. My most important project was not going to be the invention of a revolutionary device, able to personalize food and drinks on the basis of a user's emotional and physiological needs. It wasn't going to be either the historical redesign of global, iconic brands such as Pepsi and Lay's. My biggest project in these corporations was—and continues to be—the design of the innovation culture of the organization, with the aim of generating an approach that is completely human-centered and design-driven. That culture can then generate the best devices and best brands, the best services and best experiences. But you have to start with the right culture. That's my aspiration; that should be my legacy. With this idea in my heart, I have put together design teams that embody and catalyze a culture of this kind. By working hand in hand with other business leaders, I have invested endless hours and resources to progressively spread that innovation culture, weaving it into the company's very DNA.

I applied the same principles of design-driven, human-centered innovation to designing and advancing this culture: I defined a *strategy* with *empathy* and began to *prototype.* I did so for ten years at 3M. And then I went on to do the same thing at PepsiCo.

In 2002, I joined 3M as design coordinator for one of the company's six markets (the consumer market), in the European regional office. Ten years later, in 2012, I left 3M as its first chief design officer, leaving behind me an established organization with design centers in the United States, Europe, and Asia, a collective of dozens of different kinds of creatives spread across a range of locations in those regions, and having won hundreds of design and innovation awards, with tangible, visible results in every part of the corporation's business.

I joined PepsiCo that same year, without a team, throwing myself onto the front lines yet again, with a design capability that still needed to be built. Indra, Brad, and I prototyped the first element of a design organization and began to spread this new culture outward. We were in "start-up mode" with a team of a dozen talented professionals based in New York City. Over the next six years, that team grew to just over one hundred people, in a dozen locations across four continents. And that culture began to increasingly influence and be integrated into the company.

Since 2018, under Ramon's leadership, and sponsored by Laxman Narasimhan, Ram Krishnan, and Jane Wakely, we moved into "scale-up mode." The group grew to more than three hundred people and continues to grow to this day, with a presence in every region of the planet and more than fifteen strategic locations. That culture is now intrinsic to the organization, running in its nerves and veins and showing up across its skin.

But this is, nevertheless, a journey—there is no point of arrival. There is always room for improvement, for continual, constant progression. This is a journey toward excellence in *the age of excellence*. A journey that puts human beings at the center of everything, not just as objects of investigation in a project but also as the project's drivers. Designing a culture for these human beings, as the enabler of everything else, is one of the most complex and important projects of all. And it is also one of the most exciting projects that one can imagine—with impacts that are among the greatest and longest-lasting.

CHAPTER 6

A NEW HUMANISM

We have seen that society is changing, driven forward by new technologies, globalization, and the digital world. Many of the old barriers protecting the generalized mediocrity that we have witnessed up until today in the mass market and in society are gradually crumbling away. We are entering into a world where we have to innovate as never before because there is no alternative, no way out: either you innovate, or someone else will *in your place*. And that someone else, sooner or later, will also *take your place*. We are entering an age of innovation—the *age of excellence*.

We went on to analyze and decipher a new way of doing innovation, whether of products or brands, that places the human being at the center of everything—a human-centered and humanistic way, because that's the only way to innovate successfully in the age of excellence. I shared with you the advantages of this new approach through a series of personal stories, and I have tried to describe some of the universal principles of this way of working.

At this point, if you are interested in diving deeper into the details of the processes, frameworks, and tools of this design-driven and human-centered approach to innovation, you will find a vast literature that deals with this topic. Shelves of books have been written on these details; there is a world of content digitally distilled from conference stages and university classrooms. This content represents the results of the individual reflections of experts, theorists, and practitioners, as well as the output of their endless debates. Indeed, when we speak about innovation, the majority of the discussion crystallizes around precisely these details: the processes, frameworks, and tools. And often—far too often—the discussion stops right there. The fundamental element, the one that really makes all the difference, the variable that is extraordinarily indispensable for the success of any given project, is often neither mentioned, analyzed, deciphered, nor celebrated.

We talk about processes, frameworks, and tools, and then in the end we don't talk about *her*, about *him*, about the *human beings* whom those processes, frameworks, and tools are meant to manage, interpret, and utilize. Or, at least, when we discuss the topic of innovation, we don't talk about these human beings enough.

We Are Innovation

The kind of human being cited in the literature of innovation is usually the object of the innovation process, a target to be studied, dissected, examined under a microscope, and displayed for research purposes. No doubt anthropological and ethnographic approaches to innovation are fundamental. And experts the world over stress this focus on the human being constantly, in the pages of their textbooks or in the meeting rooms of the companies that invest in their services. As highly paid consultants, they repeat to these companies the same thing, over and over again: "Get out of this meeting room and go out there, into the world. Get to know the people who buy and use your products; meet your users, talk to them. Let me show you the process to do this."

But there is another kind of human being who is usually omitted from the cultural debates about innovation as expounded by experts and theoreticians, as well as in practical and strategic discussions in the meeting rooms of companies big and small. I mean the kind of human being who is effectively in charge of coming up with new ideas, who is supposed to observe, analyze, think, prototype, and produce: the human entrepreneur, the innovator, the dreamer, the designer, the marketer, the researcher. And then there is the human being who has to sponsor the approach, fund it, build it, lead it, inspire it. These human beings are the CEOs, the business leaders, the investors and shareholders. And, finally, there are those human beings who are in some way, however marginally, in contact with the innovation processes, who collide and interact with these processes, sometimes facilitating them and sometimes even blocking them.

What we don't talk about often enough are the characteristics of all these people—how they think, act, and make decisions; the dynamics of their interactions, the expressions of their mindsets, the consequences of their collective cultural habits, which are in direct relationship with an organization's ability to effectively innovate. And yet, this is the key variable for the success of any given project. Too many books, companies, agencies, universities, and leaders treat innovation exclusively as a process. But a process is only a tool, and a tool without a human being to use it is simply meaningless. A tool will never produce innovation; it is the human being who does so, by posing the right questions; finding intelligent answers; generating creative connections; transforming information and intuitions into concepts, prototypes, and products; taking the initiative; running risks, with optimism and courage, with passion and resilience.

A tool is like a brush: put it in Picasso's hands and then put it in the hands of your tax adviser, and the results will be dramatically different—at least, so long as your tax adviser is not the reincarnation of Picasso. A brush is necessary to be able to paint, just as the canvas and colors are, but all these are simply instruments: it's the artist's talent that makes the difference. Nevertheless, there are institutions that pay millions of dollars to hire consultants with the goal of making a better brush for the organization, with the finest wood and the very best bristles, made from the pelts of badgers, mongoose, squirrels; conical, flat, forked, jagged, fanned; usually sourced at prohibitive prices. Time and capital are invested in discussions, presentations, projections, and predictions. And then they forget to speak about Picasso, how he thinks, how he sees the world, how he holds the brush, how he finds inspiration, how he deals with the errors on his canvas, how he engages in a dialogue with the world around him, how he analyzes his subject, how he expresses himself, why he does all of this and more. In many organizations, paradoxically, the conviction is that it is much more difficult to produce the right kind of brush than to find, train, lead, inspire, and retain the Picassos.

That's what has happened in recent years to processes such as the celebrated "design thinking," beloved by so many and rejected by others, a source of huge commercial success for some and a horrendous failure for others. Those who have attacked design thinking have simply been taking aim at the brush. In truth, design thinking was a good brush, for the most part. What needed first to be understood and eventually to be criticized or celebrated was, instead, the way that the brush was being used in each individual project and company. Was there a Picasso behind the brush, or simply an accountant who had taken up painting as a hobby?

To be clear, most of the enterprises out there today are not clueless, and their human resources departments have brilliant minds and important resources, dedicated to deciphering the ideal leadership values, the characteristics of the best innovators, and the culture of a winning organization. But then, when business leaders begin to discuss the strategies necessary to drive forward more radical innovation projects, they turn almost by default to the familiar and stable ground of tools and processes, usually introducing into those processes *any* talented people who have demonstrated some kind of merit over their professional careers. And most of the time, these talented people have a homogeneous, similar background: each has an MBA, a Type A personality, degrees from top schools, ambition, an impressive analytical ability, a great understanding of processes and data, and a talent for numbers. The basic idea is that if this kind of person has had success in previous roles and is smart and motivated enough, then the person will also understand how to deal with this new challenge called innovation. But frequently this simply isn't the case, and these people fail.

In this new age of excellence, practicing innovation requires a unique, different, and extraordinary kind of talent. You need a person who can work with analysis and creativity, rationality and curiosity, objectivity and emotions, numbers and brushes, with the head and the heart. And you need someone who embodies all of these abilities in an extraordinary way. Innovation is complicated; it's difficult and demands a special breed of talent. It's rare enough to find someone who has the necessary levels of analysis and creativity in a healthy balance. It becomes even more difficult to find someone who balances these qualities in an exceptional way. And yet, that is the human being innovation requires.

Studying the Process Won't Make You an Innovator

If you want to re-create what people such as Steve Jobs, Henry Ford, Richard Branson, Jeff Bezos, and Bill Gates have generated with their enterprises, it isn't enough to simply study their playbooks, processes, and tools. You have to study their hearts and minds, their behaviors and obsessions, decisions and doubts, questions and answers, successes and failures, time and timing. And of course, you also need a healthy pinch of luck! How can we attract people like Steve, Henry, Richard, Jeff, and Bill to our teams? How can we try to become like them? How can we inspire that talent in and extract it from our employees? How can we incentivize people of this kind when they join us? How do we understand them, motivate them, give them a chance to express themselves? These are the great challenges of innovation that we need to focus on, after having designed processes, tools, and organizations— or even before we do.

The big enterprises have solid, sophisticated, almost scientific processes for attracting talent, growing people within the company, and transforming them into future leaders and CEOs. But these processes have historically privileged the left side of the brain, with its analytic and rational thinking rather than creativity, intuition, vision, and imagination. For this reason, when trying to strategize innovation, those organizations often end up living under the illusion that the same army of left-brained people fostered for leadership roles can now also successfully manage the new challenges of the innovation world.

In a cultural context of this kind, it becomes very clear why it's much more reassuring for many of these organizations to debate processes and tools rather than discussing and reviewing the indispensable soft skills of their team members—the quality of their imagination, their optimism, their intellectual curiosity, and mental agility. And thus these organizations end up hardly ever discussing the aspects that really make the difference between success and failure in every process of innovation, however solid the process might otherwise be.

Over the following pages, I will discuss exactly this: the priceless role of the human being, the most important asset for driving real and meaningful innovation. Up to this point, we have spoken of the *human being for whom we innovate*, the human being who, finally, needs to be put at the center of everything. Now I want to change perspective and investigate instead the world of the *human being who innovates—the innovation driver.*

On this journey, my aim isn't to establish absolute and indisputable truths; I'm neither so ambitious nor so arrogant as to attempt such a goal. I want merely to share with you what worked for me, in the hope that this experience can help and inspire other people who are beginning to go down a similar road—people who understand that tools, data, and processes are extremely important but aren't enough; people who know that everything starts with a human being, and everything returns to one as well, in a virtuous cycle, *from people to people.*

Searching for Unicorns

I joined 3M in July 2002. After just a few months, I began putting together the first nucleus of my design team in Milan, and in 2005 we started building a team in Saint Paul, Minnesota. In 2009, while continuing to consolidate the groups based in Italy and America, we were getting ready to form new teams in Shanghai and Tokyo. It was then that I realized that a problem was becoming increasingly pressing. I was looking for the best talent I could find on the market, and I'd given a series of very precise indications to the human resources team about the kinds of technical skills I was looking for. I then integrated into these directions some general advice about the kind of mindset and attitude that I needed candidates to have. We were also leveraging external recruiters, some of the most famous in the design world, the very best available in the industry. The headhunters and our own HR team were searching for designers, going through profiles, pre-interviewing them, and then proposing them to me. Over the years I found myself looking over thousands of curricula and project portfolios, and once I had selected the best candidates, I conducted hundreds of interviews with people who, on paper at least, embodied all the right criteria.

By following this structured and strategic process, I managed to find amazing talent—but I also met with many people who, despite having all the right technical characteristics I was looking for, didn't possess the other gifts that I believed were indispensable in the extremely complex world of innovation. I am talking about a series of "soft skills," both intellectual and emotional, that are intrinsic to the very essence of the *serial innovator*—a way of thinking, feeling, and acting that, over the course of my professional life, I have found to be fundamental for navigating the intricate world of business on the powerful yet delicate wings of imagination and creativity. These are traits that I found in people who were able to reach extraordinary heights, both personally and professionally, but that I haven't seen in people who have fallen along the way. Over the years, I have hired amazing talent who embodied these qualities, and I have also hired professionals who didn't possess these skills. But these errors of evaluation have also been steps along a natural learning curve, part and parcel of the intrinsic complexity of the recruiting process, and have turned out to be a blessing in disguise, because by antithesis and contrast these errors helped me understand, better and more deeply, the key characteristics of the ideal innovator.

In 2009, in view of an acceleration in hiring connected to the growth of our teams around the world, I realized that the time had come to reduce every form of inefficiency in our recruiting processes. Over the years, I have learned to give to our HR team and recruiters increasingly detailed indications not only about the technical requirements of a role, but also about the emotional and intellectual ones. But this approach wasn't effective enough. One of the main problems I found was connected to the fact that I wasn't just hiring simple designers—that is, professionals trained to imagine, design, and create products, brands, and experiences. The role I was giving to our community of designers at 3M—and then later at PepsiCo—was much more diverse. The role was based on the fundamental pillars of the discipline but then expanded into areas that had been little explored until then, at least not in a constant and consistent way, in organizations of the complexity I was in and in industries for which design had not previously represented a primary competitive advantage.

First of all, we needed designers with a *holistic approach* to the discipline, embracing all branches of the profession, from graphics to product design, to digital and experience design, all the way to strategy and beyond. This meant coming into conflict with the hyperspecialized world of traditional design.

In the second place, we were positioning design on the same level with *innovation*, interpreting the two terms as synonyms, something that required design leaders with a very particular mindset. That mindset is commonly practiced in many design universities but is not explicitly taught or formalized in a specific educational path, and thus is not always embodied by every designer.

Finally, we were introducing a new and different way of working, which demanded that the designers would be able not only to do their design work but also to *explain the value of their work* in a way that could be understood, appreciated, measured, and leveraged by other communities—business and R&D above all. The designers also needed to speak the language of those communities.

We thus needed people who could move with flexibility within a system that wasn't entirely ready to welcome them, who could leap over every hurdle, getting into the processes and conversations in a proactive way, positively and empathetically. We were innovating in terms of not only the products and brands, but also the very organizations themselves and their culture: this was our big metaproject, which transcended all the other projects and, in a certain sense, embraced them all. Doing all this meant that our designers needed to be very special people with a whole set of characteristics that were far from ordinary. The keyword was "extraordinary." Being extraordinary couldn't be exceptional; it had to be the starting point.

To make things as clear as day, I decided to draw up a list of all of the qualities that I believed were indispensable for finding one's way through this complex context, and I shared it with the HR department. These considerations from 2009 then formed the basis for two important articles that I wrote for the journal *Design Management Institute Review*, as well as the content for countless presentations at conferences around the world.[3] This public, published approach had two aims. On the one hand,

We are entering into a world where we have to innovate as never before because there is no alternative, no way out: either you innovate, or someone else will *in your place*. And that someone else, sooner or later, will also *take your place*.

I wanted to produce a document that could be shared with any recruiter working with us, in an efficient and consistent way—an official manifesto describing the mindset I was looking for in our designers. On the other hand, I wanted to communicate this profile of people to the whole world, so that those who were interested in joining our team could use the manifesto as a mirror, to evaluate independently whether they were right for the challenge.

This list then became a live document: over the course of the years, it has remained unvaried in its essential elements, but it has evolved in form and tone, enriched by important additions inspired by experience in the field. In the pages of this book, it can now find a new life, in an original, previously unpublished way, enlightened yet again by that therapeutic process of analysis and reflection that writing a book represents. It is a list that I drafted while thinking of the designers I was hiring, but it can be applied in its entirety to any innovator, from any cultural or professional background, whether in marketing, finance, science, medicine, law, communication, music, sport, or any other area in which one wants to innovate—including one's own life. Indeed, it's a list that was profoundly inspired by the children I was planning to have one day in my future. The list was made for them, as a compass for their lives, personal and professional.

Without doubt, one of the greatest challenges that I have had to deal with over the years has been the utmost difficulty of finding people who possess all of these characteristics—the key characteristics of the ideal innovator. I have realized this over time, month by month, year by year, when I found myself rejecting dozens upon dozens of profiles proposed by our recruiters. Often these were people who were exceptional on a technical level but lacked a whole series of other gifts.

A few years ago I was chatting with some members of my team at PepsiCo about this difficulty: Did we want too much? Were our ambitions too high? Were we looking for profiles that simply didn't exist? We reached the conclusion that maybe we were looking for impossible profiles. But nevertheless, we would never stop looking! We wanted to find unicorns, those mythical, incredible creatures who are rare and difficult to capture or even to spot. That description perfectly depicted the kind of people we were looking for. Since then, we have called these people the *unicorns*. We were on the hunt for them, using the net of our imagination, ambition, vision, and fantasy. And we would never rest until we had hundreds of unicorns in our company, enlisted in our army of dreams.

We Can Learn How to Become Unicorns

Over time, I realized that this list was not only fundamental to our talent search, as an official filter to scan and evaluate the candidates we were considering; it also provided us with a very precise tool to be leveraged in a variety of other ways.

First of all, it represented a collection of skills that we could all aspire to, aim for, and align ourselves around. It constituted a kind of personal and collective compass to better ourselves.

Second, it served as a point of reference for our teams when coaching and growing our talent—for everyone, but especially for the high-potential people and the younger individuals, who were "raw material" to be shaped in ideal ways to become the best version of themselves and the perfect leaders of the future.

Finally, the list became a lens to better find and identify the right partners in other departments, in agencies, in the companies of our customers—anyone who could be a potential coconspirator, ally, or sponsor; people our organization needed, across every discipline, to drive true, tangible, and impactful innovation.

And through this process, we also realized that the talent of these unicorns was not just something people were born with. It was also characterized by a set of skills that could be nurtured, grown, educated, and amplified. We will talk more in depth about this topic, but first, let's define the key gifts of these innovators.

The Skills of the Unicorns

I divided the skills of the unicorns/innovators into three groups.

The Entrepreneurial Gifts

- They are visionaries, experimenters, and executors.
- They are original and have a unique perspective.
- They are intuitive and analytical.
- They are proactive, look for the root cause, and go the extra mile.
- They are on top of trends—and eventually trendsetters.
- They are people in love with people.
- They are risk takers but cautious too.
- They are aesthetes with an aesthetic sense.
- They are holistic designers.
- They are both business savvy and tech savvy.

The Social Gifts

- They are kind, sincere, and trustworthy.
- They are in love with diversity.
- They are empaths and have an elevated emotional intelligence.
- They are dialectical conductors of multilingual orchestras.
- They are respectful.
- They are charismatic storytellers.
- They are generous mentors.
- They avoid taking themselves too seriously and know how to have fun.

The Enabling Gifts

- They are curious.
- They are humble but confident and self-aware.
- They are attentive listeners but quick to decide and act.
- They are optimistic and resilient.
- They are comfortable with discomfort.
- They are change agents.

Let's go through all of these characteristics one by one.

THE UNICORN'S ENTREPRENEURIAL GIFTS

The unicorn's *entrepreneurial gifts* are the set of skills that directly impact our ability to build an innovation strategy. In other words, these traits shape the way we manage a whole series of variables, processes, and situations that range from a single innovation project all the way through to an entire business strategy or a personal life project.

Unicorns Are Visionaries, Experimenters, and Executors

Unicorns think big. They think above and beyond. Unicorns dream. They look at the world with curious, searching eyes; they understand weak signals and decipher "wicked problems"; and by drawing on deductive reasoning, they form possible hypotheses of better worlds. Unicorns are able to imagine potential future situations that are rich with meaning for their companies, for themselves, for a specific community, or for society as a whole and then set out the best path for realizing that vision. Unicorns experiment, learn, build. They are always capable of moving in a flexible fashion, following the compass of their dreams but adapting the route according to what they learn along the way, because they have an innate capacity to move with a perfect balance between dream and reality, vision and execution, synthesis and analysis.

That act of balancing is what makes an innovator such a rare creature: many people are able to dream but are terrible at carrying things out, and so the dream remains merely—and sadly—just a dream. How many people, throughout their lives, dream about a better product, a better service, a better job, a better city, a better relationship, and then never try? They don't experiment or follow through on their plans. They remain paralyzed in that dream, entangled in ambition without execution, suffering from inertia without changing anything. Dreaming is simple; transforming that plan into reality is difficult.

Think of how often we read on social media about innovation projects launched by great visionaries, followed by congratulatory comments from dozens of people who don't lose the opportunity to remind the world that the commenter had the idea years before or presented that same concept only recently to a company that obviously hadn't understood the idea. *Companies that lack vision! Ignorant companies!* Is this really the case? In all likelihood, the truth is somewhat different.

The big difference between innovators and dreamers is that while both dream, innovators then have the ability to transform these dreams into reality; dreamers don't manage to go beyond the boundaries of the oneiric dimension—or the concept phase. The difference lies in what Aristotle defines as the movement from *potentiality* to *actuality*. To reiterate: dreaming is simple; making things happen is complex. A dream, an idea, a discovery in the world of business and science, even when it is potentially doable, remains only an idea, a concept, or an invention if it isn't then realized. Innovating means transforming an idea into a solution that is actualized and successfully arrives on the market. A solution has to be appreciated by the public as relevant and bought by people because it is meaningful. There are billions of dreamers on this planet and very few innovators. Many people—far too many—aren't able to make their dreams real because of inertia, fear, inability, or comfort, or simply because they don't truly believe in their dreams. Sometimes the only real pleasure people are looking for comes from the easy and fleeting act of dreaming in and of itself, with nothing proceeding from it.

A great number of people, on the other hand, are excellent executors—they know how to make things happen—but they lack the ability to think big. If they are given the right indications, then they can do great things, but to complement them, they need dreamers. And often, therefore, the dreamers, to make their big visions come true, team up with the executors. This is the history of many great business partnerships, composed of a visionary thinker and a pragmatic entrepreneur and operator who carries things out at the enterprise level, or by a creative designer and an enabling technician at the project level. The ability to marry imagination and execution in a perfect equilibrium is the turning point in innovation.

Innovators imagine a house in new and surprising forms, on the edge of what's feasible, and then begin to build it brick by brick, challenging the laws of physics, moving in balance between the possible and the impossible, shifting the barriers of what is even realizable, redefining the known and shared boundaries of the very concepts of technical feasibility and aesthetic plausibility. The innovator is Gaudí and his Casa Batlló in Barcelona, made of fairy-tale shapes; the innovator is Frank Gehry with his Guggenheim Museum in Bilbao, modeled on the wind; the innovator is Rafael Viñoli with his skyscraper at 432 Park Avenue in New York, made in a shape that challenges the rules of engineering; the innovator is Bjarke Ingels with the tetrahedron of VIA 57 West, redefining the skyline of Manhattan. The innovators are all those architects who have reinvented the canon of design by realizing their dreams in their buildings.

Too many people spend their lives building their metaphorical houses instead, with neither dream nor personal plan, following standards established by other people and, brick by brick, erecting rows of houses with predictable geometry, all the same, taken for granted, aligned around the status quo.

When I joined 3M, I had a dream: I wanted to have an impact, to influence things, to develop the way innovation was done in that company, drawing on a new approach in design and strategy focused entirely on the human being, typical to the world of design thinking. I was twenty-seven, and I was based in Milan, a place at the extreme periphery of the "American empire" of that US company. In my first annual performance review, the moment when management evaluates your work over the previous twelve months and interrogates you about where you see yourself in the future, I stated that I imagined myself leading design-driven innovation for the entire multinational corporation. I was only twenty-seven, not yet an executive, in a midlevel position in one of the company's six businesses (the consumer market), in one of the five regions (Europe), in a company with sales in two hundred countries and about ninety thousand employees around the world.

Today I know that, back then, many people hadn't taken my dream seriously; they had laughed at it, perhaps with affection for that slightly idealistic young man full of fantasies, perhaps in disdain at the arrogance and assumptions of a junior employee. If I had to count the number of people who didn't believe in my dream at the start, I would still be counting. And yet, that dream came up again and again, year in, year out, formally stated, in black and white, during my performance reviews. It was a dream. And a dream, by definition, has to be naive in some intrinsic way; otherwise, it isn't a dream at all.

My dream wasn't to become the company's *chief design officer*, nor was it to be successful or make money. My dream was to create value for society and for the company through my ideas and actions, by generating something that remained over time, that was greater than myself, making use of the design platform that I loved so dearly and for which I had become an ambassador. This dream translated itself into a vision, then a plan. And then I began to execute the plan, experimenting step by step, building one brick at a time, learning from my mistakes, capitalizing on my successes. In my mind, I had my own Casa Batlló, rather than a row of similar houses in a suburb of Milan.

Ten years after that first boyhood dream, I left 3M as the chief design officer of the multinational corporation, having built a new company department from scratch, with design centers in Milan, Saint Paul, Shanghai, and Tokyo, and having launched hundreds of innovative projects on the market. Above all, I left a legacy that other designers and business leaders have continued to invest in and grow after I was no longer there. It hasn't been easy. Dreaming is easy; executing those dreams is hard. And that's probably why many people prefer to dream without acting.

This was my greatest success, building something that could last and grow after me. If design at 3M had crumbled as soon as I left, it would have been my greatest failure. Everything began with the naive dream and ambitious vision of a young man who wasn't even thirty. Since then, every time that I find myself talking with young people starting out on their own journeys, I remember this important truth that I understood long ago: *Don't be afraid to dream big—you should always dream! If you don't have a dream, you'll never be able to make it come true! Dream and then act!*

All of the great innovations that have changed the world began with a dream. And then they have grown through experimentation and execution.

Unicorns Are Original and Have a Unique Perspective

"Be yourself; everyone else is taken," said Oscar Wilde more than a century ago. Each one of us is in transit; every one of us is undertaking a long journey called life, searching for our identity, for our own place in the world, for our own essence. This search is, in truth, a process of introspection and gradual awareness that matures over the course of our whole existence. We are like Michelangelo's *Prisoners*, his uncompleted statues in eternal tension to free themselves from their blocks of marble. We are born out of rough stone and then, holding the chisel of life made of experiences, observations, and reflections, we begin to remove the material, to shape our figure, artists of our own existence. And step by step, we begin to take form, increasingly defining ourselves in a more finished image. But life is an infinite process of definition. We begin as raw marble, and we die *almost* finished. We always—some people more than others—remain in positive tension, striving for something more, for greater form, for greater consciousness, with a beautiful, eternal thirst to better ourselves.

Throughout this life journey, we are surrounded by billions of other "unfinished" individuals: the people who share this planet with us. We study them, analyze them; they provide inspiration, because in our process of taking form, we draw on the forms of others as references, examples, metrics. Indeed, in order to define who we are, we need a context of reference that gives us something to measure ourselves by.

Sometimes, however, some of us decide to give other unfinished people a role that goes beyond parameters and inspiration, transforming them into modern saints to be idolized, into images to be celebrated, figurines for imitation. These unfinished persons are friends, influencers, celebrities, and colleagues whom we raise up on pedestals and passively try to become. They are the people whose opinions, behaviors, thoughts, outfits, and actions become models that we follow blindly, without perspective. In some circumstances, some of us decide to give our own chisel to the artists surrounding us, to these unfinished people who are still sculpting themselves. These unfinished people might be our parents, our friends, our bosses, our community—if we give them this role and power, we are then sculpted by their ideas, expectations, and desires.

How many of us, over the course of our lives, have made choices under the pressure of society's expectations? We may do so even with extremely important life choices, such as how to live our existence on this planet, whom to marry, what profession to undertake—or maybe daily choices, such as the reply to give in a meeting, what dress to wear to an event, what food to order for dinner, what to do for a given project.

In 1951, the psychologist Solomon Asch demonstrated the potential of social pressure with an experiment that has gone into the history books. In a series of tests, he put eight subjects—including seven accomplices—into a room to perform what was described to them as a simple exercise in visual discrimination. He then showed them two cards. On the first there was a line of a particular length, while the second had three lines of different lengths. He asked the subjects to identify which of the three lines on the second card had the same length as the line on the first. He started with the accomplices, who began one by one with replies that were in general wrong and made little sense but that all agreed with one another. The true subjects of the experiment, when they were finally asked to reply, in a whole series of cases ended up giving incorrect answers, confirming the replies of the majority. And these subjects did so despite knowing full well that the reply was incorrect because the correct answer was so clearly obvious. Only a very small percentage of subjects resisted the group pressure, maintaining their own original perspective.

In other words, trying to conform with the community of which we are a part is a widespread and very human instinct. It gives us a sense of safety and reassurance. It's almost anomalous not to do so. And yet, the people surrounding us should be used only as points of reference as we form our own unique, genuine, and distinct point of view. The more we chisel away at the metaphorical stone from which we are born, the more we can become an exclusive work of art—magnificent and unmistakable, with incomparable features, forms, finishes, and details, all different and never seen before. Would we prefer instead to be one of the little statues that are all the same, lined up on every segment of our journey, conforming to the mold of expectations and conventions? Let's build our own original perspective, our conscious point of view about every aspect of the world, founded on data, information, emotions, intuitions, and experiences, all accumulated through observation, reflection, dialogue, and those processes of continual and incessant discovery that make up our lives.

Let's explore these still undefined, undiscovered lands with passion. They are places where trends converge, collide, and overlap, where the standard canons of modern society begin to slip away and meet with the unexpected, the unusual, the different. And it is in that gray zone— formed by the overlapping of black and white but itself neither black nor white—where we can find our identity, extracting it from the raw material of which we are made, transforming, in an Aristotelian way, our *potential* into *action*, just as Michelangelo did with his *Prisoners*, a powerful metaphor of such a transition. Real innovation has always been made by individuals who have a unique point of view, who see the world with different eyes, who have the capacity to take on postures that no one else has assumed before, and who are not afraid to do so—with awareness, ease, and respect.

Unicorns Are Intuitive and Analytical

Unicorns don't run away from the magic of intuition; they recognize the miraculous role of that mysterious spark of a palpable idea that they feel coming directly from their hearts and guts. And unicorns understand what this means for the journey of innovation. Unicorns celebrate immediate cognition; they nurture perception and trust their instinct. In the business world, governed as it is by data, algorithms, and processes, intuition is often set aside; it isn't given a chance to rise up, to breathe; it drowns under the weight of numbers, data, and statistics, the constant fear of anything that looks like a risk, anything that isn't objective and quantifiable. Innovators are able to identify opportunities by making use of their intuition, but they also know how to deconstruct these intuitions and opportunities through an analytical process, adapting them to the world of business, making them usable through systems and processes—because intuition in and of itself, without a capacity for analysis, has no relevance for the world of innovation.

The seventeenth-century Dutch philosopher Baruch Spinoza, engaging in a millennia-old debate that began with Aristotle, made a distinction between "intuitive knowledge" (*scientia intuitiva* in Latin), through which you understand an object immediately, and "reason" (*ratio*), which allows you to perceive an object through a rational process. Reason cannot easily grasp the unity of things because its task is instead to grasp divisions and put things in order; it is intuitive knowledge that must identify unity despite multiplicity. The superiority of intuitive knowledge to reason resides precisely in the ability of the former to perceive the world in its entirety through an "intuitive" insight (from the Latin *intueor*, "to look") without losing sight of the infinite differences that make up the world. In reality, Spinoza held that intuitive knowledge was nothing other than executing at a great speed, almost unconsciously, a process of reasoning that reason did more laboriously. But however our brains reach the conclusion, there is a vast difference between the two faculties: one is immediate, rapid, instinctive, and difficult to explain; the other is organized, structured, constructed through a noticeable and shareable discursive process. In today's business world, discursive reason clearly holds pride of place because it allows you to establish correct causal connections, proceeding through speech and discussion, which can be clearly demonstrated and understood by everyone. Intuitive knowledge—as Spinoza used the term at least—is instead considered to be intangible, subjective, difficult to decipher, and, as a result, risky.

"The intuitive mind is a sacred gift, while the rational mind is a faithful servant," stated Albert Einstein almost three hundred years after Spinoza, in an extremely lucid and clinical take on the world.[4] And yet, we have created a society that honors the slave and has forgotten the gift. It's fundamental, through the processes of innovation, to give space to the *gift* of intuition, because unexpected visions arrive from intuition, visions that observe the whole image and grasp opportunities otherwise invisible to those lost in rational discussion of individual elements.

As Spinoza makes us see, intuition is not an accidental and emotional act, nor a mysterious variable to be feared, nor a dirty mark on the clean canvas of reason; it's a kind of holistic and hyperaccelerated discursive process. The great challenge in the world of business—and consequently also the great opportunity—is to find a perfect balance between intuition and analysis. We should use analysis supported by discursive reason in two ways: on the one hand to define the area in which intuition can express itself, and on the other as a tool to decipher what intuition has managed to see and understand.

In my work at PepsiCo, I can exploit my intuition within the limits dictated by our strategic business frameworks and financial analysis of the opportunities at hand. For example, I can unleash my intuitive ability in the food and beverage category, looking for increasingly healthier and more sustainable products. Analysis defines the field of action, but then within this field I am free to allow my creativity to explode, and indeed I have to protect my intuition within those limits. I must protect it from a system—characteristic of any enterprise—that finds it difficult to work with unproven hypotheses, with flashes of genius, with visions that don't arrive through deduction. And yet, providing space to intuition is absolutely essential.

Once hypotheses have been identified intuitively, you need to apply the analytic process again to break the hypotheses down, understand them, evaluate them, share them, and utilize them. Using desirability, technical feasibility, and economic viability as lenses and filters, intuition has its own way of emerging in all three dimensions. You can have intuition in the zone of desirability, identifying an unsolved user need; or in the zone of technical feasibility, with the invention of a new technology; or finally in the zone of economic viability, through the creation of a business model that has not been explored up to that point. Once I've had an intuition in one of these zones, I then have to reconnect it with other variables using an analytical and structured process, creating connections of cause and effect. Through that process, other intuitions may be generated, other hypotheses may be shared, and you can keep going along this balanced pathway of intuition and analysis, prototyping and validation, divergence and convergence, gradually developing the idea and transforming it into a product.

Analysis without Intuition

Over the years, I have met a great number of people assigned to innovation projects who lack any talent for intuition. They are exceptional in their analyses, in their sophisticated discursive reasoning, with their convincing PowerPoint and Excel presentations, all made up of numbers and processes, erudite terminology and impeccable logic. Their approach is often structured and academic, and thus it sounds solid and credible. But they lack that spark of magic; the approach stops at the surface, on that surface of a logic without any soul. Their analysis is a simple and simplistic mathematical formula that always provides the same solution, a portrait that lacks all the gradients necessary to make it a work of art—three-dimensionality, depth, poetry, life. Yet such analysts are celebrated because they are understood; their reasoning is easily accessible, shareable, untouchable—at least, right up to the point that those processes end, the solutions go to market, the results arrive, and the success doesn't. The solutions are not that innovative, and people don't embrace them. But at that point, most of these leaders have already moved on; their careers are on the rise, and the blame is laid on other variables, individuals, and criteria.

Intuition without Analysis

Over the years, I have also met innovators who are all intuition and no analysis. Their brains are able to produce a magma of incredible ideas, a constant flow of visions and opportunities, but they lack the analysis necessary to give these visions flesh—to decipher them, share them, and sell them. When I have had people like this on my teams, I have usually been able to help them with analytical tools, a good structure, and the right language. The results have been brilliant. Analysis, structure, and language can be learned if you have the right intellectual basis. But intuition can't be learned that easily, and in the world of innovation, you simply can't do without it. You need both intuition and analysis. And the real innovators, the unicorns, are perfectly at ease with the conflict between intuition and analysis and resolve it instinctively; it's in their nature.

Unicorns Are Proactive, Look for the Root Cause, and Go the Extra Mile

Unicorns don't expect a brief, task, or request to arrive. They make their own briefs, find their own tasks, formulate their own requests. The majority of briefs, tasks, and requests that we receive throughout our lives, above all when we don't yet have a reputation as innovators, revolve around the stable grounds of the status quo, of what is already considered feasible, believed to be plausible. If requests like these are not questioned, they will simply produce solutions that keep on conforming to that status quo. An innovator, on the other hand, always tries to identify the root causes that gave rise to the brief in the first place.

If you're asked to build a bridge, try to understand what the real need is. If what's required, for example, is a way of moving from point A to point B while overcoming some obstacle or other, try to understand whether this is really necessary (maybe the users can solve their problem without moving away from point A!), and if it is, then ask yourself whether a bridge is truly an adequate response. Any other professional will design a bridge, reacting to the brief and maybe designing a beautiful structure, with some ingenious functionality—but the only thing they will create will be a bridge. It will still be a bridge even when, eventually, the bridge turns out not to be the best response to the primary need that generated the request. Innovators, on the other hand, invent a catapult, a helicopter, a boat, or some other unheard-of vehicle that allows efficient, secure, rapid, and comfortable transport from A to B. The innovator innovates. Henry Ford famously said, "If I had asked people what they wanted, they would have said faster horses." Henry Ford simply didn't ask. He gave people the car. Henry Ford wouldn't have designed another bridge.

Innovators proactively move the boundaries of their brief, investigating the root causes, redefining the fundamental questions, without expecting someone to ask them to do so. Innovators don't follow a task blindly within the limited area assigned to them. In my design group, having initiative and being proactive are two of the qualities that I most value. I chose my direct collaborators, one by one, by weighing these common denominators. For me and my team, it's fundamental to have this approach in the company because our tasks are to identify opportunities that have never been considered before, transforming what was previously seen as impossible into something feasible, and to push the definitions of the possible to ever greater extremes, beyond the limits of the plausible.

Over my whole professional life, I've never developed my work within the limits imposed on me or expected of me. Not once—not even by mistake. The most significant stages along this journey have been two rites of passage: joining 3M and then moving to PepsiCo. When 3M Italia hired me as a young man, I had a well-defined role: managing design for the consumer and office business in Europe. I joined the corporation with very different ideas for myself, however; I wanted to introduce a new culture of design in the organization and evolve the way the company did innovation on a global scale. This was my personal brief. And I was motivated by the understanding that the root cause of the company's "design problem" in Europe couldn't be traced back to some incompetence of a designer who may have worked on the product portfolio before I arrived. The real problem was that the whole organization lacked design culture. I would never have been able to produce high-quality results in the local market, project after project, without integrating design culture into the enterprise's DNA, right at the heart, in the US headquarters. And so, right from my first day on the job, I worked toward a deep transformation of the creative culture there, even if most of my colleagues and supervisors didn't connect the dots right away. On the surface, I was just working on the projects that had been assigned to me and my teams. But over just a few years, the results began to show in a very clear way to everyone.

I was called into PepsiCo to elevate the role of design from simple packaging to a brand experience, managing a team of a dozen people in New York. Today we have dozens of design teams and hundreds of creatives around the world, and our design mandate is multidimensional and holistic, from branding to product, from communication to experience, from strategy to innovation. This is the role that I designed for myself and my team. I took the briefs given to me by 3M and PepsiCo and completely reinterpreted them. I didn't want to just respond to pre-established briefs, to just satisfy the expectations of my superiors, to just meet my official annual goals. I wanted to produce real, sustainable value in my time at 3M and then at PepsiCo. That's what I owed to the people who hired me, to my supervisors, to my CEOs, to my companies: to do what was right for the organization, to contribute to its growth and success in the long run. And at both multinationals I found partners, from the top executives to middle management, who understood the value of this approach and gave me the chance to apply it. But without that basic proactive nature, without the obsessive, stubborn, philosophical search for the root causes, the face of design in these corporations today would be very different from what it effectively has become. Who knows, in some version of the world it might even have been better—but there is no doubt that it would have been different.

Ramon Laguarta, when he became PepsiCo's CEO, crystallized this culture in a leadership principle that he co-created with all of us on his management team. This principle was to "act as owners," and it was an invitation to everyone employed by the corporation, whatever their role, to behave as if they owned the company, or the business, or brand assigned to them.

Let me translate this way of thinking in the context of our innovation world: it means that, for example, if your role is working on a series of products associated with the Pepsi brand, your responsibilities should never stop with concluding a particular project or sending off the job. The innovators are the people who follow the product generated by that project through its whole life cycle. While working on the next project, they have an urgent and instinctive desire to go to a grocery store and see how the previous product is doing, how it's been put on display, how it's presented, how it interacts on the shelf with the other brands, how it reacts under the pressure of new brands arriving to market—and then how it is used at home, in a restaurant, on the go.

Innovator-owners—proactive, entrepreneurial innovators—suffer when they see that the product they have designed is not "performing" in the store; they study the user's frustrations and find a way to get in touch with the sales team and the retailer to understand what's going wrong in the phases of sale, purchase, and use, or they contact the marketers to convince them to launch a new project to correct the current situation. And innovator-owners are also the people who, when they arrive at the shelves and see that everything is going well, are able to analyze the competition and proactively identify other opportunities. From these observations, a new innovation project is born.

Innovator-owners, finally, are also the kind of people who systematically go the extra mile. They are people for whom the project, brand, or business is so important that they aren't satisfied with the ordinary but always try to go beyond, to exceed it, to redefine it, constantly taking a further step that others wouldn't have even dreamed of pursuing.

Let's imagine, for example, that the goal assigned to someone is 100; going the extra mile means proactively raising the bar to 110, 130, 150, or more, whenever possible. All the other competitors will try to arrive at 100, but the innovators will run to make that extra section. Perhaps some will reach 80 or 90, some 98 or 99; very few will ever get to 100. But innovators who reach their own personal objective will be the only ones up there.

Reaching 110 is simply a mindset. It's the will to always go further, the desire to astonish the user, to please your listeners, to inspire your investors, clients, supervisors—sometimes even yourself!—with completely unexpected solutions and results.

Most of the time, this approach doesn't require extra resources, time, or effort: it simply requires a different way of thinking, one that always defines goals above the norm, beyond expectations, higher than the usual standards. In nearly every project throughout my life, I have imposed aims that are higher than the expectations of whoever is around me, and this has become my norm. And this norm, in most instances, doesn't require greater effort; it's simply a different way of thinking.

When I was asked to manage design for a multinational company but limited to the consumer business unit in Europe, I began by planning the diffusion of design throughout all the company's business units, in every region of the world. When I was told I would have a dozen people in my team to spread a design culture through a corporation, I began by thinking how to construct a dozen teams of hundreds of people in order to reach results that no one expected. When I'm asked to redesign a product, I think about how to reinvent the entire family that the product belongs to. When I'm asked about a packaging project, I begin by studying how to develop the entire brand instead. And obviously, I always start from the root causes, and I constantly ask myself whether it's right to take this road. I try never to think in a broad and proactive way simply for its own sake.

This doesn't mean that every time, even when necessary, I have the option of redesigning entire brands or reconceiving entire product portfolios right away. But the ability to think about the root causes and be ready to go the extra mile helps me to manage the current project in a slightly different way, as a step toward a different goal, a platform to realize a bigger vision. This is my normality—every day. And when your normality becomes what's abnormal for others, it evolves into something extraordinary. Then, there's a good chance that your results, sooner or later, will be extraordinary too. Everything begins from your standpoint, your way of thinking, your way of dreaming.

Unicorns Are on Top of Trends—
and Eventually Trendsetters

Unicorns understand trends in a deep way, in their bones; they live them firsthand. Unicorns belong to a category of human beings who are naturally in tune with what's going on. They intuit a trend while it's still developing; sometimes they are even part of creating that trend. This is partly an innate gift, which can then be nurtured and amplified through another natural trait—curiosity, and the consequent desire and ability to listen, explore, observe, and learn.

There are people who possess a spontaneous sense for what the world desires when the masses still haven't caught on. They are those friends who put on a hat that no one understands yet but that, in a few months, will be in every fashionable wardrobe in the country; those acquaintances who consume a new drink, buy a new electronic gadget, listen to a new music genre, drive a new kind of car, or share a new book, even before anyone's talking about it—and well before that drink, gadget, music, car, or book becomes a mass trend. They are the pioneers, who have an extraordinary sense for where things are heading.

I love to surf. Surfing is fun. But it's not easy. When I'm in the water, sometimes I see surfers who, standing on their own board, even surrounded by dozens of other people in the middle of the sea, manage to spot the wave before anyone else, right on the horizon; and before anyone else, they put themselves in position, turn around, and begin to paddle, to be the first to get the lick of the wave and all its force. And while they're paddling, the others don't understand why; they think it's just a waste of energy, because they aren't able to see the wave arriving with the same lucidity. A trend is designed on a chart like a curve; a trend is a wave. The innovator—at least the good innovator—is a surfer of trends, the kind who gets the wave before anyone else! This is real innovation, the kind that unicorns do.

Unicorns Are People in Love with People

Many companies around the world have a shared, constant, and prioritized mantra: "customer satisfaction." I can still recall the day at 3M, many years ago, when it was announced that it would be the year of "customer satisfaction." At the time, I found myself reflecting a great deal on the meaning of these words, "satisfaction" and "customer." And the conclusion I reached was that a true innovator doesn't care much about mere customer satisfaction—because a true innovator goes far beyond this. A true innovator *loves* their customer!

Maybe this claim will seem somewhat romantic to some and to others a little gratuitous, perhaps even inane. But the impact of the idea is really very important, fundamental even, epoch-changing. First, try to translate the concept into your own life before moving it into the world of business and innovation: What do you do when you want to satisfy someone? In all likelihood, you do everything to find concrete, real solutions for that individual's needs. But when you love someone—whether that person is your parent, your wife, your husband, your children— then you try to do much, much more. You don't limit yourself to simply satisfying their needs; you enter into the sacred grounds of magic, the memorable, the extraordinary, the surprising. You astonish them and spoil them with the unexpected. This is precisely how unicorns, real innovators, think and act.

True innovators are human beings in love with other human beings. They are in love with every human being for whom they create, design, and dream. They put people's desires and needs before everything else; this is how they make magic. Brands and technologies become enablers and amplifiers; business results are a collateral effect, even if they are obviously also sought and essential. But what has absolute priority for real innovators is the creation of exceptional, unique, precious solutions full of meaning and relevance. These solutions are spontaneous, authentic, unbiased acts of love—love for the user, for the human being, for society as a whole.

Unicorns Are Risk Takers but Cautious Too

The act of innovating implies taking risks. There simply is no innovation without risk. Risk is nothing other than the potential for a decision to produce an undesired effect, one that has an impact on our stability, our security, and that of the goods and people who are important to us. Translated into the world of innovation, risk can take countless forms: it's a product with an innovative functionality that people might not appreciate, an object's look and feel that are perhaps a little too far ahead of the times, a business model that isn't sustainable over the years, and so on.

Uncertainty relating to one or more variables is basic to innovation. When all the variables are known and under control, then the idea already exists and has been realized by someone else. This is not, therefore, innovation. The unknown is a constant in the processes of innovation, rendering them risky by definition. Every company sets up a whole series of other processes to manage risk and dampen its potential impact. But if you're doing real innovation, that risk cannot be entirely removed. Consequently, those enterprises that are more disposed to innovation need talent also disposed to taking risks.

Every company has a level of risk tolerance, which matches that of its own management team. The lower the risk tolerance of the company's leaders, the lower the company's risk tolerance is. The reason for being risk averse in a business can be traced back to the same matrix of cause and effects: you want to reduce to a minimum the probability of compromising your assets (both material and immaterial) as well as the potential of breaking promises made to investors. The higher the risk, the higher the chances of failure; but risk often also corresponds to a higher level of eventual returns.

Every individual, when faced with any choice, weighs up the benefits and threats, both real and potential. Those individuals who are naturally predisposed to taking risks are those who, faced with a choice between two situations—one ongoing and the other new—prefer to manage the *potential* "pain" generated by the new situation if things go wrong, rather than continuing to manage the *certain* pain generated by the current situation.

A common example, which many of us have probably experienced at least once in our lives, is that of being offered a new job. If we are unhappy in our current situation—if we are suffering because we are not appreciated by our boss or don't share the company's values, or because we don't love what we are doing every day—then it's very likely we will be disposed to taking the risk of changing positions. The new position could be an ideal one for us, but it could also turn out to be ill-fitting;

nevertheless, if the potential suffering of the new situation is preferable to the actual suffering of the current position, then we'll run the risk of change. This is the reason that, in situations of crisis, people are often more ready to take risks: there's a high chance that the current pain is greater than any potential pain in the new situation.

This is also the primary reason that, consequently, great crises and great risks often give birth to great innovations. This is true of our own lives as much as it is for companies, industries, and society as a whole. The wisdom of centuries carried in everyday speech teaches us that you have to reach rock bottom before you can get up again. That rock bottom is the final crisis that shifts the bar of potential suffering: actual pain in those depths is so extreme that any potential pain in a different situation can only be deemed lesser. Risk is thus lowered or even made null and void.

If, instead, we are happy in our current working position but are attracted to a potential improvement in a new position, then the decision becomes more complicated. The reason for this difficulty is that in this situation the perceived risk is high: in the current moment there isn't pain, while in the new situation there is no real guarantee that there won't be pain. Whoever chooses a new job in this scenario is the kind of person for whom the suffering cause by a missed opportunity—in relation to the permanence of the current position—is greater than the suffering provoked by the potential failure of the new situation. This kind of person, who is naturally predisposed to taking risks, has a lower level of fear of failure in comparison with others, because this kind of person tends to be intolerant of the inertia of the status quo.

There are people for whom the present represents a zone of peaceful, enjoyable comfort—and then there are people for whom the present, with its status quo, is a place of disquiet and tension. I am one of the latter. The majority of successful companies are, on the other hand, at ease in the hyperefficient situation of their own prosperity and find it difficult to engage in an act of destabilization in the name of the uncertain benefits of a different situation. In contrast, companies in crisis, at risk of closure or failure, will be more ready to run the risk of change and innovation, sometimes even in very radical ways, in order to survive.

Innovators are people who love risk because they have a gut instinct for evolution, progression, and change. But they also know how to manage risk with intelligence. They aren't gamblers. They are spontaneously inclined toward taking risks because they are spontaneously predisposed to the most impactful, overwhelming form of innovation—but they manage this innovation with planning and cunning, keenly evaluating all the variables.

Innovators climb the most difficult mountains, the ones no one has climbed before, the ones people are scared of taking on—but they make use of a harness, they employ a safety net, they study every rock and passage, they have good shoes and anti-slip gloves. Innovators have the courage, desire, and determination to climb that mountain—a courage, desire, and determination that many do not have, because the journey is a risky one. But they are also cautious. Being disposed to taking risks does not necessarily mean taking a blind leap; you need to move forward in an intelligent way, which means evaluating the potential situations of failure, imagining the effects, being ready to deal with them and with the outcomes, with a plan in your head and in your heart. This preparation for managing failure is indispensable because when you run risks, it's statistically certain that sooner or later those risks mean you'll fall—and when you do, you need the intellectual, spiritual, and emotional wherewithal to get back up again. But if you take risks in an intelligent way, then sooner or later, the results will come. And the final balance between success and failure will have a positive ending.

This is the reason that, for any organization interested in innovation, it's vital to nurture a culture that doesn't punish the errors generated by calculated risks. You need a culture that allows, manages, and celebrates risk. You need talent ready to take risks in an aware fashion, management that gives people the freedom and possibility to do so, an environment that doesn't crucify those who commit errors in this arena, and a whole series of processes that are able to make the best use of these errors, learning from them and sharing these lessons with the whole community so as not to repeat them. Great CEOs are leaders who know how to manage risks and errors in the right way, creating the right kind of entrepreneurial culture. The CEOs I've worked with—George Buckley at 3M, Indra Nooyi and Ramon Laguarta at PepsiCo—have each, in different ways, shown themselves to be individuals who have understood this principle in a very deep way. My own existence in these companies, and the development of design organizations that are unique for their mission and makeup, are the tangible results of this capacity.

My advice for people who want to re-create this kind of culture in their own organizations is this: look at innovation with the eyes of a scientific researcher. Scientists know very well that in order to arrive at any invention, patent, or discovery, they need to run hundreds and hundreds of experiments. The problem of the business community is that, during the processes of innovation, these experiments are often given the wrong name. What science calls *experiments*, business calls *errors*. It's once again a problem of terminology. Specific words are the reflection of a specific culture and its powerful amplifier. Imagine a scientist who is told, "Find a cure for cancer. Your deadline is in six months. And please do it without the inefficiency of all these experiments—without errors in the process." Financial algorithms and business culture don't like experiments too much. And yet, the reality is that without experiments—what are *erroneously* often called *errors*—you will never be able to produce anything radically different. For this to happen, every business needs to consider the risk of experiment or error within its business models and establish a series of processes and systems to extract lessons and insights from these errors, so as not to repeat them, and to take them into account in future innovation processes to produce more intelligent, sustainable, and solid results.

Unicorns Are Aesthetes with an Aesthetic Sense

Unicorns appreciate beauty; they understand its virtue and know how to generate it in a refined and elegant way. *Intuitive appreciation* and *intellectual understanding* are two complementary and important dimensions of this gift.

Intuitive Appreciation

Appreciating beauty means looking for it, enjoying it, celebrating it, surrounding yourself with it. You see it in the choice of objects that people make for themselves, from a pen to a car, in the way they dress, how they furnish their homes, in their offices, their attention to detail about everything surrounding them. They curate their vision both in an overall and a particular sense. The specific styles they choose have little importance—what counts is that their choices are always the result of their own original points of view. There are many people who simply don't have this ability or, rather, don't have it in all of its expressions. You might say about these people, "they don't have (aesthetic) taste."

Attraction for the beautiful is an instinct defined within parameters that can be clustered into three groups: they are partly biological, universal, and objective; partly historical, cultural, and relative; and partly individual and subjective. Natural beauty—such as a landscape, a puppy, a sunrise—is appreciated universally and timelessly, in a generally unanimous way. Artificial beauty, however—that is, something created by people, such as a dress, a building, a work of art, an object, packaging—is appreciated through a varying hybrid of universal canons on one side and cultural and individual criteria on the other.

The beauty of a sunset in the African savanna has been marveled at in the same, universal way throughout different historical epochs, hundreds of years ago and in our own era, by people from very different backgrounds. But a human creation such as the Sydney Opera House—today prized by everyone as one of the Australian city's most splendid and iconic buildings—was bitterly contested when it was constructed in 1956. The times simply weren't ready for this kind of language in that region of the world, in years when Australian aesthetic culture clearly was not—in many ways—aligned with the European and specifically Scandinavian culture of its Danish architect, Jørn Utzon. There are canons of universal beauty, often associated with nature, and then there are other canons that evolve with the historical, social, and cultural context.

Then there are all those variations within the same historical, social, and cultural context that are connected to personal taste. Let's imagine two individuals with different tastes within the same context, faced with the same object. We might think of two people, one with "good taste" and one with "bad taste," who are asked to judge the ugly packaging of a well-known brand of cookies in front of them: the person with good taste will understand what's going on and describe the packaging as ugly—that is, not enjoyable, imbalanced, unattractive, perhaps even *kitschy*, as the critic Gillo Dorfles would have defined this characteristic.[5] The person with bad taste will simply not realize any of this.

You may be asking yourself who decided a priori that this packaging was ugly. We could run through a whole series of shared and universal canons, as defined by philosophers thousands of years ago, such as Pythagoras's harmony of parts and Heraclitus's dynamic balancing of otherwise discordant elements. We could look at the design principles of alignment, balance, contrast, proximity, repetition, proportion, and positive and negative space. We could check the hierarchy of each visual element; the accuracy of scale; the choice of finish and materials; the design of lines, forms, and volumes; and the selection of patterns, textures, and colors.

There are people who aren't able to grasp a certain harmony and balance on first sight, in a natural and intuitive way. It's as if these people have a kind of aesthetic myopia: they can make out the universal beauty of nature or the familiar beauty of objects and buildings that are universally prized on a mass level, but they don't have the critical capacity to see beauty in high definition in all other situations; they see things as if through a haze and thus simply aren't able to evaluate their beauty. The ability to recognize beauty is to a certain extent innate, but it can also be trained and learned through technique and experience.

The eighteenth-century philosopher David Hume defined individual taste as a kind of value judgment generated when you're exposed to beauty. Beauty generates these emotional reactions, which in their turn generate value judgments that make us appreciate a given product X as being more beautiful than another product Y. Hume maintained that "beauty is no quality in things themselves: it exists merely in the mind which contemplates them; and each mind perceives a different beauty." But he clarified that there are also "certain qualities in objects which are fitted by nature to produce those particular feelings" (that is, the pleasure of beauty, the displeasure of deformity).[6] This is where the universal canons of beauty come in. In other words, for Hume, good taste is the individual ability to perceive, to a higher degree than others do, the details of beauty as defined by shared biological and cultural parameters.

The same is true, for example, of the ability to taste wines, to appreciate and distinguish each note and flavor: not everyone has the same talent or ability. The aesthetic sense and the ability to taste wine are, to some extent, spontaneous and natural; there are people who by their very nature have a greater sensibility than others do. However, these senses can also be trained and nurtured through education, observation, and practice. I have experienced the truth of this myself.

Looking back over these first forty-seven years of my life, it is clearer to me than ever how much my aesthetic sense—its sensitivity and sophistication—has gradually evolved over time. In some way, I believe that I have always possessed a decent dose of basic taste, but who knows, perhaps I'm wrong; many people think they have good taste when in truth they don't. Perhaps I didn't have any natural good taste but was then helped, influenced, and unconsciously trained and inspired by my first months of life, through the deep aesthetic sense of my parents, especially my father, an artist and architect. But what is extremely obvious to me is the evolution of that sense of taste over the course of my life. Studying design at university; the countless projects, errors, and gradual improvements in those projects; the continual interaction with mentors, teachers, supervisors, and colleagues in the world of creativity; keeping constant company with stylists, architects, designers, and others with a high aesthetic sense typical to the world in which I have grown professionally—there is no doubt that all of these experiences have contributed to fine-tune my taste over the decades, developing it, improving it, making it more accurate, more confident, more precise. This has been a constant and daily labor—consistent, careful, obsessive; sometimes conscious, sometimes unconscious.

One aspect that I find fascinating is that in each phase of my life I was convinced that I had a sophisticated aesthetic sense, and yet, today, I know that my taste twenty years ago was not as refined as it is now. So it's fairly clear to me that in another twenty years' time, I will probably have a still more refined aesthetic sense, trained by decades of further experience, than I possess today. Most people tend to believe that they have good taste, even when they don't.

We must be
students *of* life,
students *for* life.

When taste and the ability to recognize beauty become important assets for a company and provide a competitive edge in the business world—and this is the case for our age of excellence, dominated by the visual culture of the digital world—then these organizations can't rely any longer on the randomness of an aesthetic sense that differs between one leader and the next. The best approach is to trust a community that has made beauty, aesthetics, and taste its cultural and educational pillars and keys to success. I refer, of course, to the design community in a broader sense.

There is a very high probability of finding people with a good aesthetic sense in this creative world for three main reasons. First, people with a more developed natural taste are attracted from an early age to disciplines that privilege beauty. Second, if you aren't able to recognize and produce beauty through your own work, then in the majority of cases your career in this world won't take off, and you'll end up doing something different. Finally, over the years, these people continuously refine the aesthetic sense that is part of their DNA through practice and experience, becoming professionals of beauty, generating a level of taste that people who have not undertaken this journey probably do not possess.

Being in touch with these communities also helps innovators who are not designers to develop their own aesthetic sense over time. And this is of extreme importance: the more people you have inside your organization who have a good aesthetic sense, the more effective your company will be in using this lever as a competitive advantage to create meaningful value for people.

Intellectual Understanding

The ideal innovator is someone who doesn't merely appreciate beauty and ecstatically and enthusiastically contemplate it. Beyond appreciating the essence of beauty, innovators also understand and rationalize its role. In other words, they are clear about the potential for beauty in our modern society and in the business world—especially in a world such as today's, permeated by a social media culture in which images and visual codes have become more important than ever before.

Beauty is an asset that generates different levels of benefit for the user: it attracts, distinguishes, facilitates, inspires, creates trust, moves people, represents ideas. In one way or another, beauty does all of these things. As human beings, we are naturally and instinctively attracted to beauty, even when we don't realize it. Without beauty, companies and brands lose this added value, often in an unconscious and gratuitous way. And yet, this happens in so many situations and organizations.

It happens when innovators, managers, and entrepreneurs don't understand beauty's value or don't assign beauty enough value. There are industries in which aesthetic sense offers an obvious competitive advantage, from fashion and jewelry to tourism, interior design, consumer electronics, and lighting; from automotives to entertainment, theater, music, sporting apparel, and kitchenware. Either you manage the aesthetic value of your products and brands in the right way, or you fall afoul of it. Other industries are arriving at this point and becoming progressively aware of the value of aesthetics. In some other sectors, this isn't the case yet, but it's only a matter of time.

In these last two categories, a range of business leaders still do not understand the virtue of aesthetics and don't think they need to invest in this as a necessary variable. But, yet again, this is merely a temporary situation. The wheels have been set in motion, and soon these people will also grasp their error of judgment. And this may happen in a more painful way, for them and for their businesses, than really would have been necessary—if they had only understood matters earlier.

Unicorns Are Holistic Designers

Let's be clear: a unicorn doesn't necessarily need to be a designer. This is obvious enough. In my life, I have met talented scientists, wonderful lawyers, finance wizards, brilliant marketers, resourceful musicians, and skilled politicians who were all unicorns, in one way or another. A unicorn doesn't have to be a designer, but does have to be a *design thinker*. In other words, unicorns need to be able to exploit the unique way in which the design community, as we have described it, typically thinks and works.

Design is nevertheless a fundamental component of the art of innovation in most products and industries, whenever there is an object to generate, an experience to construct, a message to plan. We've spoken about this at length earlier in this book.

If a unicorn belongs to this community—that is, if the unicorn is indeed a designer—then for that designer, it will be of the utmost importance to have a holistic approach to the discipline. Unicorns who are not themselves designers will need a designer in their innovation process. And in that case, these individuals will need to entrust themselves to a designer who in turn has a holistic approach, rather than a merely traditional designer, focused on one of the professional specialties, from graphic to product design, strategy to fashion design, interior to digital or experience design.

Let me explain what I mean by the term "holistic" in this context. Design is a vast domain, even if many people don't realize this. Talking about "design" is like talking about "medicine." Medicine has a whole series of specializations, from cardiology to oncology, gynecology to orthopedics, pediatrics to anesthesiology. Doctors each have their own specialty and don't work in other fields. Would you let a gynecologist treat your heart? Would you have your knee ligaments reconstructed by an oncologist? And just as in medicine, there are huge differences between cardiologists, oncologists, gynecologists, and orthopedic surgeons, so too, in the cosmos of design, there are vast differences between industrial designers, brand designers, strategic designers, fashion designers, interior designers, food designers, experience designers, and digital designers—even without taking into consideration their cousins, the architects, artists, animators, photographers, and directors. An industrial designer is rarely an expert in typography. A graphic designer doesn't know how to use 3D modeling software. A fashion stylist doesn't have the tools to create objects. The digital designer doesn't design strategies. These disciplines have had parallel lives for years, separated into their silos, from the academy onward—and above all in the hyperspecialized Anglo-American world.

But today, matters are changing. Or, to put it better, society is changing, the way we innovate is changing, the way we imagine and launch products is changing, the way we build a brand is changing, the way we communicate is changing—and design has to change as well. In a world like today's, where brands are on the digital stage twenty-four hours a day, innovators need to know how to plan and manage all aspects of brand performance, from the object to packaging, from communication to experiences, in both the physical and the virtual world.

At PepsiCo, for example, we constantly find ourselves defining how the Pepsi brand behaves in the most diverse kinds of situations. One week, we might design the brand's presence on a shelf in Walmart for an everyday shopping experience; the next week, we'll design what the cola of the future will look like; the following week, we'll be imagining how Lady Gaga could interact with the brand at her upcoming Super Bowl performance; perhaps the week after that, we could be drawing an $800 hoody for a collaboration between Pepsi and Dsquared2; and the next month, we'll find ourselves planning the hoody's online promotion for both the Chinese and American markets at the same time.

If Apple had designed only a beautiful iPhone, and the design of the packaging, the digital interaction, the retail experience, and the online communication platforms had not all been aligned to that quality level, then the iPhone itself would have suffered and would never have met with the extraordinary success that it has enjoyed. Every touchpoint of the brand is connected and needs to be designed with consistency and sophistication, telling one common, holistic story.

Social media has amplified this necessity to extreme levels. In the past, a company could control how a brand was expressed, with careful art direction across a few well-defined channels. Today, on the other hand, everyone can share their experience with the brand across the democratic stage of the digital planet; every moment of excellence, along with every error and incoherence, is constantly on display, amplified and made visible as never before.

Pepsi is always Pepsi on that stage. And therefore it must behave in a way that is coherent with itself, on a global level, and that simultaneously works in the local context. And the brand has to do this at every touchpoint, in every field. It doesn't matter whether what you are looking at is a photo of a can snapped in Carrefour in Buenos Aires or a limited edition bottle on the catwalk in Milan, a cooler in a village on the edge of Nairobi or a licensed jacket in the Harajuku shopping neighborhood of Tokyo. The brand must look consistent in every expression and manifestation, independent of its location, and at the same time it needs to be in total synergy with the environment in which it is immersed. Otherwise, it will be perceived as inauthentic and disengaged.

The modern innovator thus has to know how to design every one of these touchpoints in a strategic, informed, and detailed way. This is no small task because designers are trained, for the most part, in a specific discipline, focusing on specific categories of these touchpoints, from products to packaging, from digital platforms to physical experiences, to mention only a few. And when these professionals enter the workforce, they usually begin a career in a specific field, the one corresponding to their training. A product designer who joins a company to perform that role will then find it difficult to become a brand designer, an interior designer, or a fashion designer. And even if the individual wants to make such a transition, that designer wouldn't immediately have the skills necessary without having studied or been exposed to the discipline before in some way during the person's career. Equally, it would be very difficult for a company to give such a person that opportunity.

There are, nevertheless, designers who—through a mix of curiosity, courage, and various circumstances (what we call life)—have the chance to train themselves in a holistic way. In my own case, it was fate that made the ideal conditions to begin a journey of this kind; my curiosity and my dreams did the rest. I have tried to decipher this journey over the years, to try to find the right indications to nurture high-potential talent in my teams in a similar way, offering them a career path that could be the most holistic possible.

My father, Eugenio, is an architect with a passion for art, both practicing it and studying it. My grandfather Emilio worked for the Italian Ministry of Aerospace but spent his whole life painting, and that's how I recall him—old, retired, constantly at the drawing table. My brother, Stefano, is an industrial designer like me, but over the years he has created multiple fashion brands and has always worked at the intersection of communication, product, graphics, fashion, art, and experience.

When I was at 3M my partner, Elisa, was a haute couture designer with Yves Saint Laurent. My wife, Carlotta, is the head of marketing in the United States for the Italian fashion label Golden Goose and contributes to keeping me constantly in touch with that world. And then there are friends, good close friends, who work in the most varied sectors of creativity. My private and personal context has always kept me linked in with different continents in the world of design. And this keeps on nurturing a very broad sense of creativity within me.

At university, I studied industrial design, a discipline that expands out into graphics, communication, and experiences in a very organic way. At the university Politecnico in Milan, we were already speaking about service design and strategic design in the 1990s, and that became my training. At the National College of Art and Design in Dublin—where I spent a year studying through the Erasmus exchange program—I was exposed to a more artisanal approach, to the culture of the prototype, to the practice of design as created in workshops and laboratories. I then got my master's degree with a thesis on wearable technologies, which brought me closer to the worlds of fashion and the most advanced technologies.

When I joined Philips Design in Milan, the team was made up of only a few people, and so even though I was working in product design, at the crossroads of technology and fashion, I was asked to play a role in every creative area so as to support the group as a whole. That period opened up windows onto a universe that I still knew very little about, that of typography and graphics, and I made sure to carefully watch the experts I was surrounded by, as well as to engage in constant, persistent practice. I wasn't scared of asking questions, even the most naive ones. I documented my attempts, tried, failed, tried again, and improved, step by step. I was experiencing what has been called, since time immemorial, an apprenticeship. The only difference, if I look back over my professional journey from those days to now, is that I have never really lost the mindset of an apprentice. I always try to preserve that mindset, and I hope that I will never abandon it. I'm always on the search for new concepts, new ideas, new tools, new methods.

When I founded Wisemad, my design agency, I had to learn to code, to build websites, to design motion graphics. And I met the world of music, entertainment, and celebrities. In the meantime, I was advancing my own projects in industrial design and wearable technologies.

Joining 3M meant returning to product design, to 3D modeling and prototyping—but it also meant encountering the professional communities of science and business. While at 3M, I realized very soon that in order to produce value for the company, I needed to leave the restrictive boundaries of product design—the role that had been assigned to me—and so I began to venture into the fields of communication, branding, experience, innovation, and digital design. Yet again, I learned a great deal by getting my hands dirty, having the courage to make mistakes, and earning my first successes. I began to gain more credibility project by project and, with that, more resources, more opportunities. And in the second half of my decade with 3M, I finally had the opportunity to begin exercising that holistic approach to design in a more visible and official way—an approach so important for the whole organization. Those years also gave me the chance to develop other important muscles, such as design leadership, design thinking, strategic design, and system and organizational design.

That's what I took with me to PepsiCo in 2012, when I moved to New York City. And my learning curve didn't stop there. Even today, I keep absorbing the knowledge of all people and communities that surround me, especially the new ones. I am a sunflower, and they are water and light to me. I look for them and I look to them, to keep growing, constantly, day after day.

Fate gave me some of the ideal circumstances to inspire this diverse journey—but curiosity, courage, resilience, and dreams have done the rest, giving me a push to launch myself into areas adjacent to my own discipline, outside of my comfort zone, while always learning more, mastering these areas, and over time making them my own. In the past several years, I have met a range of designers who have developed similar multifaceted career paths; today, some of them are on my team, and others are partners and friends in agencies, corporations, and start-ups. But the percentage of designers with this holistic education is still very small.

For anybody interested in becoming a holistic designer, this is my advice. Choose a design school and select a specific design discipline—whatever you love the most. Then, in parallel, expose yourself proactively to other design disciplines right from the start of your academic career, with an infinite and insatiable curiosity. And when you get your design degree, well, that's just the beginning. It's essential to understand that any formal educational course can represent only a fragment of a much longer journey of discovery—as long as our entire existence. We must be students *of* life, students *for* life.

If you're a designer, choose companies that give you the greatest possibility of interaction with a full range of design disciplines and exploit those contexts so that you never stop learning. If you work in other disciplines, try to do the same in your own field. Even if we are extensively talking about design in these pages, this approach applies to essentially any other profession.

At PepsiCo, my mission has always been to provide all our talent with this kind of opportunity. To this end, over the years I've hired some of best designers in the world from across the fields of design: product, graphic, digital, experience, strategy, and innovation. These are professionals with very different backgrounds and levels of experience, hailing from more than forty different countries, working together, side by side, on the most varied projects, experimenting, evolving, growing, learning from one another, mentoring one another, all in a holistic way. I have always tried to create the best context in which to amplify individual learning, transforming the workplace into a laboratory for collective cultural growth. And all those people who are authentically interested in this multidisciplinary approach have leveraged this opportunity.

This context, however, is still only a platform, in the same way as an academic environment is. It's a useful and valuable platform that inspires and stimulates, multiplies chances and generates synergies—but it is, nevertheless, still only a platform. A platform is like a gym full of equipment: the place and the tools cannot build your body. It is we ourselves who have to go in, use the tools, and exploit the place to the best of its possibilities. And even if we have been assigned machines to work on our quads and our triceps—because that's our training and objective—we still have access to all the other equipment to work on our dorsal, pecs, abs, and any other muscles we want to develop. But it's up to us to try out the equipment, to talk to the people who know how to use those machines well, to experiment and learn.

The same thing happens in the design and innovation unit in PepsiCo: it's each and every person's responsibility to leverage the possibilities that they have access to every day in that context. An industrial design project will always need the best industrial designers on the planet—but a graphic designer who's in charge of the visual strategy of that project, and in parallel is also learning to design in 3D, can make a contribution, prototype ideas, and generate concepts by turning for assistance from the experts. And that graphic designer can thus learn, grow, improve, and increasingly take steps toward the well-rounded dimension of holistic design. The same thing can obviously happen with a product designer who wants to work in graphics.

It goes without saying that, over the course of the years, I have learned a great deal from my teams. Throughout my whole career I have always made sure to surround myself with exceptional talent, not only because I needed these people to achieve the goals that I had set for myself and for the companies I have worked in, but also to be able to keep learning from these talented professionals. At PepsiCo in particular, I've been able to attract and hire some of the biggest names in design in the world, including heads of design in various other multinational corporations, as well as managers who used to run agencies and consultancies supporting some of the biggest companies on the planet. I've been taught so much by my teams, and I continue to be inspired by them every single day.

Innovators need to have a holistic design approach. If you're a designer and want to innovate, define a career path and a personalized course of learning for yourself that allows you to form an all-around approach to design. If you remain anchored to one dimension of the discipline, you can still undertake a wonderful professional journey, full of satisfaction and success—but, in that case, most of the time, to change the world you will need to put your professional skills and talents at the service of innovators who can leverage design in a holistic way.

If you're part of the business community—if you're a CEO, an entrepreneur, a leader in marketing or R&D—make sure you collaborate with designers who have this approach and experience. Too often— far, far too often—I've seen companies hire designers with the wrong backgrounds, people who are one-dimensional and too focused on just one area, unable to establish broader, relevant connections with other disciplines that are indispensable for generating the proper innovation strategy for a business. And the designers have thus failed in their roles. Those companies have then accused design itself of this failure, without realizing that they have only themselves to blame for having chosen a designer with the wrong background.

In February 2019, I visited the Triennale Design Museum in Milan for a very sad event: the funeral service of Alessandro Mendini, one of the greatest Italian designers of all time, who had recently passed away. As soon as I stepped into the spacious room where the body had been laid out, I saw something extremely peculiar that I will never forget. The family hadn't put his photo on the stand next to the coffin in the usual manner. They had decided to display a sketch of a fantasy creature instead. It was a self-portrait that Alessandro had made in 2006. On the drawing, he had written the following note: "I am not an architect, I am a dragon: the head of a product designer, the hands of a craftsman, the chest of a manager, the stomach of a priest, the feet of an artist, the legs of a graphic designer, the tail of a poet, the body of an architect."

I find this description extremely powerful. Designers of the world, if we want to do innovation, we all need to aim at being dragons. Nondesigners of the world, go hunt for dragons and form alliances with them!

Unicorns Are Both Business Savvy and Tech Savvy

If the unicorn is a business leader, then the gift of being business savvy should be taken for granted. If the unicorn is a scientist or an engineer, then the quality of being tech savvy applies automatically. But aside from their professional background, unicorns need to understand and appreciate to a decent degree both of these parallel worlds of business and tech. Designers, engineers, scientists, artisans, and technicians who have pure genius and creativity but lack an understanding of the world of business aren't unicorns. They might be fantastic creatives or extraordinary technnologists, able to generate exceptional concepts, inventions, and patents; but unicorns are something else. They are the people who transform these ideas into a product that reaches the market, creating value for both the user and society. Innovators will partner with such creatives and technologists on their own projects.

Business leaders or designers who do not understand the science and technology relevant for their own industry are not unicorns. They are perhaps the people who execute the strategy as defined by the unicorns. A given technology might range from data science to artificial intelligence, from manufacturing processes to material chemistry and physics, and much more. You don't need an MBA or a PhD to understand these aspects. What you need, once more, is a good dose of curiosity, initiative, resilience, and a desire to roll up your sleeves in order to learn, to throw yourself into new areas, to grow, experience by experience.

3M and PepsiCo have been my MBA and PhD. I can share my vision and ideas with thousands of CEOs and entrepreneurs from the stage of the World Business Forum, or with thousands of researchers and scientists at the World Innovation Forum, because PepsiCo and 3M's leaders in marketing and technology have been my mentors, and the projects that I have worked on with these leaders have been my school. The publications of experts across the world have been my textbooks, the resources available on the infinite network of the internet have been my research base, and my thirst for knowledge has been my drive and stimulus. And in all the projects of my life, I have put to the test—often in ways that were uncomfortable for me—everything that I have continued to learn from disciplines adjacent to my own over the years.

I have many, many friends who have become multidisciplinary in similar ways, but through very different journeys. The possible pathways take many different routes.

The designer and innovator Kevin Bethune, chair of the board of directors of the Design Management Institute, on which I sit with him, is one of those friends. I had the privilege of interviewing him about his professional journey for my podcast *In Your Shoes*. Kevin began his own career with a degree in engineering and a position in that field with Westinghouse Nuclear. As often happens in the professional world in the United States, he decided to pursue an MBA in finance, strategy, and entrepreneurship (from Carnegie Mellon University) in order to advance and consolidate his career. Once he got the degree, he was hired by Nike in Portland. It was there that he began to appreciate the world of design, realizing how in truth this had been a passion of his since he was a child. At Nike, he found a series of leaders who offered him—a process manager—the chance to experiment with design, giving him the opportunity to design shoes for the Air Jordan brand through a personal project outside his working hours. Some of those shoes reached the market, and Kevin understood that design could become a real profession for him. He thus decided to go back to university once more, this time to get a master's of science in industrial design at the ArtCenter College of Design in Pasadena, which guaranteed him a more formal education. And from there, he began a brilliant career that saw him become, over the following years, the leader of Boston Consulting Group Digital Ventures and then the founder of his own consultancy, Dreams • Design + Life.

Kevin began with engineering and business and then shifted to design; I began with design and then utilized the knowledge of business and technology that I had gained in the field. Kevin chose a more formal and formalized path; I had chosen a more informal and unstructured one. Who knows if there was also a certain "Italianness" about my way of doing things and a certain "Americanness" about his? But putting stereotypes aside, despite our different routes, we share an approach that is essentially identical. Our keywords are "curiosity," "thirst for knowledge," "enthusiasm," "passion," "resilience"; we share a desire to act with speed, incisiveness, and determination. This approach inevitably led us to the same crossroads between different worlds—between business, technology, and design—and this was how we found ourselves in the same place, that cultural "piazza" where roads meet up from every direction: the crossroads of innovation.

If innovation is made up of the ingredients of desirability, technical feasibility, and economic viability, then every innovator is a chef who knows how to taste those ingredients and recognize them, to use them and mix them in the best way possible to generate a perfectly balanced and memorable dish. The journeys to becoming this chef are very personal and unique; but the ingredients are well known, and it is up to each of us to decide how we want to acquire and blend them.

CHAPTER 8

THE UNICORN'S SOCIAL GIFTS

The unicorn's *social gifts* are the set of traits that are indispensable for working in an effective way with other people, moving with ease in a dense network of social relations. These gifts can apply to our interactions with our teams, colleagues, bosses, senior management; with customers, external partners, investors, and anyone else with a role in a business ecosystem; and also with family members, friends, acquaintances, and others surrounding us in our private life. These are fundamental characteristics for doing innovation holistically, utilizing a community's collective know-how, and avoiding dangerous roadblocks on the way.

Unicorns Are Kind, Sincere, and Trustworthy

Unicorns possess humanity, generosity, and sensitivity. They are transparent, sincere, honest, and inspire trust. They are kind. Any innovator should be a good person. Not all of them are, obviously, but this is the kind of innovator I look for, the best kind, the ideal kind, the unicorn. This is the innovator that I want for the world! If the aesthetic measure that we've spoken about earlier relates to what is beautiful, then the ethical one is about what is good. Having leaders with good hearts is thus clearly an ethical asset for a company. This should be enough to close the discussion; but, obviously, in the world in which we live, we see some people, every day, who aren't kind but nevertheless hold positions of power, in many fields and situations—and thus also in the world of innovation.

The idea of the kind leader might seem a little idealistic to many, simply gratuitous to others, and to some simply meaningless. I would like to say something to all of these people.

First, if you believe that kindness is not a necessary ethical value in the business world or is insignificant, then, quite simply, this saddens me, and I'm sorry for you, your company, your community, and the people dear to you. But even if this is what you truly believe, these gifts nevertheless have a reason to exist that might still be relevant to you.

It's only recently that I've realized the incredible business value of kindness and trust, which until a few years ago was for me only an ethical value that I took for granted, a filter that I used automatically to select collaborators and friends. The people who surround me in my private life are, in general, kind people. I have a priori rejected the unkind, negative, malevolent, untrustworthy, and insincere people. I simply don't manage to relate with them in any way, and usually I don't even have to really make the choice: we don't get on with each other—case closed.

At the same time, I have always looked for kind people for my team. My group is made up of hundreds of individuals spread across every continent, and I can't control every single hire, but I do have daily and direct supervision over my closest collaborators, as well as an important part of the second level as well. And I'm completely intransigent about this point: having a kind soul, being sincere, and looking out for others is indispensable. This applies to my collaborators and to their teams. This way of being thus permeates the entire design department, like a cascade. When someone without these characteristics finds a way into our ecosystem, usually that individual doesn't last long in the organization, because they don't find fertile ground in our group culture.

Let's now talk about the importance of this gift. I have about a dozen people who report directly to me. These are kind, transparent, honest, respectful people who love working together and trust one another. Passing time together is a pleasure; it warms your heart and does you good. This is the first, most visible, and most immediate value: kind people surround themselves with other kind people and love sharing spaces and moments. In contrast, who would want to spend the majority of the time in an office with malevolent and insincere people who can't be trusted? If such a person is imposed on your team, you try to avoid that individual as much as possible. This creates a form of inefficiency; team members avoid one another, they find it difficult to work together, and consequently they don't create synergies and aren't productive.

Now, if there's a member of your group whom you don't trust, what are the chances that you'll delegate to that person the team's success—and therefore also your personal success—by counting on the person to effectively play an assigned role in the group? The chances are very low, obviously, because clearly it would be too risky to trust that person. And so you try to protect yourself beforehand by creating a series of backup activities to neutralize the risk, defending yourself and your team in case that individual doesn't do what the person is meant to do. This then triggers a whole set of redundant activities, which in their turn impact the organization's productivity in a deeply negative way. For example, imagine how inefficient it would be for your company if a global business leader led a project that was supposed to be activated in every market in which the enterprise operates, but then the leader of the Chinese (or American, Italian, South African, or Mexican) team went ahead with another project in parallel, simply because that person wanted to make sure there would be a plan B in case the global project didn't succeed as intended—a triumph of inefficiency. Sincerity, transparency, kindness, and reciprocal trust would have avoided such a situation. Now multiply this problem for the number of people and teams you have in your organization, and you will understand very quickly the scale of unproductivity that the wrong culture can generate.

You might be asking why kindness is a part of this: surely you may trust a bad but talented person in your group to do what the person is supposed to do. The big difference is that kind people have not only their own futures at heart, but also those of other people on their team. Sooner or later, if they need to, bad individuals will put their own interests before those of their organization, and they will do so with few scruples—especially when others are in difficulty. Kindness is not a guarantee of trust and transparency, but it raises the probability of these, as well as guaranteeing a set of other benefits. Kind people don't take advantage of moments of difficulty but are ready to help the people surrounding them, in those moments more than ever. Each of us faces a mathematical certainty in our lives: sooner or later, these moments of difficulty, in our private or professional lives, will come. And in those moments, we need a hand from the people around us; we want their support and comfort. If that happens, all of us benefit: we do, the team does, and the company as a whole does, too.

In the most difficult moment in my private life, my work team picked me up, held me, protected me, and saved me. Without their kindness, things would have gone very differently. That moment opened my eyes more than ever, not only to the ethical and personal value of kindness, but also to its business value.

What makes the presence of just a few negative individuals within a community of otherwise positive people really very dangerous is the ability of those few individuals to generate and expand their negative energy within the group, creating unnecessary short circuits, separating kind people from one another, fragmenting existing synergies and trust, and creating disconnections that otherwise wouldn't exist. And this negative energy, yet again, impacts the team's productivity, as well as creating an unpleasant working environment and consequently lowering the group's engagement overall.

Too many companies, too much of the time, overlook this aspect and reward professionals who have produced brilliant business performances despite their personal and interpersonal behavior. Individuals who generate results at the expense of their team's health represent a cancer within a company, a slow and invisible sickness that destroys the organization from within, without too many symptoms, working through a body that seems healthy until it's too late, right up to the point when the metastasis has spread everywhere.

Kindness and trust produce efficiency and productivity. In a team of innovators, synergy, collaboration, and co-creation are the basic conditions for the success of the group and the project, and kindness and sincerity are precious values. I know that my team members can trust

Listening is a precious act. People should listen more in this world. Listening helps you to think, to reflect, to correct yourself; it makes us better.

me, and I can trust them. I know that there's a strong synergy and that the common interests of the group, of the company, of the collective vision, of the shared dream, take absolute priority. We are kind to one another, there's a positive vibe, the air is clean, the atmosphere is healthy, and we're ready to support one another. And if sometimes we argue—just as in a family, between brothers and sisters—then we also know how to make things up in the end, with a pure soul and a candid heart. Kindness meets with productivity, sincerity with efficiency, ethics with performance.

Unicorns Are in Love with Diversity

Unicorns thrive on diversity. Rather than being afraid of it, they purposely seek it out. Diversity is above all a mindset, entirely focused on the recognition and celebration of the unique character of every individual and on the consequent inclusion of this uniqueness within our communities. These criteria might be gender, race, ethnicity, socioeconomic status, age, sexual orientation, physical ability, or religious and political beliefs. But, within each of these categories, there is an infinite diversity of thought, feeling, style, and behavior. Imagine how reductive it would be to believe that everyone belonging to a gender—women, for example—all had the same way of thinking. Imagine how reductive it would be to believe that all Christians or all communists or all African Americans were similar, with the same behavior and style. It would represent the triumph of the stereotype. And it would be deeply disrespectful to both the community and the individual concerned.

True diversity is much deeper. It's the diversity that you find within every category, the kind that distinguishes each person as a citizen of the world, as a unique and irreplaceable being. This is a precious, real, concrete, widespread kind of diversity that should be celebrated, nurtured, explored, and amplified.

Innovation is a process that begins with empathy and is based on the ability to observe the world around you through an unusual and unexpected perspective in order to grasp moments, form ideas, and see things that no one has seen, formed, or grasped before. It should be clear, then, how important it is to have diversity in a team working in the field of innovation. Someone who has a background different from my own perceives, analyzes, and interprets the same situation from a different point of view; the union of our perspectives through dialogue and respect provides the potential to forge an entirely new and unheard-of perspective. That's where first intuitions and hypotheses come in, activating the journey of innovation: precisely from my perspective colliding in a positive way with yours, generating another one that is entirely new.

These two people could be a Latinx person and someone from East Asia, a person of color and a white person, someone with an analytic approach and someone with an intuitive one, someone who's sedentary and someone who's sporty, an older person and a younger one, a designer and a marketer, a heterosexual and a homosexual, a woman and a man, a wealthy person and a poor one, a Jew and a Muslim, an introvert and an extrovert. In order to facilitate this kind of opportunity, we need to design organizations with a diversity of backgrounds and thought, encouraging a diversity of opinions and styles, integrating them into a healthy, dynamic, and balanced dialogue.

Diversity, even before it is reflected in physical and visible differences, has to first be a trait of the group's culture. Otherwise, our teams will have different aspects, but their way of thinking, and the results of their actions, won't reflect that apparent diversity. Diversity in innovation needs to be wide-ranging and authentic. It can't be reduced to a few stereotypical categories; it has to sustain a truly diversified culture. This is the only way to generate real value through innovation processes—for our organizations, our business, our society as a whole. And this authentic interpretation is also the only true way to embrace the more traditional and visible forms of diversity.

Nevertheless, there are minorities who have been discriminated against over the course of history in incomprehensible and atrocious ways. And this aspect, when we talk about diversity, can't be overlooked and forgotten. It needs to be vividly impressed in our minds. As leaders, brands, and companies, we have an ethical and social responsibility to give these specific communities an amplified voice and shine the light of visibility. This should be the duty of every individual on this planet, but it's especially the duty of people who have the resources and platforms to do so in a tangible and impactful way. True diversity, integrated into a company's culture, is a moral duty and a fundamental driver of innovation.

In our design team, diversity is a mantra, completely organic and inscribed into our genetic code. On the one hand, it's supported through a conscious and structured program of recruiting, retention, and career growth, which creates a lucid, explicit, and conscious focus on systemic social problems; on the other, it is so natural for our working environment that it functions on an unconscious level—it's in our very way of being and existing. We have more than forty ethnicities represented in our Design Center in New York alone, with a complete balance of women and men, as well as individuals representing the LGBTQIA+ community and a variety of religious faiths, socioeconomic backgrounds, political affiliations, and lifestyles.

And yet, there is still a long way to go before arriving at an ideal situation, in order to rebalance the distortions of history, prejudice, cognitive biases, and structural hurdles that are all too real—evident social barriers extraneous to the healthy safe space we are building. What we should never forget is that diversity and innovation cannot be separated. Innovators don't fear diversity; they love it with a visceral passion. Practicing innovation without diversity of thought and action is like exploring a jungle with a blindfold on, or swimming out into the ocean with stones in your pockets.

Diversity is one of those areas in which doing the right thing from an ethical point of view corresponds completely with doing the right thing from an economic one, because diversity is at the basis of innovation and progress. Not engaging with diversity is myopic, ignorant, and senseless. When you understand this fundamental principle, everything should become still more simple, obvious, and clear.

Unicorns Are Empaths and Have an Elevated Emotional Intelligence

We have already spoken about the importance of empathy and its role in the innovation process, along with strategy and prototyping. Innovators have to be empathetic toward the users they are designing for, or rather have to be able to understand these users in a profound way, seeing things from their point of view, putting themselves in the users' shoes.

But this is only one aspect of the empath's role in a professional team. Empathetic innovators are individuals who also understand the people around them in a visceral way, within the context of the company and the external world, from their team to their peers, the supervisor to the sponsor, the client to the investor, the consultant to the journalist. This empathy is one sign of innovators' emotional intelligence (their EQ, or emotional quotient). This is a gift that allows innovators to be lucidly aware of themselves in relation to others, establishing relations on an emotional and spiritual level with their neighbors, immediately understanding who is in front of them, reading the room on every kind of occasion. People with high emotional intelligence are emotional bridges, facilitators of dialogue, connectors of souls.

Over the years I have sometimes hired leaders who were wonderful designers, sophisticated thinkers, sharp strategists, and good people—but who didn't have an elevated emotional intelligence. Unfortunately, without this general skill, and in particular without empathy, all the rest is in vain, because in the world of innovation and more generally in business, the ability to engage others on an emotional level, both within and outside your organization, is indispensable. The world isn't a one-man or one-woman show. We are in the era of the *one-team show*. In our design organization, we even created the hashtag #oneteam to synthetize this idea. Empathy is the glue that makes a team stick together.

Unicorns Are Dialectical Conductors of Multilingual Orchestras

Dialogue allows the glue of empathy to take hold, enabling the surfaces to connect and dovetail, smoothing over the edges for a perfect fit, flattening out collisions that then sound like music. Unicorns create dialogue, harmony, melody; they are conductors of different elements that are reconciled in perfect balance. They are facilitators, interpreters, generators of synergy. Their art resides in the rare and sophisticated ability to know how to listen, to unite—to rebalance matters through transparent conversations, unexpected discussions, and surprising resonances—throughout the multidisciplinary, cross-functional processes of innovation. The scientist concentrating on the microscope and the marketer in love with the spotlight, the legal department and the creative studio, the leaders managing the resources of a company, both human and financial—all of them have to be brought together, to take up their own instruments and play in unison. Knowing how to do so in a seamless and effective way during the innovation journey is an art and gift. And it requires prodigious orchestra conductors.

To act as such conductors, innovators need to be polyglots. They need to speak a range of languages—the language of marketing and anthropology, design and science, finance and law, and more besides—all while maintaining a coherent and constant message but adapting its codes in accordance with the audience, in order to be understood by every professional community, acting as a universal connector and translator, jumping seamlessly from one area to another. This kind of ambiguity is the innovator's very essence.

As a designer I've needed to learn the language of finance in order to make people understand the value of what I was creating and to give me access to the economic resources I was looking for, in exchange for a clear return on investment. I've needed to learn the language of human resources so that those colleagues would support hiring the best creative talent, positioning them at the right level in the organization, paying them on a par with those in other, more established roles (such as marketing and research and development), retaining and incentivizing them with the right tools and resources. I've needed to learn the language of R&D, to work with engineers and scientists on the feasibility of our visions, to not accept replies such as "you can't do that" from manufacturing sites or research centers, in order to get closer to lab technicians and make them fall in love with forms and poetry that transcend the functionality of an industrial product. Being ready to learn different cultural languages was partly a mindset that I developed at school, through a curriculum ranging across different disciplines, but above all it's something I've learned in the field, driven by a thirst for knowledge, curiosity, and empathy toward others—my neighbors and those different from me.

Dialogue is a fundamental tool for all of this. This is why the unicorn is also *dialectical*. In ancient Greek philosophy, dialectics (from the Greek *dialeghestai*, "to discuss, to reason together") identified the search for truth through the dialogue of two speakers with different theses. In the *Phaedrus*, Plato compares dialectics to two opposed but complementary processes. The first consists in "perceiving and bringing together in one idea the scattered particulars, that one may make clear by definition the particular thing which he wishes to explain"; the other consists in "dividing things again by classes, where the natural joints are, and not trying to break any part, after the manner of a bad carver."[7] For Plato, in other words, dialectic represented a privileged road to arrive from a multiplicity to the unity of an idea, which is both the origin and final goal of consciousness. A unicorn is able to connect all disciplines, all points of view, all backgrounds, in a supreme and final synthesis in harmony with the needs and dreams of the human being for whom the unicorn is designing. And unicorns are simultaneously able to divide up their own vision, intuition, and dreams into intelligible and accessible fragments for a community with different cultural strands. Unicorns can establish a dialectical and profound dialogue with every kind of professional group searching for truth and are able to connect all communities into a unique, mutually cooperative conversation. In this sense, dialectics is a preparatory and enabling *social gift*, at the service of the *entrepreneurial gifts* of analysis and synthesis.

Unicorns Are Respectful

In the realm of innovation, as well as in business and indeed the world in its entirety, respect for others should be a common denominator for how everyone thinks and acts. Unfortunately, this is not always the case, especially when individuals or communities have points of view that are different from our own.

Let us take, for example, two macrocommunities of which we have already spoken at length in these pages: those of business and design. Designers often hold that they understand what society wants, what is beautiful and useful, what's on trend and what creates value, and they generate product and brand concepts that, in their opinion, align with that kind of ambition and expectation. Just as often, you find designers who think that the world of business, especially in some industries, is unable to understand these ideas, to appreciate their essence and qualities, systematically compromising the integrity of their incredible visions for the most futile and incomprehensible reasons. "This guy in marketing doesn't understand a thing!" How many times have I heard that sentence? It's what many designers think. At the same time, the sales and marketing communities often believe that designers are merely creatives, ignorant of the real needs of business, unable to grasp the rules of branding, limited and superficial in their perception of strategy. "Designers are basically stylists. Let's just leverage and channel their creativity, and keep them far away from the business world before they do any real damage!" That's what many business leaders think. And yet, when a smart designer and a smart business leader finally find a way to listen to each other, to open up, to respect and understand each other, they often find aspects of each other's worlds that make them change their ideas.

Let me share an example from my past at 3M. Around 2003, I was very close to a colleague who had gained the position of Six Sigma Master Black Belt. "Six Sigma" is a management discipline focused on generating efficiency in the processes of an organization, utilized over the years by a range of corporations, including Motorola, General Electric, Microsoft, and General Motors, just to name a few. The Master Black Belt at 3M was a role held by high-potential employees on a two-year rotation, in order to train them in these methods, giving these employees the opportunity to apply the methods in real projects in the field. This colleague, Marco (a pseudonym), was intelligent, strategic, a quick thinker, and generous with his smiles. He was very aware of the important role of design and had fully understood the discipline's potential at 3M. At that time, he wasn't working on any particular product development project or managing a particular brand, but he often came to me to share his passion for what I was doing, his understanding of the impact that still needed to be revealed, and his willingness to draw on this as soon as he was in a position to do so.

A few months later, the moment came: Marco became manager for the office business unit in Europe (commercializing Post-it Notes,

Scotch Tape, multimedia projectors, professional lighting, workspace solutions, ergonomic products, and much more). It was the occasion that I had been waiting for patiently for years—we would finally be able to radically change things in that business!

But over the next few months, I realized that that acceleration in the use and impact of design simply wasn't happening—and that it wouldn't be happening any time soon, either. In every other instance, as the designer that I was, I would have thought Marco was just another marketer, among many, who didn't understand our community's professional approach. But this case wasn't like all the others, and so something different happened.

There was a fundamental difference from all the other preceding situations: I knew Marco well, and I knew that he understood the value of design. *I respected him!* I always respected the other marketers on a human level in the past, but as a designer I usually didn't respect their ability to understand our creative vision. In Marco's case, however, I respected his intelligence, his strategic thinking, his empathy—but also his grasp of design. And so I began to ask myself questions that I hadn't asked before, questions that many designers (or other professionals in other contexts) never ask themselves during their professional lives. "Why was this sensible and intelligent marketer not making use of design, even when he understood its value?" That question, generated out of a position of respect, was a fundamental turning point for my entire professional life—and not just for me.

I found the answer by looking further into the goals that the company's upper echelons had assigned to Marco and trying to understand what limits, hurdles, and difficulties he might face in reaching them. In other words, I tried to put myself in his shoes, through empathy (it's not a coincidence that fifteen years later I called my first podcast exactly that: *In Your Shoes*). Empathy generates respect, and respect generates empathy.

As is so often the case for business leaders in many companies, Marco's role was being measured over the short term. Within the first year, he needed to generate a defined revenue, with a defined profitability, and earn a defined market share, with specific and limited resources. These goals and resources and this timeline had been assigned to him considering the current business model and strategic levers and not taking into account any other disruptive activity. This model implied that any long-term investment not forecast up front would carry the concrete risk of negatively affecting Marco's ability to achieve his business goals in the short term. And design was a long-term investment by definition. Accelerating the use of design would have then impacted on his annual performance, his compensation, and his overall career. And in some cases, in some companies, in some business cultures, missing a target and failing a year can even mean losing your job. This obviously has an effect on someone's private life—for example, the person's ability to maintain a certain lifestyle, to support a family, to guarantee a good education for children, and so on. The repercussions, in other words, are serious and real. It's no wonder that many professionals demonstrate caution when it comes to the decisions and choices they make throughout their careers.

The situation was made even more complicated by another variable: the majority of the managers in most organizations are evaluated on the basis of their own performance on a yearly basis, but innovation projects have much broader temporal horizons, seeing the first effects years after their kick-off. If these managers regularly rotate through positions every two or three years as they progress in their careers, then they have no official incentive to develop long-term innovation programs, leveraging their current budgets and putting at risk their short-term goals, to create winning solutions that will benefit their successors, not themselves. If the managers do so nevertheless, as does happen in a variety of situations, it's because they are aware that this is their duty as leaders in their organization. But the company essentially doesn't provide them with any concrete stimulus for long-term innovation, which relies entirely on these managers' sense of responsibility if it is to happen. Good luck with that!

As the psychologist Abraham Maslow wisely noted, the primary instinct in the majority of people has always been to guarantee themselves stability and security. This need is at the base of his pyramid of needs. The desire to innovate as the form and expression for other needs, positioned higher in the pyramid, is in second place. If the first layer isn't there, it's difficult to rise up to the second. And even if some fearless, less risk-averse individuals do exist, such people are few and far between. The world's companies cannot entrust themselves to anomalies in order to generate innovation.

In Marco's case, as in countless other situations since then, I realized that in order to promote the use of design in the company, there was little sense in continuing to push managers to act in a way that was reckless and self-destructive for them, going against structural obstacles much larger than they were. I needed instead to work with top management, in sales and marketing, human resources and finance, in order to redefine objectives, allocation of resources, incentives for long-term projects, annual compensation criteria, and strategies for entrepreneurial innovation. Being responsible for design at 3M didn't mean simply managing design projects, as they were asking me to do, and then complaining if business leaders didn't work the way we wanted them to. That responsibility meant, first and foremost, designing the conditions, culture, processes, and metrics for making those projects possible—even if nobody was asking me to!

And, indeed, the big challenge in this case was exactly that: the focus of that metaproject—culture, processes, metrics, organization, and business goals—wasn't really my responsibility; it was a role shared by a whole series of other departments. I could only try to influence them—not an easy task! But that's what I decided to do. And that's why, over time, I became chief design officer of that corporation instead of being fired a couple of years after I joined: I did what the company needed me to do, instead of doing what the company was (at first) asking me to do. My respect for Marco had helped me to understand better what my role in the company could be and should be. And it changed my professional life.

Respecting individuals with a different point of view from your own creates exceptional value, allowing you to transform your perspective through the conscious effort of trying to understand other people's. And this has two potential consequences.

On the one hand, it allows you to realize things that you'd never understood before, as was the case with my working relationship with Marco. This realization then helps you to reach a new awareness of yourself—of your role and your potential—and helps you to evolve, to adapt, to improve, to build new bridges, new bonds, new collaborations, new partnerships that you wouldn't have embarked upon otherwise. It's a win-win situation.

The other possible outcome is that respect allows you to understand in a deeper way how other people think, their drives, culture, difficulties, and fears, allowing you to identify the real causes of their inability to understand the value of what you're offering them. This helps you to adapt your language, codes, and content, the form and essence of your communication, without distorting the message or meaning, in order for that message to become more accessible, better understood, and more relevant. In this way, other people will finally have access to your perspective; they will appreciate it, and they will become allies. Yet again, it's a win-win situation.

In both instances, respect allows you to evolve together, opening the doors to new opportunities for both sides, improving matters both individually and collectively, growing and empowering one another. Respect is one of the fundamental engines of growth. This is true for the world of business and innovation, but it clearly has an extraordinary significance for our whole existence.

If people respected one another more—meeting each other halfway, talking despite their differences, appreciating each other for those differences, growing together through those differences—then we would probably have a better world. If individuals with different political views or religious beliefs, different skin colors or sexual orientations, didn't fall into the trap of lacking respect, on both sides, then we could get back to civil conversation, and we would have a more peaceful, happy, inclusive society, one more inclined to progress, innovation, and collective evolution.

Even when you have the right perspective, when you defend your values, when you fight for the right cause, lacking respect for people who are different from you is a sterile, harmful, dangerous attitude, because it produces divisions and fractures—and, in some contexts and situations, can even generate hatred. And hatred, as well as being an evil cancer for society as a whole, is also the most ferocious enemy to innovation and progress.

Unicorns Are Charismatic Storytellers

Unicorns are storytellers. They are able to express the value of their ideas, fine-tuning their message and their codes of communication in order to reach the hearts and minds of whomever they're speaking to. Unicorns use their stories, language, words, gestures, pauses, and glances in order to inspire and influence, to excite teams, colleagues, clients, investors, and the media. Unicorns tell stories, and they do it with extraordinary charisma. This is a fundamentally important gift. In a world in which our audience's attention is constantly challenged by external factors, by every kind of pressure, by a myriad of content, the ability to enchant someone with your story is a precious quality to make sure that people follow your vision with concentration, determination, diligence, coherence, passion, and joy.

I have been storytelling my entire professional life, from the very beginning. It's always been a passion of mine. I have done so with speeches, conversations, articles, and posts, in conferences, meeting rooms, magazines, and social media—and now with this book.

It's not been easy; it's been very complex indeed. But it's been fun too. Most of what I was able to build over the years has been shared through stories, and progressively, each of those stories became the foundation and the amplifier for more dreams to build and more projects to execute—and ultimately for more stories to tell.

Unicorns Are Generous Mentors

Unicorns have an intrinsic and genuine passion for spreading knowledge and culture. They do so every day, generously, without expecting anything in return. And they do so for the pure pleasure of sowing the seeds of culture throughout their organizations, their communities, and then the whole world. This mindset has a vital role in the context of a company because it exponentially amplifies the sharing of know-how and consequent learning, making the enterprise progressively stronger and more stable.

To be an innovator you don't need to be a mentor, nor do you need to be generous—but if your team is composed of people of this kind, it will have an exponentially greater potential to grow and succeed. A generous mentor is like the fertilizer that allows your plants to grow faster, stronger, healthier, richer in taste and nutrients. These are the kind of innovators I look for and want on my team.

There are many different ways to be a mentor and also to access these incredible individuals. We'll discuss these ways in more detail over the following pages.

Unicorns Avoid Taking Themselves Too Seriously and Know How to Have Fun

Unicorns know how to laugh, to be ironic, to make fun of themselves. And they know how to enjoy themselves, too. Science reminds us that smiling and having fun—two distinct but often connected actions—have exceptionally positive effects on personal and group health. Smiling and having fun can increase levels of serotonin, the hormone that regulates our mood; diminish stress; impact positively on our energy levels; amplify our ability to manage challenges; free our minds by empowering focus and memory; increase trust and connection between people; help sleep patterns; and create greater efficiency and productivity throughout the whole community. In brief, the ability to smile, laugh, and have fun is good for you and for your team. It's an innate and individual ability, but it can be facilitated within a group of people by creating the right culture and applying the correct tactics.

I never miss an opportunity—context permitting—to share a joke with my organization, to use irony to ease the tension, to steer through stressful moments with some laughter. I use my social media platforms to communicate with my own team, with my colleagues and partners, and with potential talent who might join us in the future—and I rarely skip over the chance to share something funny or amusing. I do so not only through my personal channels but also when using platforms on which fun isn't the standard, such as the professional platform of LinkedIn.

Smiling and fun are tools that I often use to avoid taking myself too seriously, to rebalance the gravity of deeper reflections with the levity of easier thoughts. Using these tools is a way to show humility, to get closer to people, and to show my human side, something that is perhaps sometimes hidden by titles, positions, images, and thoughts, which don't entirely communicate my real self. And it's fun for me too!

Even though the ability to smile, laugh, and have fun is a personal and individual gift, as the leader of organizations made up of hundreds of people, I do everything I can to generate situations that can promote that kind of collective culture. I want to come into the office and see people smiling; I want to see them enjoying themselves. I want to avoid the dull gray monotony of sad workplaces, made up of people who are emotionally stuck and take themselves too seriously. And I'm fully aware that their smiles are also signs of productivity, efficiency, and constant and consistent effectiveness, generated by people who love what they do and enjoy doing it.

At PepsiCo, this kind of mindset is something we protect and celebrate. And it's been the topic of endless conversations, efforts, and plans with my team, and particularly with Leighsa King, our vice president in charge of business, culture, and strategic transformation and one of my most trusted advisers (thank you, Leighsa!). A few years ago we created a Culture Club, led by Richard Bates on top of his daily design role: a small group of people whose mission is to think up, generate, and manage initiatives that forge, maintain, and protect our organization's creative culture. One of the team's goals is to program entertainment activities for our department, often bringing together learning and fun. We've organized costume parties and competitions and bowling championships; we've done ax throwing, magic-potion tasting, and visits to amusement parks. I've shared trips with my leadership team in hot air balloons, in small boats, and on horses—and we've seen wonderful places. I've even learned how to make a chunky knit blanket! During a virtual class online, together with our designers connected from several countries around the world, I was able to make one by myself, in less than an hour, and it became a beautiful holiday gift for Carlotta. You should try it; it's easy.

That's what we do. And we do it all for pleasure and with pleasure. We've never taken for granted the importance of these moments because we know how difficult it is to organize such experiences with your colleagues, for a whole series of reasons.

The first difficulty is that often, you simply don't have colleagues with whom you want to spend recreational time; this is the unfortunate truth in many organizations, big and small. And it's also one of the many reasons that I've always used the list of characteristics in these chapters as a filter for hiring collaborators. If your team is made up of positive, kind, sincere, empathetic, generous, intelligent, funny people, who want to smile and enjoy themselves, well, then you'll also enjoy spending time together. If you don't have this kind of people around, then all those moments of downtime—dinners, team-building exercises, and more—will simply be torture for many of you and a loss of money for the business.

The other difficulty is that enjoying yourself at work is often seen as taboo, as a result of the distorted and erroneous conviction held by some that these moments of entertainment during working hours throughout the year can somehow impact negatively on team productivity. The reality, instead, is the diametric opposite. Those moments of real living experienced together, far away from working situations, not only do *not* represent a loss, but actually constitute an exponential amplification of the organization's productive potential. These moments help to build priceless bonds and connections, cementing the team cohesion that can overcome any obstacle in day-to-day work, generating a deep reciprocal trust that is too often is missing in professional environments, and accelerating the production of that empathy, sympathy, passion, and inspiration each one of us needs when working in a complex organization, engaged in the sacred journey of innovation. These moments speed up the team's productivity and nurture the quality of the team's performance, both in the short and long term.

It's true that this isn't easy. In order to generate this kind of opportunity, you need the right people, the right leadership, and the right culture. We need to take care of this culture, cultivating it day by day, week by week, month by month, 365 days a year. Try to do so: it's worthwhile, and it's fun!

CHAPTER 9

THE UNICORN'S ENABLING GIFTS

The unicorn's *enabling gifts* are the set of characteristics that give an individual, on the one hand, the necessary structure to work effectively and successfully—know-how, culture, mindset—and, on the other, the drive and energy required to move forward in the prickly and unexplored territory typical of innovation, both in business and in life.

Unicorns Are Curious

When someone asks me where I find inspiration, my reply is always the same: I begin from inside myself. I have a natural motor of innate, insatiable, unstoppable curiosity for everything around me. Curiosity is a portal to access knowledge and an instigator for inspiration. Unicorns are curious—it's a minimum common denominator for the tribe. Curiosity is the desire to observe, to know, to investigate, to question, simply for the sake of knowing. If you think of the etymology of the word "philosophy" (from the Greek *philosophia*, conjoining *philein*, "to love," and *sophia*, "knowledge"—"the love of knowledge"), then in a certain sense curiosity is the most *philosophical* of the unicorn's attributes.

Curiosity is effectively the basis for that investigation of the world typical to philosophy. Curiosity consists in approaching every conversation, interaction, and experience with eyes full of a child's wonder, always on the lookout for the root causes that move all things, never taking anything for granted—always, constantly, incessantly asking yourself *why*.

The nineteenth-century Italian poet Giovanni Pascoli crystallized this sublime ability in his poetical work on the young child (*il fanciullino*).[8] We all have this child inside of us in the first years of our lives, but many of us then lose this child along the way, as we grow up. This child allows us to observe the world with innocence, poetry, with a passion that is always fresh and new.

I came across Pascoli and his inner child back in 1993, at my school desk in Varese. It was an extraordinary revelation because I suddenly became fully aware of the power of the inner child in myself, and I've never abandoned him since. Ever since then I have celebrated, nurtured, and protected him. I nurture his curiosity, I celebrate his potential, I protect him from the erosion of the years, from the attacks of a culture that is imposed upon us, from the so-called common sense of the adults surrounding us. True curiosity, the curiosity of the inner child, is what allows you to appreciate everything around you with new eyes, constantly renewing every experience.

Have you ever seen, for example, the infinite beauty of the microcosm that we're immersed in, the infinite variety of forms, colors, tones, and patterns that come together in nature, right in front of our eyes? Often the grains of sand on our beaches are not mere grains, but tiny shells with magnificent forms and unusual colors, losing themselves through their tiny scale, skipped over by our distracted gaze, becoming *only* sand and nothing else. Have you ever seen close up, perhaps with the help of the macro lens of a camera, the stupendous and unexpected colors of an ant, of a dragonfly, of a whole series of insects that live between the blades of grass, that perhaps you see but don't really look at every day on your way to work? You don't need large swaths of countryside to discover such wonders; even the small patch of grass in front of your house can reveal incredible surprises. Have you ever seen the elegant movements of a caterpillar or the wonderful patterns on a spider's skin? Most of these little spiders seem all the same, all brown and black, but in fact they have the most delicate details designed by Mother Nature across their abdomens, composed in blues, yellows, oranges, greens—saturated tones, perfect definition, high resolution. And from far off, we lose sight of these masterpieces. We are blind to the beauty of the microcosm, not so much because a few feet of space stand between these creatures and ourselves, but rather because of the light years of distance artificially generated by our distracted minds. And nature is not the only place where we have this problem.

Have you ever looked up in the air while walking in the canyons of your city? New York is often lived at eye height; many of us lose the wondrous forms, generous decorations, and unexpected colors of the architecture above us. You merely need to throw a glance to the sky to have your head struck by lightning, to be excited again every day, appreciating a new detail, a new story, a new experience. And it's simply enough to then lower your gaze and to look around you again with the same focus in order to admire a myriad of other details as clear as they are invisible to our careless eyes. Stop and look at the manholes of South Street Seaport in Manhattan, with the fish carved in bas-relief, each one thought up and designed by someone, trampled over by thousands of people every day, thousands of people who don't even notice or appreciate these marvels. Or slow your steps down and enjoy the forms and colors of the city's fire hydrants. A few years ago, I photographed hundreds of them, amazed by the variety of these objects that are dotted through the streets of the Big Apple. I saw dragons that cry, laugh, kiss each other, embrace each other, wink at each other. I was excited by what I discovered, so excited that I then shared the results in a series of posts on my social media platforms. I was excited by a series of fire hydrants that I had seen a thousand times before on my daily walk through the city but had never really stopped to look at with care, attention, and curiosity. I was as excited as a *fanciullino*—a little boy!

Our minds are sometimes lazy and sleepy, sometimes hyperactive and distracted, but when curiosity catches them they get excited, focused, feverish. Every day, we meet dozens upon dozens of different people; we pass them by, taking them for granted, without ever truly looking at them, without asking ourselves why they behave in a certain way, why they dress as they do, how they communicate. And this doesn't just happen with passersby but all too often with our neighbors as well, with a colleague, an acquaintance. Too often, we don't truly understand these other people; we stop at the surface, thinking that this surface is a sufficient representation of the substance beneath.

But in truth, every person is a book, a novel, full of thousands of pages, rich with images and words. And our lives are an immense and labyrinthine bookstore, where we see hundreds of different books on the shelves every day. Often—far too often—those books remain on the shelves, mere wall decorations for our existences. We look across the spines distractedly; sometimes we judge the book by its cover. Most of the time we don't stop to check the cover or even the title; we don't take the time to leaf through the pages, to lose ourselves in the stories they contain—surprising, touching, enlightening stories. Those books remain simply spots of color that populate our world.

Have you ever asked yourself why someone you know is shy? What is really behind that shyness? Is it just the individual's character, perhaps a difficult past, an experience that changed the person's life? Does this person need help? Or can this individual perhaps help us, we who sometimes are too outgoing, too extrovert, too boisterous? Why is one person kind but his brother not, despite their being raised by the same parents? Why—generally speaking—do women put on a certain kind of makeup, but men don't? Why do we say words like "hello," and why do we move our hands to greet each other? Why does a gesture in Italy have one meaning but in England another? Have you ever asked yourself that question typical of children—"Why?"—and then again "Why?" and yet again "Why?" It's a very powerful technique because it allows you to get down to the roots of every kind of behavior, to grasp the origins of the most different kinds of occurrences, providing you with the tools to decipher so many other situations, experiences, approaches, and emotions. Feeling wonder before the world and always asking why, without taking anything for granted, is a precious approach I have used countless times throughout my life.

This way of thinking has not only helped me in my professional path; it's also been of use in my private life. When someone has hurt me, disappointed me, or abandoned me, for example, I've always asked myself,

"Why?" And when I've found the first response, the most superficial one, I've then asked myself yet again, "Why?"—and there's another response, something deeper. And then I come again to the next "Why?" and so on, until finally I get to the real root cause. And often, in the depths of that new perspective, I have realized that the pain that's been inflicted on me wasn't intentional, that perhaps it was just collateral damage from an act that didn't really concern me or that began in some other trauma or pain that had nothing to do with me. There's an important difference between someone who harms you in a targeted and conscious way and someone instead who does so unconsciously, by accident. In the latter case, understanding, accepting, forgiving, and forgetting is much easier.

When we consider those root causes, our actions and reactions can always be channeled in a more efficient and effective way. Everything begins with this innate curiosity, this insatiable thirst to understand, to grasp, to know. Curiosity, when paired with respect and empathy, is a powerful asset in the life of anyone who wants to grow, progress, and innovate.

All the unicorns I know share this trait. Curiosity is the fertile ground where we plant the seeds of knowledge. It's the currency used to acquire as many seeds as possible, the water that irrigates them, the fertilizer that nurtures them, the eye that sees them grow, and the body that enjoys their fruits.

Never be ashamed of your curiosity. Too many people are scared to ask, "Why?" They are in fear of demonstrating a gap in their knowledge, of exposing the fact that they haven't already understood everything, haven't seen everything, and still have something to learn—especially when they are in management positions or when they've reached some form of success in life. Wise people instead know the limits of individual knowledge. "I know I know nothing," said the *knowledgeable* Socrates thousands of years ago, according to Plato. The unicorn's only concern is not the embarrassment of showing some lack of knowledge but the eventual inability to access the knowledge of others through curious questions and dialogue. Too many people don't understand that the prowess of asking questions with intellectual and spiritual curiosity is one of the greatest forms of intelligence. It's a tangible expression of self-confidence and self-awareness, and it's one of the most powerful catalysts and generators of knowledge.

Someone who isn't curious is simply arid, infertile—a tree destined to dry up under the sun, to wither away with time and disappear. Lack of curiosity is a formidable inhibitor of innovation.

Unicorns Are Humble but Confident and Self-Aware

Unicorns have a basic humility that derives from their own inner consciousness. They are able to recognize their own limits in an honest and transparent way and to avoid falling into forms of pride. They are individuals who, when they meet people who have knowledge and abilities different from their own, do not close themselves up in the armor of their arrogance, because unicorns don't fear the impact of that diversity on their own ego, their image, their position. Instead, they recognize the potential for growth and improvement intrinsic to the exploration of areas beyond the boundaries of their own limits and comfort zones. Unicorns are professionals who do not fall into the trap of contempt. First, it isn't in their nature, not even on a basic level—it's not in their DNA, not codified in their cultural matrix. Second, they understand that condescension, in all its forms, is sterile; it doesn't procreate but instead blocks the seeds of innovation. A humble approach connects and flows, removes obstacles, breaks energy free, and opens doors, hearts, and minds.

I have met many arrogant people over the years. At first, I tended to respond by becoming irritated, thoroughly so, right down to my bones. With the passing of the years and the acquisition of some wisdom, I gratefully realized that that emotion had changed. I began to feel sorry for these people—not in a way that was arrogant in turn, but with a sincere feeling derived from understanding the extent to which these individuals were wasting their potential. When I interact with arrogant people, I can almost feel in the air the quantity of knowledge and inspiration to which they don't have access and will never have access throughout their lives, blocked as they are by those walls of pride their weak and insecure ego is hiding behind.

Curiosity is the fertile ground where we plant the seeds of knowledge. It's the currency used to acquire as many seeds as possible, the water that irrigates them, the fertilizer that nurtures them, the eye that sees them grow, and the body that enjoys their fruits.

On the contrary, when I have met individuals who are both successful and humble, from every kind of background—from music to design, from business to science, from movies to fashion—my heart expands, my mind opens up, my horizons broaden. They inspire me so much! It's hard to describe. I've had many such encounters in New York, and it's no accident that the city is one of the most prolific innovation laboratories in the world. I've found a widespread humility in this metropolis, at least in the environments I spend time in, those of innovators, entrepreneurs, and creatives—the environments of unicorns. This humility derives from self-confidence combined with the awareness of being surrounded by countless people who, in one way or another, have the potential to be more interesting, intelligent, brilliant, resourceful, wealthy, equipped, or connected than ourselves. This awareness doesn't weaken unicorns; it deprovincializes and revitalizes them, giving them more charge, more energy, more motivation—because they don't view such individuals and their gifts as threats but simply as a wonderful opportunity. Conscious humility is an extremely powerful tool for innovation, evolution, and progress.

Unicorns Are Attentive Listeners but Quick to Decide and Act

Unicorns know how to listen. With age, with the positions we achieve, with successes in life, we risk listening less and less. God knows how many times I have slipped up in this way myself. How many times have I shared and talked more than I have listened and absorbed? How many times have I met wonderfully brilliant people who were perhaps less eloquent than myself, and for this reason I haven't managed to benefit from their knowledge? Some years ago, I finally understood that listening was as important as sharing. I had to force myself to listen more so that I could grow more, and faster.

From that point on, I have become increasingly intolerant of a breed of people I already didn't understand: the ones who feel the need to speak merely to fill the empty void of their own silence, to show that they too have something to say, on any topic whatsoever, almost as if to legitimize their position during a meeting. Imagine how much deeper, more productive, stimulating, and informative all our conversations would be if we eliminated those pointless words from our society, mere mechanical stimulation of the vocal cords with no real purpose or benefit. Our words should never be redundant or an end in themselves, shared merely for the objective of showing off an opinion or justifying our presence.

Listening is a precious act. People should listen more in this world. Listening helps you to think, to reflect, to correct yourself; it makes us better. Too many people love listening to the sound of their own voice filling a room and their own insecure soul, rather than listening to other people's content. I love listening to my teams. I have always tried to create a culture in which the designers surrounding me feel free to criticize, to disagree, to contest matters, to share their own ideas—especially when their ideas don't coincide with my own.

But watch out: listening doesn't mean not acting. Too many times, too many people are paralyzed by listening. They listen too much, and then they don't act. They watch, analyze, absorb, reflect, and then don't act. And they fall into *analysis paralysis*. This is a classic problem in many organizations, in which individuals use this approach to put off important decisions and delay critical activities, in the hope of running away from risks they don't want to take, slowly drowning in overreflection and hyperaccumulation of data and insights.

Listen, observe, analyze, learn, and then, at a certain point, decide and act. And do it with adequate speed and extreme accuracy. Progress, innovation, and success are directly connected to the ability to know how to manage *listening, deciding,* and *acting* with perfect balance and timing. One of the most serious structural flaws in big enterprises is a lack of people who take on the risk of making decisions and acting on them. Action is extremely important, and the speed of that action is similarly fundamental.

I understood this sacred truth very early in life. I learned it, not from a school blackboard or in a company meeting room, but on a suburban soccer field. I understood it through a completely unexpected analogy, through a completely unlikely mental connection, transferring a sporting experience into the world of innovation. When I was just over twenty, I played on a good team, in a category just a step below the professional one. Every now and again I played against AC Milan, in training games at Milanello. Our team was made up of players who were very good at footwork; many of us had great technique, and we were well trained, with four sessions a week as well as Sunday competitions. We were also paid. In short, our approach was similar to that of a professional team. But there was a big gap between an Italian Serie A team—one of the strongest teams in the world (and I'm saying that as a Juventus fan!)—and our own team from an inferior category. There was a vast difference that can be described with two key words: "action" and "speed." When I found myself faced with Maldini, Albertini, Costacurta, Desailly, Boban, and Weah, the speed with which they touched the ball, made a pass, moved around the pitch, and put the ball in the net was simply stunning. I don't know whether it seemed more as though we were in slow motion or as though they were moving at double speed. They looked at the field, identified their adversaries and teammates, thought how to mark them, decided where to put the ball, and then acted, kicking the ball exponentially faster than we did, but with an extreme precision and accuracy. It was killer playing.

I remember my astonishment when I realized for the first time the importance of this variable. On that pitch in Milanello, you didn't need a genius to understand it; it was entirely obvious to all of us, and yet, up to that point, I hadn't understood, probably because on TV and in the stadium I hadn't had the chance to compare the professionals in action with players who were little more than amateurs by comparison. Over the years, while reflecting on the concept of strategy, analysis, decision, action, and speed, I've realized that what happened on that sporting field was exactly analogous to what goes on in the world of business. The two worlds follow the same rules: the best leaders are the ones who listen, think, decide, and act with exceptional speed and perfect timing.

The innovator isn't just someone with the right idea; the innovator is also the person who decides to act on that idea, who develops and launches it before anyone else, with the greatest efficiency and quality. The ideal company is not simply the one with the perfect strategy, but the one that adapts this strategy to evolve with the market and society, with extraordinary velocity, refined agility, and sublime timing.

Listening, deciding, and *acting* constitute the magic triad. Over the years, I have often made the mistake of trying to strategize more than necessary, slowing things down; I've also made the opposite error, of being forced to act in haste, without taking the time to listen and think things through. Finding the right balance is the gift of a great thinker, a great strategist, a great leader—and the ideal innovator. The ability to *listen* is a gift that we make first of all to ourselves and then to others. The ability to *decide* when to make decisions is an art that you refine over time and through experience. The ability to *act rapidly,* faster than anyone else, is a craft that you learn in the field, with training and toil, forged through both successes and failures.

Unicorns Are Optimistic and Resilient

Optimism reduces the stress produced by complexity and increases the level of individual performance. Science tells us this, but it's also something we can feel ourselves, in our bodies, in our hearts. It's much easier to deal with complicated situations if you have a positive outlook. In that long journey we call life, each of us is bound to find closed doors, obstacles, barriers, and difficulties of every kind. It's part of the game. If we decide to innovate along the way, to change, to evolve, to overturn the status quo, then those barriers suddenly become even higher, thicker, harder to overcome.

If you're making something that no one has made before, then you're sure to face resistance. If you don't, then it's very likely you're not doing anything new. But unicorns don't give up or get discouraged. They keep on going despite everything and everyone, with a natural, organic, and permanent optimism. This optimism is the source of their energy; it's the drive for their dreams. Dreams are their compasses and optimism the gasoline. My journey—as a designer through the strange world of business, as an innovator in the realm of mass market efficiency, as a young boy in the world of adults, and as an Italian from a simple suburban family through the high ranks of US corporations—has not been without difficulties, doors closed in my face, metaphorical punches in the stomach, whacks on the back, microaggressions, and macroambushes. Optimism, passion, resistance, and persistence have been fundamental qualities for me, allowing me to keep going without hesitating, as solid as a tank.

How many times have I gotten angry, suffered, and been disappointed by situations that have come up along the way! But then, most of the time, those emotions have gone away shortly after they arrived, in the space of a few hours or a few days, thanks to two fundamental superpowers. First is the power of optimism, which has allowed me to constantly find a positive angle in every moment, even in the deepest crisis, always managing to see the glass as half full. And second is the power of my dreams, which I hang on to tenaciously—those dreams that have always given me a route to follow and a light to aim at, even in the darkest circumstances of my life. The resilience that I have called on to face the world is the product of a magic mix between my dreams and my optimism.

When I find myself dealing with moments of particular difficulty, I use a technique to activate my inner optimism and reawaken my dreams. I take a metaphorical journey through an imagined landscape in my mind, a hill that rises up over time and events, a hill without time and events, and I look at the situation that I'm engaging in as if it were a distant valley, taking a thousand steps away, putting things in perspective. In other words, I try to visualize my pathway, remembering where I started, putting the goal on the horizon, and grasping what steps have been taken up to that point. From the vantage point of this analytic hill, through reflection and meditation, you can see everything with much greater clarity. Often we are so lost in the forest of our daily lives, tangled up in the vines of particular episodes, blocked by the mud of everyday difficulties, that we are no longer able to remember the journey we're on; we don't manage to appreciate with the correct perspective the road taken up until that moment, and we forget the results we have already achieved. That progress and those results give you the strength to continue with more enthusiasm than before: in that goal placed on the horizon, you find your motivation, and along that path—now seen in perspective—you find the next steps with greater lucidity. Optimism and resilience at this point are simply the results of a new awareness.

Perspective is all the more precious because it helps you to concentrate on the journey instead of on the obstacles in front of you. Once you look at things with some perspective, it becomes easier to understand how that daily obstacle, the battle that has been lost, and the unexpected defeat often don't really represent steps backward but are actually parts of pushing onward toward the final goal. I never tire of sharing this approach with my teams, especially the younger members who often get demoralized by the new barriers and hurdles they meet along the way.

Let's give a concrete example to explain the approach. Think of how many times you've driven forward an exceptional creative idea, but the idea has then been rejected by managers who lack vision or courage. Those managers have then launched to the market a compromised and mediocre version of your concept. Think now of how many times it's then been the case that, a few months later, a competitor has arrived on the scene launching something similar to your original idea and has done so in a successful way. When something like this happens, there is a high probability that the business leaders who didn't understand your original idea and the people around them will realize that what you were proposing was actually a winning concept. Sometimes, they will admit this directly to you; most of the time, they won't. But they will know.

This has happened to me a few times over the past twenty-five years (and when it didn't happen, often it was because my original idea wasn't really as exceptional as I thought it was). For people in your organization to see that your rejected concept was a winning one has a special value. It helps you to exponentially amplify your credibility, with an even greater impact than would have been the case if your idea had been accepted and launched in the initial phase. It essentially demonstrates your ability— and that of your team—to identify creative opportunities even when your partners haven't yet spotted them. You provide your partners with another set of eyes, complementary to theirs, giving them the chance to envision solutions that they themselves would otherwise miss.

Often, though, when in the middle of an episode that we are living as a defeat, we aren't able to see things this way. It seems in the moment that we're going backward, when instead we are actually advancing toward our goal. Everything just needs to be put in perspective.

Innovating in a highly complex world is like scaling Everest: From the base camp you climb up to the intermediate point. From there you don't go up immediately but instead go back down to the base camp again, to adapt your body's cravings for oxygen to the conditions of that extreme altitude. The next day you go up to the next point and then back down again. This is how you proceed for weeks, moving the upper point increasingly higher but doing so gradually, alternating the ascent and descent. These multiple journeys back down, from a higher base to one at a lower altitude, are the necessary steps to get to the final goal, despite the perception of regressing. Going in reverse physically is part of the holistic motion toward the final objective. But if you don't take in the whole vision, made up of the entire journey and the final destination, then those reverse movements are experienced as simply backward motion, nothing else.

In both our private and professional lives, all those times when we think we're not getting ahead, that we're regressing from the steps already taken forward, we need to put things in perspective, visualizing the end goal and trying to understand how that section of difficult road—so uphill, impervious, discouraging, and incomprehensible—is in truth helping us to advance in the direction of our dreams. This transforms those moments into fragments of learning, phases of consolidation, accelerations in credibility, changing them into part of an exciting journey. From this perspective, we find energy and positivity to proceed with resilience and optimism.

Unicorns Are Comfortable with Discomfort

Unicorns are at ease in what I call suspension: they are comfortable with change, in those undefined areas that displace everything, in unexplored territory, in dimensions that are yet to be understood. When most people want a precise definition, a role and responsibility, a label and a playing field with well-defined boundaries, unicorns prefer to make their own role, to design their field of action. They love exploring virgin territory; they find comfort in constant evolution. This is far from an obvious gift, because this human instinct comes up against the shared search for stability and security, one of our primary needs; the lack of that stability and security creates discomfort for most people. It's natural.

Like most people, I, too, have always loved certainty, stability, and the comfort of security, but I have never viewed security and stability as the final port where I can stop and sit down with ease and pleasure. Instead, for me, security and stability are platforms, springboards to leap from to reach other platforms, which in their turn are also safe and secure.

That moment of leaping into the void, suspended between one platform and the next, has always fascinated and excited me. In that leap, I taste all the air of life on my skin; I feel the adrenaline of dreams. It's this dynamic transition that makes me feel alive. Many people fear this leap because they don't know where they will find the landing point on the other side. If our current platform is stable and secure, it will be difficult to abandon it; if instead it's precarious and uncertain, it will be all the simpler to take the leap.

Yet again, this is the reason that moments of great personal and professional change, such as moments of innovation for individuals, companies, and societies, often come out of great crises. It takes courage, optimism, and vision—as well as the necessary security measures and safety nets—to overcome the fear, to enjoy every moment of that jump into the sky, propelling yourself into new horizons. This is the only dynamic of innovation. This defines the ideal innovator, crystallizes what a unicorn is. There is no innovation without discomfort. We have to be at ease in that discomfort if we want to innovate.

Unicorns Are Change Agents

Unicorns are obsessed with change—not change as an end in itself, but change that is constructive, that aims at evolving the status quo in order to improve it. Unicorns' very natures drive them to analyze the world that surrounds them and constantly ask themselves how they can redesign it to make it perfect. They are animated by a positive tension with what Plato called the world of ideas, the world of absolute perfection. And given that this perfection cannot be reached except by God—or, if you don't believe in God, then by what God represents—innovators are destined to constantly move toward that goal, in their private and professional lives, without end. They are constantly propelled onward toward the intuition of new possibilities, toward the search for intelligent solutions, toward the idea of better worlds.

Looking back over my life, I realized some years ago that I have never had a specific goal in mind, a final and concrete objective to reach. I've always been switched on by a constant tension with the infinite. Whenever I reach an objective, I have been conscious of the fact that this was only a temporary step, one of the many stable and secure platforms from which to then launch myself, to fly toward the next objective, always moving the limits higher and higher, continuing along this journey toward a better condition—for me, for my teams, for my community, for the brands and organizations I'm working for. This is why I have never felt that I have truly "arrived." This is, and will always be, a journey that doesn't end with the next step, because that step will always look forward to the next one, constantly, continually.

In a world where any system proceeds through inertia—maintaining, in the absence of an external force acting on the system, either a state of rest or uniform motion in a straight line as Newton demonstrated—I have always tried to put external forces into the system, creating discomfort and interference in the organizations where I have worked. I have always been obsessed by the idea of triggering a dynamic of constant evolution. This obsession has often been the source of both joy and pain for many of my collaborators and myself: every time we reach one of our goals, I'm already thinking about establishing a new one, higher and higher.

Unicorns are in love with meaningful change. They are agents of change, sponsors of change, because they know that change contains the seed of progress.

Design Thinking Needs More Unicorns

Unicorns, with all their attributes described in these pages, are ideal creatures. They are models to aspire to and to inspire; they are exemplars to try to emulate during the arc of our personal and professional journeys. The long list of the unicorn's gifts deciphers an innovator's way of thinking, deciding, and acting. In other words, this list defines the *how* of innovation.

What we have described as the human-centered (or design-driven) approach to innovation defines, in contrast, *what* the ideal innovator needs to do, in bringing together empathy, strategy, and prototyping; embracing desirability, technical feasibility, and economic viability; and being inspired by the principles of meaningful design.

In order for the human-centered approach to innovation to be successful, you need both the *what* and the *how*. You need a design-driven process, but you also need the brilliant minds and knowing hands of the unicorns. The reason that experiments in this approach to innovation often fail is that people concentrate too much on tools and processes, on the *what* of innovation, without equipping themselves with the *how*—in other words, with the right talent, possessing the right intellectual and emotional abilities to come up with the right questions, generate the right responses, and then imagine, design, and produce the right solutions.

The need for both these elements also explains why many designers in the world are not innovators, despite having been educated in design-driven innovation. The reason is that they have been trained in the *what* of innovation, which certainly provides an important starting point. But this training does not necessarily give you the *how*.

Design thinking is fundamental for doing human-centered innovation successfully, but it's not enough. The winning innovator is someone who exploits the typical way that design thinking works, but who does so in ways that only a unicorn can. And this ability derives from a delicate mix of innate talent, on the one hand, and education and training on the other. This is a type of education that schools often can provide only in part. It's a training that comes from living life itself, from fortuitous encounters, carefully planned meetings, lucky circumstances, personal curiosity, and the right mental attitude.

CHAPTER 10

FIGHTING THE DICTATORSHIP OF THE NORMAL

Being a unicorn is difficult, complex, and tiring. Being different isn't easy. Not fitting into the norm isn't easy. Being in suspension, in evolution, in an obsessive tension with something that is always better isn't easy. Constantly questioning yourself—getting out of your daily comfort zone, continuously evolving—isn't easy.

Over the pages that follow, I want to recount to you some fragments of this complexity, as I've lived it, in my attempt—intimate and private—to grow into a unicorn and to then become the best unicorn I could imagine. I want to share this struggle with you, this multidimensional tension, and the way that I've tried to resolve it. I'll do so through stories, memories, and anecdotes, taken straight from the deep pockets of my personal baggage, from my childhood to the present day.

Living in Suspension: The Difficulty of Being a Unicorn

Some years back, my parents knew someone whom I only vaguely recall. His name was Roberto, and he was a mystic and a preacher. Sometimes he came to our house, and it was always interesting listening to him chat with my mom and dad. There was something mysterious, intangible, and fascinating about that man with his long white beard and abundance of words. One evening we—my brother, my mom, my dad, Roberto, and I—were all at the dinner table. And Roberto asked a question: "What do you think is the farthest distance in the universe? The greatest distance that you can possible imagine?" Roberto gave us a moment to think. You could feel the deafening silence in the room as our brains whirled around, looking for the right answer, weighing up the potential responses.

In reality, Roberto didn't want a reply; it was simply a rhetorical question. He was creating a state of suspense, an emptiness in atmosphere and time that he would soon close with his message. But then I decided to dive into the void, and I threw out a reply: "It's the distance between the heart and the mind," I said. Roberto looked at me with astonished eyes, smiled and then laughed, and said, "Yes, that's quite right!" He then ran a hand through my hair and ruffled my locks to congratulate me. Roberto's wonder quickly spread across my parents' faces as well, but in them it soon transformed into pride. I was sixteen, and that moment remained forever impressed on my heart.

I remember that moment, first, because I had felt the pure and genuine happiness of a young man who had managed to give a good answer in front of his parents, the kind of reply "grown-ups" gave, legitimated by an expert from outside our family unit. It was one of the very first "grown-up" replies by a teenager who was shifting from adolescence to maturity. The response was a metaphorical first step into the world of adults, made in view of my mom and dad. Our first true physical steps aren't something we can recall—we are too small—but that first cultural step, in a family for whom culture was as important as walking, had the same magical flavor for me.

The second reason that moment became memorable to me is also the reason I'm telling you this story. I had begun to adventure into the world of philosophy at my high school in Varese, and I was immediately struck by the unavoidable dichotomy that I had found in the discourses and thoughts of philosophers, intrigued and fascinated by that eternal tension between heart and mind that had marked the great flow of humanity's thought for millennia. Roberto's question that evening, in that small kitchen in the Bustecche neighborhood, was touching an intimate yet universal tension generated by the contrast, through encounters and conflicts, between science and religion, between rationality and romanticism, between instinct and reason, between passion and process: a tension that I have carried in my soul throughout my entire life, to every corner of the planet, navigating along the subtle boundary that separates those two different dimensions.

I have been attracted in a visceral way by the seduction of emotions, creativity, and intuition, celebrating their virtue and potential, pushing them to the limits in my life experiences, experimenting, building, destroying, in the name of the most extreme myth of love, in all its aspects. But I have always appreciated, respected, and embraced the potential of rationality, of the intellect, of reflection and reason as safety nets, as background, as fields of action, as cultural foundations, as navigational devices. Often with passion, sometimes through suffering, I have lived suspended between these two dimensions throughout my life, reconciling them, mixing them, amalgamating them, feeling their inner tension and learning to tame it, to channel it, to give it meaning. Rereading the long list of unicorns' gifts and virtues, you will find a common thread: everything moves within this tension, which unicorns try to resolve through the demiurgic act of innovation.

Innovation is precisely this: knowing how to grasp people's rationality and emotions, their needs and desires; how to manage a pathway comprising intuition and reason, brilliance and processes; and, finally, how to imagine and produce solutions that respond to these dreams and needs, in a perfect balance between form and function, a perfect synthesis between heart and mind.

The innovators live suspended between these two zones. They understand both, they love both, they draw on both—with intelligence and with passion. They find their ideal dimension and optimal equilibrium within that tension. It is the same tension that has animated the cultural debate of all humanity since the dawn of civilization, the tension that has torn apart consciences, has struck history itself, sometimes has inspired progress and at others has clipped its wings. Unicorns are the people who manage this dichotomy better than others do and who reconcile it on a daily basis, through their own thoughts, decisions, and actions. In a unicorn, this tension is resolved with harmony.

Finding that balance is far from simple, though. One of the main reasons is that we are dealing with an equilibrium that is completely dynamic and very different from the static nature that is imposed upon us by the communities we're living in. Unicorns are usually very different from what our society expects and from what it defines as normal. They live on the edges of distinct worlds, moving between one and another, or simply inhabiting the middle worlds—worlds that are sometimes hybrid, sometimes multicultural, sometimes unexpected, sometimes unexplored. And if, over the course of unicorns' lives, this abnormality has the potential to become a formidable competitive advantage, distinguishing them from the norm and raising them up to the point of being accepted and celebrated once they have reached maturity, nevertheless, in the process of personal growth, this diversity can also be a source of suffering. It can be punitive, it can risk alienating unicorns, suffocating them, choking them. Society tries to tame this kind of diversity; it tries to normalize it, to flatten it out. And thus, if unicorns don't have the strength to protect this diversity, the ingenuity to impose it, or the awareness to resist, then their gifts risk being tamed, normalized, and flattened out by the system that surrounds them. Over the course of my life, I have experienced this myself, in different ways.

I grew up in northern Italy to parents originally from Rome, a city where the southern part of the country begins. My mom was born there in May 1946; my father was born during World War II, three years earlier, in the small town of Altopascio, near Lucca, in the Tuscan countryside. But his family moved back to Rome soon afterward, and that's where he was raised. As a child, my north Italian accent was broken up here and there by fragments of idioms and accents from Rome. Instead of "coltello" (knife), I said "cortello"; for me, a small bread roll was a "rosetta" and not a "michetta," as they would call it in Varese. I pronounced the letter "s" like a "z," and my vowels had a distinctly Roman color to them, all very strange and amusing for northerners. When I met my school friends' grandparents, I didn't understand them; they spoke a local dialect that was almost incomprehensible to me, which seemed to me to be closer to French than to my own language. I remember as though it was yesterday the day when my uncle Renzo, my aunt's Milanese husband, asked me during a Christmas lunch whether I felt northern. I told him, to his great surprise, that no, I didn't feel I was either from the north or from the south: I was in the middle. Certainly I wasn't from the south, nor from Rome. Rome isn't really the south either: Rome is Rome, just as New York is New York. That I wasn't from the south was undeniable. When we went to the seaside in July for our summer vacations, to a small town on the coast of Lazio, Tor San Lorenzo, my northern accent was unmistakable and out of place in the ocean of Roman sounds we were surrounded by, reminding me and the world around me that, despite everything, social imprinting and your cultural context beat your DNA in many ways.

This beginning, straddling different cultures without really belonging to one or the other, surely marked my early years, my way of thinking, giving me an important model for the rest of my existence. I was completely at my ease suspended between these cultures; I didn't suffer from a lack of belonging. Or better still, I probably felt that I belonged to something hybrid, something that was mine alone and no one else's.

Perhaps due to this cultural diversity, perhaps because of my family education, or maybe due to my genetic code—or a cocktail of all of these things together and much more besides—since I was very young, I have often found myself having to deal with what we would call today *my different point of view about the world*, ranging from the smallest situations up to important decisions. There was normality, and then there was my own point of view. Sometimes it was aligned to that normality, and sometimes it was not. But it was mine, only mine, always mine. It wasn't planned or strategic; I didn't look for it, brag about it, or study it: it just happened. It was just like that. Normality was what a whole series of people—teachers, neighbors, friends, the local priests, the entire community, society as a whole—expected of me and what they expected of everyone. And then there was my own way of seeing things, which was often quite different, always supported and sustained by my parents, sometimes consciously, at other times less so.

This mindset would manifest itself in many different ways, many times in the smallest details. When I was very young, for example, I began to hold my pencil in a fashion that was "different" from what was considered *normal*, grasping it between my middle and ring fingers, instead of between the index and middle fingers. I began to use the pencil this way, and that's how I managed to draw well. Over the years, my inclination for drawing began to be recognized by people around me, and at school I received exceptional grades in art class. I took part in drawing competitions, and sometimes I won them. I loved experimenting with new materials, from graphite to watercolors, chalk to oil paints. I played with pyrography (the art of decorating wood with burn marks by applying a hot metal nib), first mimicking what my dad was doing and then independently trying the technique out on new surfaces, so that I could be the innovator of the family, using fabrics and leather, belts and jackets. I drew because I enjoyed it and because it came naturally to me. Who knows whether I enjoyed myself because I was good at drawing or whether I was good at drawing because I enjoyed myself? Probably the two things are completely interconnected. Either way, I did everything with a pencil, a pen, or a felt tip held in my hand "incorrectly," according to others.

I was unaware that this way of holding my pencil or pen was "abnormal" until one day that I recall very clearly, with the clarity of an emotional shock that burns into your heart when you are young. That day my mom came home frustrated and annoyed after a meeting with the schoolteacher. During the meeting, the teacher had complained to my mom about the fact that she had never corrected how I held my pencil when I was younger. *It was clear that I was a child who hadn't been brought up well by my parents.* And how could it be otherwise, from the standpoint of normality? My mom, who had dedicated her life to her children, who had sacrificed everything for us—including her own job—and who had celebrated the virtue of education, culture, and knowledge her whole existence, was being criticized for not having educated me.

Who Decides What's "Normal"?

In truth, what my mom had done was simply not to educate her child according to a series of norms that society wanted to impose on her. She hadn't corrected how I held my pencil. My mom, a sensitive and passionate person like myself, felt offended and attacked. Her reaction in that moment, calm and dignified but clearly wounded, remained impressed on my green mind and in my childhood heart. What does "normal" mean? What is the "normal" way of holding a pencil? Who decided that one way is normal, and why should it be the same for everyone? Was the norm invented to produce excellence or simply to flatten everything out in the name of efficiency and stability?

And what happens if that normal produces mediocrity instead? If by holding the pencil in a different way I was able to produce excellent work, with naturalness and without effort, then why should that way of holding the pencil be considered an error?

Back then, I didn't realize the impact that these gut reactions would have throughout my life, but I understand today more than ever that they were early signs of a way of interpreting the world that was entirely mine: yet again suspended between, on one side, normality—which in many ways I supported and which was part of my desire for integration and belonging—and, on the other, the originality of my own point of view, which was part of an opposing instinct.

The real magic—for which I can thank God alone—is that as a child I was, for the most part, ignorant of the fact that my perspective, so often different and anomalous, might be unique: I simply had that way of thinking, and it seemed to be the most natural thing in the world. This meant that I didn't try to change it, vainly searching for some form of acceptance and integration. And above all, this ignorance allowed me to be original in a peaceful way. "Happiness consists in the ignorance of the truth," wrote the poet Giacomo Leopardi.[9] I was certainly ignorant of how different some of my behaviors and opinions were, and in that phase of my life this was of huge assistance to me. My domestic environment, where that originality of thought was stimulated, protected, and celebrated as if it were the most natural mindset in the world, was probably the source of my inner peace, along with a blessed natural unawareness. Only a couple of decades later, I began to develop a new awareness about the meaning of that diversity, but with this new consciousness I also developed the wisdom to selectively ignore irrelevant social pressures, to conserve yet again some of my existential calm.

I wore my watch on my right wrist instead of on the left. At first, I did so simply because I found it comfortable. But later, it became something that contributed to defining me. I was the only one who wore a watch in this "not normal" way. And yet, I also looked for fashionable shoes or a sweatshirt produced by a trending brand, because while I loved distinguishing myself, I also felt the common desire to be integrated into the group, the community, the society in which we live.

I didn't frequent the local church in my neighborhood, the Bustecche, and I used to travel miles on my bicycle every day to reach the church in a different area, at Bizzozero. I had to obtain special license from the parish priest to do so. I got on better with the boys in that neighborhood, and that environment inspired me. I was the only child attending that church, out of hundreds, who didn't live in the neighborhood. Yet again I was caught in suspension, this time between neighborhoods. I was different because I came from "outside," and at the same time I tried to make myself belong to this new context. I always maintained this aspect of originality. I was both Bustecche and Bizzozero. And at the same time, I didn't completely belong to either one place or the other.

Abnormality was, quite simply, often my normality. It was what I desired, and I wasn't afraid of any obstacles in my way. Ever since, I have followed my dreams, supporting my desires without thinking twice, like a child set free in a field of grass, living in the naive conviction that anything is possible. If that was what I wanted, that was what I'd do. The passing years and the facts of life have moderated this belief intellectually, but emotionally that flame is still alight within me, and it will never be extinguished. A good dose of unawareness and naivete is necessary to dream and then to make those dreams come true.

I could keep going with many other anecdotes, but the point would always be the same: since my childhood I've always been comfortable in a state of becoming, floating between different worlds, between the normal and the different, between belonging and uniqueness, between integration and originality, bringing together choices and aspects of my life that have defined and distinguished me in a unique way, along with ones that instead have helped me to become part of the social fabric.

That diversity has often given life and space to expressions of marginalization and discrimination, because people—all of society—often fear whatever is different from them, whatever isn't the norm, and tend to reject diversity. How many times have I been mocked, set aside, or left out, because of my diversity? I have experienced this from the beginning of my life, starting, for example, with the fact that when I was a child, people from the south were not loved in the north of Italy. Racism against southerners, who were labeled with discriminatory words such as a *terrone* (a classist and pejorative neologism that etymologically means "somebody working the land"), was the norm. Faced with these difficulties, I have reacted in different and even polarized ways. On the one hand, I have drawn on a set of practices and tools to deal with the contrast, to build bridges with the world I live in, while on the other hand I have often found myself at ease in that difference, enjoying my diversity and everything that made me unique and even special. I have searched for diversity; I wanted it.

I have obviously never suffered from the extreme persecution that those in some communities live through because of the color of their skin, their country of origin, their sexual orientation, their religious or political preferences, their different physical abilities. I didn't fear for my life at every step and every corner. Who knows how I would have reacted if I had belonged to any of those communities? I don't think those situations are really imaginable for someone who has not lived them in the first person, and surely they are not situations I can compare to my own. But my small diversities—geographical, cultural, and intellectual—have nevertheless been a source for attacks and aggressions originating from the same cultural matrix: ignorance and fear.

Transforming Diversity into a Competitive Advantage

In order to manage these situations better, I have always tried to work on my strong traits, transforming points of uniqueness into potential assets, showing how my diversity could in truth become a unique advantage to the community I was living in—and thus, in the end, in one way or another, could become a unique advantage to myself as well. My childhood and my adolescence were my training ground, which helped me to think in limbo, suspended between different, often conflicting worlds, and to accept others' diversity, to celebrate my own, to investigate everything that might be considered abnormal with a certain honesty—having an original and unique point of view—and then integrating this into the community through an open, authentic, and transparent dialogue. Over the years, with an ever greater dose of awareness, I have taken this mental attitude into the world of business as well.

Today, in my midforties, I realize more than ever before that this proclivity for being suspended between different dimensions has been one of the greatest drives in my professional life. And one of the main reasons for the particular advantage of this approach to life lies probably in the scarcity of this mindset in the modern world. We live in a society that the Argentinean psychoanalyst Miguel Benasayag has defined as the "dictatorship of the normal," a reality where "everyone wants to be normal," where "there is no longer a creative, joyous marginality."[10] From Benasayag's enlightened point of view—and my own as well—"the problem is the normal people, we need to free them. To be normal means being passive, to function as little as possible." In his *Elogio del conflitto* ("In Praise of Conflict"), he writes that "the incredible armada of psychologists" want to transform "multiplicity into unity," while for the psychoanalysts, conflict "is a consubstantial dimension of human subjectivity."[11]

The psychiatrist Giancarlo Dimaggio, in an interview for the Italian magazine *Sette*, associates Benasayag's theories with the words of the Mad Hatter, in the 2010 Disney adaptation of Lewis Carroll's *Alice's Adventures in Wonderland*, when he says to Alice: "You used to be much more *muchier*, you have lost your *muchness*."[12] There is so much truth in that fabulous neologism. We all need to be more "muchier," accepting our own personal "muchness" without anxiety, as a form of growth, discovery, and evolution, and appreciating the collective "muchness" as a form of social wealth, communitarian potential, and group inspiration. This "muchness" is none other than what we today call "diversity."

The first twenty-five years of my life, before I entered the professional world, gave me fundamental lessons and experiences and provided me with the intellectual and emotional tools necessary for later navigating the infinite complexity of that professional world in a more natural way. Looking back, I can see an important thread running through everything that I experienced in those years and up to today. This subtle thread that connects everything is the concept of *suspension*.

I experienced this suspension between normality and originality, between cultures, between approaches, geographies, societies—always in a state of becoming, always in tension, always traveling, attracted by the unknown, by discovery off the beaten track. In these unexplored territories, I could find myself, design my identity, express my point of view about the world, and form my own unique reality. I have been suspended between Varese and Rome, between Italy and America, between design and business, between analysis and risk, between integration and diversity, between normal and abnormal, between creativity and rationality, between today and tomorrow. With my pencil held in the wrong way and my watch on the wrong wrist, with my Roman accent in the north of Italy and my bucolic spirit enchanted by the city lights, I have navigated the world and my life, sometimes suspended by chance, other times by circumstance, and then ever more often by a specific conscious plan.

Many people find themselves uncomfortable in a situation that is undefined and in flux; they need the stability of a label, a pigeonhole to place themselves in, a community to belong to. I have always had an almost physiological need to print my own personal label, to construct my own pigeonhole, to forge the community I belong to. And I have always done so through opposing dimensions. The Greek philosopher Heraclitus, in the fifth century CE, observed that "if there are opposites in the universe, worlds that seem not to reconcile themselves—such as unity and multiplicity, love and hate, peace and war, calm and motion— then the harmony of these opposites cannot be found by canceling out one side, but through letting both live in a continuous tension. Harmony is not the absence but rather the balance of contrasts."[13]

Over the past twenty years I have been an anomalous designer, a figure the design community didn't fully understand for a long time; it's only in recent years that this community has partly understood and accepted me. The reason was that I was suspended between the worlds of design and business, and it was difficult to identify and fit into the traditional categories of either professional community. Even today, some designers mistakenly call me a marketer because they ignore the kind of design I do. And yet, I certainly don't belong to the traditional marketing community. The marketers, the proper ones, see me as an alien on vacation in their world. They like me because, even though I come from Mars, I speak their language; I understand them, I appreciate them, and I give them a set of useful and innovative instruments that I have brought with me from my distant planet. But in their eyes I have green skin, scales, and antennae. I am a designer, a creative, a being visiting the marketing planet, an ambassador with a diplomatic visa.

It's a Pirandellian situation: I'm a *character in search of an author*, a designer impersonating a businessman too.[14] In the end, I always remain a designer—a pure and true designer, a designer in every cell of my brain and heart. But I constantly live suspended between design and business, in a virgin territory, trying to create value for both communities. The great difference between me and Luigi Pirandello's characters is that I feel great in this suspended dimension—because it's in this dimension, where his characters lose their identities, that I finally found my own!

The great Italian designer and my good friend, Fabio Novembre—in an interview he gave in my very own Varese in 2018—defined this dimension, through a metaphor that has remained branded on my heart and mind because he sublimely, romantically, and poetically defined what's happened over the past twenty years. I'll quote him word for word: "Mauro's great lesson is the following. For me, you know why they say I'm a young designer? Because I'm the last of the Mohicans. That is, I followed a well-beaten track and I followed it well, and I'm considered one of the great ones. But I took a well-worn road! Mauro went out to find a track that didn't exist, he went to cut his way through the forest. And that's a huge thing to do. Can you imagine this young guy, only twenty-seven years old, at 3M, ready to begin that kind of climb?"

I will do everything I can to educate my children to grow up fascinated by the unknown, by discovery, by unexplored territories, by the culture of suspension. Through example, education, and experience, I will try to give them that virtual machete that they can use to make their way through the jungle they choose, beating new and unexplored pathways. I will watch them from afar, letting them discover, experiment, allowing them to fall, to make mistakes, always ready to run to their help in moments of need, while I will continue to make my own path, opening up new sections in my own personal jungle. Suspension, discovery, and the unknown are my unavoidable destiny, where I find all the energy I need to survive, to be happy, and to fly.

The concept of *suspension* is a fundamental filter that blends all of the ingredients that define the recipe for the unicorn. In this dynamic, constant, changing suspension, I have searched for myself—and this is where I found my unique and distinct identity.

All those who want to innovate have to find themselves at ease in this constant state of suspension. To everyone who lives this on a daily basis: Don't fear it, don't flee from it, don't give in to the pressures of a society that always wants to make you normal, to tame you, to force you into a definition, a label, an accepted and shared dimension. Don't be afraid to live in suspension; don't be afraid to be different. And to anyone who is the leader of a company, a community or a team and wants to innovate: Remember to look for this abnormality, this suspension, this diversity. Celebrate it, nurture it, amplify it.

Can You Make a Horse into a Unicorn Through Education?

Many of the anecdotes shared over the preceding pages are stories that concentrate on my early years of life. And they recount a natural tendency to *be a unicorn*, a tendency that has nevertheless been formed, directed, and molded by the culture in which I was immersed, especially by the culture of my family and my social context during those years.

Over time, I have found myself speaking about the unicorn's gift on countless occasions, in the most varied contexts, in different forms, and often I've been asked questions that perhaps some of you are also asking yourselves while you read these lines: Is it possible to educate someone to become a unicorn? Can you train a unicorn? In other words, is it possible to identify a set of individuals and coach them in a strategic and systematic way to become unicorns?

My reply is always the same: yes and no. To be a unicorn, a real unicorn, a pure one—to possess the long list of personal gifts shared in this book and to demonstrate each of these virtues in an exceptional way—is, in part, a natural talent. So to a certain extent, people are born unicorns. This doesn't mean, however, that if someone isn't a natural unicorn, that person can't try to become one. It only means that if someone isn't born a unicorn, then that person doesn't start with all of the characteristics that give a unicorn that extra gear for innovating in an exceptional way.

Being a unicorn is a talent just as, for example, the most obvious and visible abilities in sport are talents. Maradona and Ronaldo were born talented athletes; Serena Williams and Roger Federer were, too, as were Tom Brady and Peyton Manning, Kobe Bryant and Magic Johnson, Sachin Tendulkar and Shahid Afridi. However much I trained, I would still find it difficult or impossible to reach the results of these superstars of sport. And it's the same in the world of business: Steve Jobs, Henry Ford, Richard Branson, Jeff Bezos, and Bill Gates were born innovators.

In the case of unicorns, these characteristics are contained in these individuals' genetic code, but at the beginning of their journeys through the world, some are still rough, and others pure energy. Some are bursts of excellence that appear in an uncontrolled way; some are flashes of genius; and others are dormant, mere potential awaiting activation. Education and training are a way to tame and awaken these characteristics. Therefore, education and training are fundamental.

Let me be very clear: this is true for people who are born with these gifts as well for those who do not have them naturally. A nonnatural unicorn who wants to become one and who has the right training and proper motivation could manage to generate better results than those of a natural unicorn who does not cultivate these gifts with the right education.

To avoid confusion, I'm not saying that a soccer player who has no natural gifts can become a Maradona through good training. Maradona's raw talent, that of a pure unicorn, can't be reached through training alone. But a normal soccer player, with a good dose of training and effort, can manage to play in a more satisfying and eventually superior way than someone who is gifted but never trains or puts in any effort.

Let's try to understand this logic in greater detail. Education has three main functions: *generating awareness*, *growing*, and *maintaining*.

There is no dichotomy between DNA and education, between genius and experience, between predisposition and training, between natural gifts and hard work; you need both.

Generating Awareness

Education first of all creates *awareness*: it makes a unicorn aware of the function of some of those gifts that otherwise the person might take for granted. Education can even make a unicorn aware of having some of those gifts, in case the individual had not already realized this.

The situation is like that of a young soccer player with a magic touch and lucid vision, who as a child thinks that all of the other children have the same control over the ball and clarity in the field, until he trains on his first team and the coach points out how extraordinary the player's gifts truly are. The match makes him realize his value and how that value can make a difference: training gives him a measure to compare himself to and makes him aware of the unique nature of his attributes.

It's the same with someone who is naturally empathetic but doesn't realize the extraordinary value of this ability to read a room at first glance, to attend to people's surface reactions, their moods, their level of interest, their function in that context, the social dynamics established between individuals in any given moment. Then, the training ground of life, or an encounter with a coach, allows the person to understand the extraordinary value of those gifts and their deep significance for innovation processes as precious tools for understanding people, both as the objects of research and as project partners.

Awareness is a fundamental step, because it allows unicorns to focus their own skills in a more intentional way, nurturing them and amplifying them exponentially.

Growing

The second function of training is precisely this: growing, fine-tuning, and perfecting these gifts.

The soccer player with good footwork who continues training, session after session, to continuously improve in technique is fine-tuning, getting closer to perfection, constantly and systematically.

This is the unicorn who is able to bring together, in a natural way, vision and execution, dream and action, but who simultaneously, through practice and education, perfects this balance, understanding how to move with agility and efficiency, refining the timing, defining the rhythm, fine-tuning the frequency.

Maintaining

Finally, continuous training and constant learning are indispensable for *maintaining* these gifts to the utmost degree, to keep them toned, brilliant, fresh, and exceptional. To do so requires understanding that life is a journey of study without end, a continuous school without limits or conclusion, where we have to act like students and apprentices for the whole duration of our existence.

Soccer players who train every day to keep their performance and technique more brilliant than ever are maintaining their gifts. So is the unicorn who never stops being curious, reading, studying, staying informed, listening, thinking, with the goal of perfecting every single gift that Mother Nature has bestowed, in a gradual and constant way over time.

In her book *Mindset: The New Psychology of Success*, Carol S. Dweck provides a very powerful term for this way of acting and thinking.[15] She calls it *growth mindset*. People with a growth mindset, even without an exceptional basis of talent, can overtake people with natural talent who do not have this same mindset, in terms of performance and results. Through self-awareness, and careful work to grow and maintain their gifts, such people can reach optimal results.

The French psychologist Alfred Binet, inventor of the IQ test, used to remind the world of a simple truth: those who are the most intelligent when they die are not necessarily the ones who are the most intelligent when they are born. The same is true for unicorns. There is no dichotomy between DNA and education, between genius and experience, between predisposition and training, between natural gifts and hard work; you need both. Genius, DNA, and nature take inspiration from environmental contexts and social interactions, which activate them, wake them up, mature them, and allow them to grow and progress. Natural unicorns without a growth mindset will end up failing to exploit their own qualities and will be overtaken by individuals who have much less natural talent but who apply the right experience and determination, with time and energy invested in their growth. A unicorn with a growth mindset is an explosive mixture.

And finally, I should clarify something: the status of the unicorn is an ambition, a tension, an aspiration toward an ideal profile. Ronaldo,

Serena Williams, Tom Brady, Magic Johnson, and Sachin Tendulkar, to return to the sporting metaphor, are not 100 percent unicorns, but they have drawn nearer to that status than many others in their fields. They are surrounded by many other unicorns who play and compete in the UEFA Champions League, in the NBA, the NFL, the Grand Slam, the Cricket World Cup, boasting exceptional performances without claiming the role of superstars. They are 70, 80, or 90 percent unicorns. In other words, we don't need everyone to become a Maradona or a Steve Jobs; we can all be incredible innovators even in our imperfect status of being *almost unicorns*. What's important is to have some basic characteristics and then continue to move toward perfection, through continuous training, with courage, passion, and devotion.

There are two characteristics among the unicorns' gifts listed earlier, however, that need to be standard in every human category, whatever role people have. These characteristics are kindness and sincerity. If all of the companies in the world—big and small, public and private—celebrated these values, then we would have more efficient enterprises, better businesses, and a happier society. The schools of our planet, as well as teaching math, literature, geography, philosophy, physics, and finance, should educate people in kindness and sincerity. And then schools should teach the ability to dream, the practice of curiosity, empathy, the art of execution, respect, tolerance of discomfort, storytelling, and all the other gifts that make up unicorns. And the schools should do so not in an accidental way, through the lucky example of a few special teachers who embody these same attributes, but in a strategic and systematic way, with textbooks and seminars, to help grow awareness of the value of these virtues both for the students and for the teachers themselves. This kind of approach to education would create many more leaders for our companies, our communities, and our society as a whole and would create better conditions for collective social progress.

CHAPTER 11

INSPIRED BY UNEXPECTED MENTORS

Up to this point, we have spoken about people in two particular roles: first, as *objects of the innovation process* and, second, as *drivers of that process*—the *unicorns*. There is, however, a third category of people who have another, fundamental role in the life of any unicorn. It's a democratic role that any individual can decide to take on in daily interactions with other people. And it's role that you can decide to assign to someone in your orbit. It's a formative role that can exponentially amplify the number of unicorns in your organization and in the world. And it's an extremely important role, because it has incredible potential for increasing the levels of knowledge, inspiration, and success of every unicorn on the planet. I'm talking about the role of the *mentors*.

The Ideal Metamentor

Personally, I've never had an *official* mentor. And yet, throughout my life, I've had dozens of prodigious mentors, although they were often unaware that they were performing this function for me. Some of them have been bosses, others have been friends and loved ones; some have been colleagues, others far-off figures, both in space and time. What I've always done—first unconsciously and then in an increasingly strategic way—is to identify the *superpowers* of particularly inspiring people and absorb their essence in every possible way, through watching them, listening to them, studying them, reading them, and talking to them, when feasible. For example, if someone was particularly strong in navigating corporate politics, I'd try to understand the person's strategies and behaviors—whether indirectly or through direct questions and discussion. If another person proved to be brilliant in the world of communication and story-telling, I would do the same with that individual. If another was a charis-matic leader, that person would become my mentor in this aspect of my life. If yet another was an extraordinary graphic designer and typography expert, I would transform the person into my mentor in that dimension.

The synthesis of these exceptional qualities made these mentors into my supreme mentor, the *metamentor*, the ideal mentor, one to whom I could try to aspire. The great difference between a perfect, entirely fantastical mentor and the metamentor is that the latter—even if still a chimera—represents a figure nevertheless composed of aspects of real people who are approachable and available, to whom you can reach out, with whom you can interact in a concrete way in the world in which we actually live and work.

Many of the mentors who contribute to defining my personal meta-mentor are individuals I have met along the way, friends and acquain-tances who are unknown to the masses of people. Other mentors, how-ever, are very well known, because along my path I have had the privilege and pleasure to befriend some people who have made great achievements in their lives, redesigning their industries with extraordinary success, making history in different and unique ways, and consequently earning visibility and fame.

From Stefan Sagmeister to Karim Rashid, from Michel Rojkind to Bjarke Ingels, from Tiësto to Kanye West, from Indra Nooyi to Ramon Laguarta, from Silvio Scaglia to Laxman Narasimhan, from Jenke Ahmed Tailly to Paola Antonelli, from Francesco Carrozzini to Fabio Novembre, from Stefano Domenicali to Anjula Acharia, from Fabio Volo to Jovanotti, from Benny Benassi to Joe Gebbia, from Davide Oldani to Franca Sozzani, from Marco Mazzoli to Denis Dekovic, from Stefano Giovannoni to Job Smeets—all these people, in their own ways, have inspired me over the years as a creative, as an innovator, as an entrepreneur. These individuals, together with a series of other, less widely known people, have become integral parts of my personal metamentor.

They are people with whom I interact and I converse, who have left something deep within my spirit. Some of them are the humblest persons I know, some are the kindest; some are extreme experimenters, some are incredibly generous; some have found the perfect balance between art and business, some are profound critical thinkers; some are wonderfully curious, some are uniquely optimistic. Collectively, the people that compose my metamentor embody every single skill of the unicorns.

Now imagine someone who has all of these characteristics—all of these gifts developed to the extreme in one single human being. It would be very difficult, probably impossible, to find such a person. But it's much more likely that you might find some of these single gifts in people close to you, in the friends and acquaintances who surround you. Anyone around you might have one or more of these traits, with peaks of individual excellence. It's enough just to open your eyes, focus your heart, and prepare your mind, and you'll begin to find them.

Look for these superpowers in the people you interact with every day, or in others with whom you come into contact over the span of your life, identify them, become aware of the luminous glow that surrounds these people, and absorb their positive energy. The union of all these figures creates what I call the ideal metamentor. These people don't realize it, but I constantly study them. I watch them and absorb and learn from them; I am inspired by them. I have identified at least one characteristic in each of them that is developed to the extreme and that has become my reference point for that gift, a kind of constant point of comparison to measure myself by. In my dialogue with each of these people, my questions and their answers have become acts of constant mentoring.

The Mentor by Osmosis

With their unique gifts, the people that compose the metamentors inspire us from a distance; proximity, physical or emotional, makes the dialogue possible, but we don't have the privilege of an intense and daily interaction with each one of them. There are other individuals instead with whom we have the opportunity to spend much more time. Usually these are family members, close friends, or coworkers. With them, we have daily exchanges and deeper connections. With their thinking and behaviors, they can inspire us organically, constantly, permeating our souls day after day, without even realizing it. Sometimes these people evolve into traditional mentors, taking on a formal role. Other times they become what I love to call *mentors by osmosis*.

My first mentors by osmosis, without any doubt, were my parents. And the same is probably true for everyone, albeit in different ways. My mom and dad taught me the essential values of culture and kindness. And they inspired me with their creativity, applied to the world of art and writing. The gods of money and success weren't icons for my parents. They neither celebrated nor denigrated wealth and fame; my parents simply didn't take these into account. Perhaps my parents feared the pursuit of money and success, somehow seeing in it a potential threat to their sons. In my parents' minds, wealth and fame came with a risk—the risk of losing your moral compass. My parents have been my mentors by osmosis through their behavior, their convictions, and their passions, but without ever applying any pressure, simply by handing down lessons from their own lived experiences.

My wife, Carlotta, is another mentor of these pure, traditional, and traditionalist values. Held by our grandparents and in eras long past, these values are difficult to find today and represent a breath of fresh air and an anchor in the storms of my life.

My brother, Stefano, reminds me every day about the importance of humility and creativity. His is the humility of an extraordinary designer, among the most extraordinary I have ever met, who never stops being grateful for the universe of possibilities in creation, experimentation, and invention, always combining agility, pragmatism, and fantasy.

But in the context of this book, one of the most important mentors by osmosis that I ever had in the world of innovation was the great Claudio Cecchetto. I want to pause a moment to talk about Claudio because of his deep meaning in my life. Let me take you by the hand as we take a journey into my past—one that I hope will help you to better understand the importance of this kind of person, the impact such individuals' teachings can have on you, and the conditions necessary for those teachings to take root.

A Turning Point

Claudio Cecchetto is an Italian celebrity: a DJ, a singer, a producer, the founder and creator of two extremely famous radio channels (Radio Deejay and Radio Capital), a presenter of TV festivals, and a discoverer and producer of an infinite list of stars—TV and radio hosts, singers and musicians.

I met him in the iconic year of 2000, at a turning point for me—I was fresh out of university with dreams in my pocket and atomic energy in my heart, in transition between the worlds of study and work. One day, a day like any other, I got an unexpected call from my friend Filippo. A former colleague of his was working as Claudio's assistant, and she could organize a meeting for us.

As enthusiastic twenty-somethings, we could have gone to this meeting with the simple idea of getting an autograph and sharing a drink with a star, someone until then we would only ever have seen on our TV screens. Many people probably would have done just that. But instead, we decided to do something different. We were going to propose a project to him. Filippo was an engineer. We decided to bring on board two more friends, designers as well, to cover all the different skills necessary for our project.

Claudio was investing in the digital world at that time—he's always been a pioneer—and had just created a partnership with Renato Soru, the founder and owner of Tiscali, which back then was one of the most important internet providers in Europe. We were young and very skilled in the most advanced software for 3D modeling and digital design. We went to Claudio's dream home on Via Meda, in Milan, with an idea that was simple and powerful for those times: applying 3D modeling to web navigation, changing completely the user experience on Claudio's websites. And we shared that idea through a presentation that spoke for itself, full of renderings and animations.

I remember entering the main hall in his house: there was a huge screen that covered the central wall, flanked by two towering speakers, while a long glass table took up most of the space in the room. Claudio was seated at the center, and we spread ourselves out around him: four young men at the court of the king of Italian entertainment. But Claudio, an experienced and brilliant talent scout, didn't see just four young men; he didn't make a snap judgment about us four youngsters without experience or look down on us with that cultural snobbery that so many successful people have. Instead he viewed us with the curiosity of the innovator, with the intelligent eye of the explorer.

Claudio had a unique awareness of the magic role of talented people, those human beings who roam free in the prairies of society, people who are invisible to the majority until the moment that an enlightened individual uncovers them, identifies their superpowers, and then gives them the platform to express themselves, transforming them into a precious resource—including for their discoverer. That day, Claudio didn't just look at the project that we were presenting to him—the project itself, probably, interested him very little. Instead, he saw four young individuals full of enthusiasm, rich in ideas, able to utilize the most advanced tools of this new digital world that he was beginning to explore.

As Aristotle would have said, Claudio saw *potentiality*, which he could transform into *actuality*. Claudio wasn't interested in finding the *action*—he was on the hunt for *potential*.

Claudio was an *actualizer of potential*: this has been his whole life, the foundation on which he has built his fortune. First by working on himself, and then by working with a whole set of people who have had a positive collision with his sphere of influence. And so—as he had probably done over the course of his life for many individuals whom he has found and launched—he asked us a question and made us a proposal. The question was simple: "What do you do?" Stefano and I were working at Philips Design; Filippo was working in a health care company; Mariano was a consultant. We told him instead that we were about to start a studio together. I don't remember who said those words, but I imagine that none of us was surprised by them: it was a dream that probably leaped out of all of our hearts, even if we still hadn't formalized it through a proper discussion. Claudio's reply was even simpler, quick and intentional. But this time it had the flavor of something incredible, at least for us four young men: "Let's make this studio together."

A month later we signed a contract that saw the birth of Wisemad, our agency with Claudio Cecchetto, in a dream house with a swimming pool, a garden, and a music studio right in the heart of Milan. I remember my boundless enthusiasm when I went home to tell my family. It was a complete dream for four kids from an Italian suburb. The business lasted only a couple of years, the length of time we were able to support ourselves financially without big investors behind us. We were flying prematurely in the completely unstable universe of the internet in its pioneering phase. We were cowboys in the Wild West, with horses, a wagon, and few provisions, out to explore the immense prairies of the digital world. These were the years of the big storms and tornadoes on those lonely prairies. It was too soon—far too soon for most people.

Nevertheless, those couple of years represented for me an exceptional schooling in life and business, and Claudio became one of the most important mentors I have ever met. Without those years, I wouldn't be where I am today. One lesson in particular became a mantra of my existence from that time on. As young men from the suburbs, out to discover the world, my friends and I were more than satisfied with the opportunity to work with a bunch of celebrities—indeed, we were in seventh heaven. From the digital content for an album by the pop group 883 to the design of Jovanotti's website, the projects were stimulating, fun, prestigious, and exciting.

But for Claudio, the projects weren't any of these things. Claudio saw these jobs simply as services necessary to generate revenue that would allow us to do something else—something that could be truly stimulating, fun, prestigious, and exciting for him, too. For Claudio, those jobs weren't the dream that we thought they were; they were simply financial enablers of another, much bigger, more ambitious dream. We met him every day in that office house. Every day we worked, interacted, and dreamed with him; and every day, in one way or another, he repeated the same thing over and again: "We need to create something that no one else has done before. I don't want Wisemad to just offer design services.

I don't care about that. Wisemad needs to generate new ideas that can change the world!"

Someone could easily have interpreted his behavior as a delusion of grandeur and could simply have continued to enjoy the satisfaction of the existing projects. I saw the light instead. Claudio's way of thinking and acting opened up a new world for me. And the door to that world would never close again. Without once using the word "innovation"—not even accidentally, not even in passing, not on a single day during those two years—Claudio was teaching me the purest essence of innovation. He was acting as a model and influence in a way that only rarely has anyone else been able to replicate over the course of my life.

He did so through his behavior, his way of thinking, his way of working—by osmosis, a process of transfer through exposure and contact. Claudio had caught the innovation bug; he was obsessed by innovation, and this was—and still remains—one of his most beautiful traits. From big projects to small daily activities, he always thought about how to do things in a way that was different—different from how it was done in the past and from how others would think to do it in the present. As soon as he built something, he thought about the next step. It was a constant tension. He always lived in the mood of a "Saturday evening in a village," to use once again the words of the great Italian poet Giacomo Leopardi.[16] Claudio enjoyed the preparations for the Sunday feast more than the feast itself. The journey of innovation excited and stimulated him; it was his raison d'être. He hadn't been designed by God to manage the results of his innovation, to extract efficiency from the systems that he created. He had been created to continue to create, to constantly live in that Saturday of construction, always heading for a new Sunday. When Sunday arrived, he had already started to think about next week, next Saturday, and next Sunday.

Innovation Is a Mindset

One of the most important concepts that I learned from Claudio is that innovation is first and foremost a mindset. Before innovation takes the form of a strategy, a project, or a process, it's something that you have in your mind, a way of reasoning and acting that becomes part of your

DNA. You just do it, in every moment of your existence, in the personal day-to-day as much as in your professional life—and the surprising discovery is that the simple effort of asking yourself to think in a different way doesn't require more energy than doing what everyone else is doing. It requires only a different way of looking at things.

Over the past twenty-five years, I've listened to experts talk about innovation in an erudite and sophisticated way; I've read dozens upon dozens of books on the topic, full of ideas and tools; I've collaborated with consultants who were paid millions and were able to hold forth about strategies and processes better than anyone. But the problem with a great many of these experts and theorists—along with their carefully tailored language and quick wordsmithery—is that very few of them have ever actually innovated in their lives; very few of them had innovation in their blood, in their guts, in their eyes, in their bones. They spoke about innovation, but they didn't actually do it. And when they tried to, they often failed. Over the years, I've become terribly allergic to these nonpracticing orators: people who speak about things without having done very much at all, who hide behind processes, frameworks, numbers, and statistics—and then grind to a halt when they have to actually innovate on a daily basis.

Claudio innovated; he didn't talk about innovation. Let's be clear: I think the ability to know how to articulate the value, theory, and praxis of innovation is an extremely important gift, especially in the world of big corporations, because it provides an essential tool for the innovator to communicate with potential partners, sponsors, and investors and to unlock their partnership, sponsorship, and investments. And this ability is fundamental. But these gifts have to be matched by the ability to actually innovate, through instinct and vision, practice and experience, intuition and sensitivity, and amplified through experimentation and learning. Too often, I've seen instead the deflationary force of this superficial oratory, lacking any substance but nevertheless putting entire organizations on the wrong track with their business strategies and innovation processes.

Over the years with Claudio, we worked on a great number of unique and interesting projects. One of the most significant was probably

Energybank, a virtual bank with its own currency—digital but real—that could be used on the internet. Energybank represented a first intuition about what today we call cryptocurrency, which would be truly invented only some years later. And then there was the power and potential of e-commerce—think of PayPal, Apple Pay, and similar platforms to facilitate online shopping. We were in the year 2000. It was too soon. Innovation is made of good ideas but also good timing. Ideas can't be launched too soon or too late. Sometimes, timing can be managed by anticipating or slowing down the launch of a given idea. But if the anticipation is by a decade or decades, then there's little to be done. It was definitely the right idea, but the moment was all wrong.

With Claudio I dreamed, experimented, and grew. I accumulated a lot of practical knowledge. I learned new tools to design websites, to do animation graphics, to code, and to model in 3D. These were all useful technical skills in that moment, but they are of little use over time if you don't keep practicing them, because the newest software and technologies keep on evolving and mutating at light speed. We should never limit ourselves to learning how to use just one instrument; we need to learn instead the mindset and method for learning that instrument. This is the most precious gift we can give to ourselves: the gift of *employability*, which is the ability to learn in a constant fashion and to transform ourselves in a flexible way, continually repositioning ourselves in the job market as an important asset, whatever our specific technical experience might be.

In those years I also diversified my experience as a product designer, experimenting in the fields of the internet and digital technologies, learning their cultures, their vernacular and grammar. And in the meantime I was advancing my own projects in wearable technologies, which I had developed for my thesis at the university Politecnico of Milan, in collaboration with fashion brands and tech companies. I collided with the worlds of entertainment, music, and celebrities—which all turned out to be of great use over time. All of these were extremely precious experiences for my journey toward becoming a holistic designer, and I faced them with enthusiasm and an open mind.

But yet again, the greatest gift that Claudio Cecchetto gave me in those years was much bigger than all of this. Claudio taught me to think as an innovator. And since then, every time that a new initiative gets going, someone gives me a new task, or I decide to do something, I always ask myself the same question: "What can I do that no one has ever done before?" Whether it's a small graphic design project or a breakthrough innovation program, I always ask myself how I can produce something extraordinary that people don't expect. And by "people," I mean both the end users and customers and also my superiors, the investors, the sponsors, the media, the world out there, and anyone else around me. This practice also applies to my private life.

This is what Claudio taught me by drawing out, through a maieutic process, something that was already there within me but that I had kept dormant, allowing it to emerge only randomly and occasionally. Claudio, as an unconscious mentor, gave consciousness to his unconscious disciple Mauro. From out of the raw material in front of him, Claudio extracted the mindset of Mauro the innovator. Once extracted, it has remained with me ever since.

The Virtual Mentor

Some years before meeting Claudio, I came across another person who has been essential for my personal growth—another individual who has been a mentor, but in a very different way from Cecchetto. I want to tell you about this man, about his role and his impact on my life. Give me your hand once more, sit comfortably, and—just as you did with Claudio—follow along with me on another intimate dive into my past. This man's name is Stefano Marzano.

I met him in the summer of 1995. I was twenty years old, and that day I was on a bus, stopped in front of the Pontiggia bookshop in the center of Varese, before setting off again on the route toward the neighborhood of Bustecche, where I lived. A few minutes earlier, I had received a call from Valentina, a friend from back in high school. Valentina knew that I had just begun to study design at Politecnico university and a few months before had told me, by the by, that her father knew a well-known designer who was working on some very interesting projects in the consumer electronic business. She was talking about Stefano Marzano.

I came across the "legend" of Stefano at school: he was the global head of design for Philips, the renowned Dutch company based out of Eindhoven. Even though I had never met him personally, I knew his work very well. His projects were shared with us by our professors, who presented them as tangible demonstrations of strategic enlightenment and praised his innovative approach. Stefano himself was presented as an exemplary kind of creative leader, one able to wed large-scale business with the most visionary and humanist kind of design, composed of empathy and emotions. During those years, Stefano was a reference point for many designers, a kind of celebrity in our world—a figure who inspired, whose example you could aspire to follow.

When Valentina told me that she knew him, my eyes popped out of my head. I explained to her what he meant for us designers, and her eyes lit up, too. Until that moment, she had only thought of him as of any other interesting family friend; now she was seeing him in a completely different way. It's fascinating how the perspective of another person can mix into our own to create a third, completely unexpected perspective, which ends up enriching us and providing new ideas. Yet again, you can see the power of diversity of thought in action.

Valentina left me that day with the promise that she would introduce me to Stefano at the first opportunity, when he came back to Italy from Holland and would pass by the family's home. That day finally came in June. I was on the E line bus just as on any other morning, my hand on the railing and my head in the sky, when Valentina called me to keep her promise. "Mauro, Stefano Marzano's coming round for lunch! Why don't you come by for a coffee afterward so you can meet him?"

I stared at my Motorola MicroTAC cell phone, which I still have today along with other souvenirs of that era, and I couldn't believe my ears. I had the chance to meet the legendary Marzano, the global head of Philips Design.

But it was a complicated day: in the afternoon I had training with the soccer team, and anyone who has ever played soccer at that level knows that training is sacred. You never miss training. I had to pass by my house to eat, and I was already on my way. But besides these other plans, something else contributed to making this meeting somehow difficult. It was much easier to simply stay on the bus, with the excuse that I couldn't accept the invitation due to my soccer training, rather than getting off the bus and going to meet a grown-up I didn't know, in the intimacy of a home belonging to other grown-ups I didn't know.

I would need to leave my comfort zone. I was twenty years old and, just as many people my age would have been, I was intimidated by this successful figure whom I'd seen on recorded interviews so many times and whom I'd read about in books and articles. What could I say to him? What would he ask me? I had just begun to study design, and he was twenty-five years older than me. Twenty-five years of experience, projects, and life! Up until then, the majority of my private and social conversations with strangers had been with people of my own age. I was at ease with them. I was even confident, most of the time. But this was an adult and a stranger, surrounded by other adults and strangers: What could I tell him? Would I seem stupid? Would I simply show myself up for not having interesting content? I could feel my anxiety. I was experiencing all of those emotions that usually we don't even consciously notice, that fly quietly through our minds, under the radar of conscious thought, and that then make us find understandable excuses to avoid putting ourselves at risk. For many people, this is a constant—a devilish, immaterial constant that forces us to miss an infinite number of opportunities.

Audentes fortuna juvat, as my Latin forefathers put it: "Fortune favors the bold." I have always found this a saying full of truth. It doesn't simply and optimistically mean that if we're more fearless, then we will have more luck, like a sort of divine intervention. I like thinking that the wisdom of this saying resides in the purely statistical fact that if you take a risk and you do so often and intentionally, then sooner or later things will go well. It's the science of probability. Instead, if you spend your time dreaming and planning better futures but then never trying, never throwing yourself out there with bravery, over and over again, then luck will never have a chance to help you out. If we try and try often enough, luck has more of a chance to meet us halfway. Statistically speaking, our likelihood of being helped by fate will increase. Or better still: the probability increases that our talent—made of courage, intelligence, and creativity—will meet with the right people, in the right place, at the right time, so that the magic can happen.

Fortune favors the bold: I put my Motorola MicroTAC to my ear and told Valentina: "Perfect, I've got nothing going on. I'm coming right away!" I got off the bus and looked for the right way to get to her family's house. And I realized that the best way was probably by foot. To get there on time, I skipped lunch. I walked; I ran. I was happy. I got to the house about an hour later with an empty stomach—but a stomach full of butterflies! I could feel the adrenaline in my limbs, which were sweating with summer heat and emotions. I hugged Valentina, shook hands with her parents—whom I was meeting for the first time—and finally I shook Stefano's hand. Her parents offered me a coffee that formally justified my presence in their home, and then I began the conversation. A conversation about which I now remember almost nothing.

What has remained impressed on my mind very clearly, instead, is Stefano's emotional profile, at least as I perceived it in those couple of hours together. I recall his enthusiasm for the world of design, an almost boyish enthusiasm, very similar to what I was used to at home, which I had seen in my father when he painted and in my mom when she wrote. The little I remember of our conversation was when we spoke about the cell phones that Philips had started developing, and how the company was coming up with innovative features including new and unexpected ringtones. In those years, Philips was producing and selling mobile phones, along with hundreds of other products in the consumer electronics business. All the ringtones on the market until then had been a monotone, just like the sounds people were used to hearing from their home phones. Stefano was experimenting with music instead: he whipped out his own cell phone and had me listen to the prototype. It was amazing—or, in the Italian expression I used with my friends that evening, "*Che figata!*"—so cool. Stefano was probably thinking the same thing about his project, given the pride with which he was sharing it. I could feel his positivity, his passion and farsightedness.

The meeting was extraordinarily inspiring. I had gotten up close to his humanist creativity, and I had felt for the first time where that kind of creativity could take someone like Stefano. I could see a link between his

If we try and try often enough, luck has more of a chance to meet us halfway. Statistically speaking, our likelihood of being helped by fate will increase. Or better still: the probability increases that our talent—made of courage, intelligence, and creativity—will meet with the right people, in the right place, at the right time, so that the magic can happen.

spirit and his results. Up until then, I had seen the successes and results of that renowned person only from afar; that day, I actually shared the physical presence of his soul and drive. So I began to follow him more closely. I didn't miss an article, I never skipped an interview, and whenever he was in Milan for one of his open talks, I was systematically present. But I went further than this: fresh from studying philosophy, I was fascinated by the exchange of letters between well-known scholars and their young disciples, between mentors and students. It was through those letters that they exchanged theories, deciphered reality, and imagined better worlds. It's through those correspondences that we know much of what we know about their thought. And so, just as the philosophers once did, I picked up pen and paper and began to write: a correspondence between designers! In truth, I didn't really expect a reply; maybe I hoped for one, but my spirit as a philosopher-designer was entirely satisfied with the possibility of writing about design, innovation, and society to someone of this caliber. If I remember well, I sent two or three letters over a couple of years—no more. And as I expected, I never received a specific reply to any of them.

At a certain point, though, Stefano decided to give me something with a much richer meaning in return, which had a very important impact on my life. On September 6, 1996, he sent me two books published by Philips, created and produced by him and his team. One was called *Vision of the Future* and the other *New Objects, New Media, Old Walls.* In these books, Stefano—along with a hybrid team of designers, sociologists, and scientists—imagined and defined the future of technology, with ideas and concepts that twenty years later have become many of the products and services we are all used to today: from the iPad to the cloud; from dematerialized music, free of any physical support (CD, cassette, or vinyl), to wireless charging stations for any of our electronic devices; from video calls to virtual reality eyewear. In those pages, you can find the design seeds for hundreds of physical objects and immaterial solutions that today surround our whole existence. I adored those books; they bewitched and inspired me, and they made me appreciate more than ever the "profession" of design and the ability of designers to imagine and conceptualize the future. Fundamentally, the books made me fall in love with what many people today call innovation and what we designers have always called design. Those were the years in which I understood that I wanted to practice this kind of design for the rest of my life—design that innovates.

Stefano's gift had another fundamental role in my life. In the first pages of one of the two books, he wrote me a dedication: "I'm also sending you this 'project document,' one of the few bilingual ones, so that you can get English under your belt." And then, in the following pages, he wrote: "PS Mauro, the text in Italian is full of printing errors!! (I'm driving some of the Dutch guys crazy), but the text in English ISN'T. Practice reading both." Stefano was pushing me to learn English with those books. Back then, I didn't speak a single word of this language. I was one of those few Italians who was still "forced" to study French in school. In those years, there were still many French teachers in the Italian system, and even if English was quickly becoming the indispensable language of the new global world, many Italian schools still offered foreign language instruction in French. At the age of ten I had, quite accidentally, been put into one of those classes. And I had never had any other choice. When, years later, I met Stefano Marzano and told him that one day I would like to work with him, he asked me quite rightly if I spoke English. When I told him that I didn't, he told me that to work on his team at Philips I would have to learn it. And at that point I understood that the English language would be not only the key to entering Philips but also the basic variable to reach the results and impact that Stefano had reached, in whatever company I worked.

It's Never Too Late—Even When It Seems Too Late

Learning English wasn't easy, though. I had a very full life already: I was going to university every weekday in Milan, with around four hours of commuting in total from Varese and back; and then there was soccer training four evenings a week, with games on Sundays—often away games—and the summer training camp. And then, of course, I had a social life as well. I didn't have a spare moment for studying English or for practicing it correctly, above all in a town such as Varese, where there weren't many foreigners. And then there was the fact that I was already over twenty years old; I was ten years behind in comparison with the majority of my peer group, who had begun studying English at school and by then already spoke it fluently, or at least in a way that sounded fluent to my inexpert ears. I felt it was especially too late to learn the language to the level necessary to use it in the professional world.

Back then, social media still didn't exist, the internet was still little known, and the pressure to learn a language that allowed you to speak with the borderless, globalized world of the web was relatively low; there was still the perception that anyone could start a brilliant career in Italy, in any industry, without necessarily needing to learn the English language. Or at least, this was the perception of people such as my family and me, who had not traveled extensively nor had an international network of friends and colleagues. But Stefano's words pushed me to persevere; they gave me the inspiration, energy, and drive that I had lacked until then. I wanted to be able to dream as Stefano did at Philips. I wanted to be able to advance similar projects, on that scale, of that magnitude, with that level of global impact. English was an essential tool for reaching this dream.

It was thus that I decided to turn down an Erasmus fund scholarship to study in Paris for a year. I waited another twelve months and reapplied to obtain a new grant for an English-speaking country. It was a risk: I was losing a scholarship for a wonderful experience abroad, in France, and there was no certainty of receiving the funding again to study in another country. There were very few places available. But I tried, nevertheless. And this was how I received the opportunity to go to Dublin. In December 1997, I left Italy for Ireland. And with Italy, I left not only my family and friends, but I abandoned the opportunity to stay with someone for whom I had very strong feelings in those years, as well as the chance to complete the soccer season in a superior category, in a new team I had signed with just that summer. In other words, that move wasn't a simple one. It implied material and emotional sacrifices. And to make it even more complicated, I was going to Dublin not to study English but to study design. And I had to do so in a language that I didn't know at all! I couldn't financially afford to lose a year of university to go and study a new language. A more intense and effective method was simply to combine learning the language with my design studies; within six months, I would need to have mastered English well enough to pass the university-level exams. *Good luck!*

In brief, it wasn't a simple decision, whatever way you looked at it. I couldn't have launched myself further out of my comfort zone.

But today, I know that that was one of the best decisions I ever made in my life. The year in Dublin was extraordinary in every way. I have shivers down my spine while I write about it. First of all, I learned English to a level that in the following years even allowed me to become an executive in multinational corporations headquartered in the United States. Beyond that, the city gave me the first taste of life beyond Italy, and this was a unique opportunity for observing my own country—and thus my whole existence in that country as well—from a completely different perspective, appreciating both its infinite worth and also noting its weaknesses. This changed my way of thinking for the rest of my life.

I was twenty-three when I left Italy. It seemed too late to learn English, too difficult to leave behind some passions and ties; but I decided to throw myself in, to try, to experiment. And it was the right choice. Without that decision, I wouldn't have accomplished what I have today—something that has given me such deep satisfaction and, in the end, such intense happiness. Never say never: it's never too late! This is what I've come to realize; this is my personal mantra. And I never stop repeating it—especially to people who at a certain moment in their lives find themselves faced with a hurdle that seems too high to be overcome, and so they decide not to even try.

When I was faced with the wall of having to learn another language, it was certainly not easy to see over the top. I needed the help of someone else, someone who ran free on the other side, to understand the world of opportunities that was just beyond the horizon, shielded from my view by these virtual bricks. I needed another human being to push me to find the right stimulus to climb that wall and conquer it. And that's what I did—I climbed, I conquered, and when I got to the top I saw that the world extending out in front of me was much more vast, beautiful, and spectacular than I could ever have imagined.

I didn't just discover English in those years; I discovered the uniqueness of Italy, as seen from abroad, and at the same time the magic of Ireland, the extraordinary beauty of a place so different from my own country. I discovered new aspects of the supreme virtue of diversity in my small university class made up of students of dozens of different nationalities, and I discovered my ability to go it alone, to support myself far from my family, cleaning dishes in the college's cafeteria, the only job I could find before learning the language. I tasted the hardship of being less popular than others in my peer group; "exotic" Mauro was good for a few hours but then became tiring, because the Irish students couldn't easily communicate with this foreigner who couldn't speak, couldn't joke, couldn't entertain or be entertained. This continued until a few months had passed, when I began to express myself correctly and became less exotic in the eyes of my new Irish friends—and more enjoyable to hang out with.

Magic Occurrences: A Successful Leader Gives Back

Stefano Marzano gave me this chance, probably without even realizing it. I've often thought over the years about what would have happened if Stefano hadn't sent me those books. This act of his cast two spells.

First of all, a very busy and successful leader, who knew me by chance, decided to invest the time to get the books, think about a note to write, write it, find my address, and send the books from Holland to a young man in Italy. Was this a huge effort? No, not really. Would many other people have done it? No, probably not. And usually they don't. The small effort of a big man had a huge impact on the life of that young student. To be quite clear: Stefano didn't really know me; at that point we'd met only once, and he'd received a couple of my letters. He owed me nothing. I wasn't from a well-off family, and I did not have the kinds of connections that were relevant to him. He had no aim or personal interest in sending me those books with the dedication. It was an act of simple kindness. I had had coffee with that man a year earlier, and that meeting had transformed him into my mentor, without him knowing, simply because I followed him, studied him, and admired his work from afar.

Magic Occurrences: A Young Man Searches for Inspiration

The second magical spell in this story of my encounter with Stefano was that a young man of twenty put in the effort to find an inspirational model and made the decision to select him as a *virtual mentor*. I say "virtual" because Stefano wasn't physically near to me; he wasn't my boss, a colleague, a teacher—he wasn't even a friend. I simply began, proactively, to follow him through conferences, publications, and interviews, studying him and learning from a distance. What made him different from a role model was that I had had some interactions with Stefano. He knew he had a fan in Italy somewhere, but he didn't need to do anything else. He was leading design in a Dutch corporation, and I was simply a young man who had begun my journey in a faraway Italian university.

In those years, I learned so much from him—silently, respectfully, observing the results of his work, the many projects, the impact of his leadership on the company, the encounters and stories of many people who worked directly with him, his words in books and discussions. At the end of my studies, four years after I met him for the first time, Stefano offered me a job at Philips Design in Milan. It was the official beginning of my professional career. I spent only a year at the company, but it was a short period of important learning. A few months later, I met Claudio Cecchetto. And at that point I was ready to fly. I spread my wings and took off. And the rest is history.

Find Your Mentors—There Are No Excuses

When I hear people complain that they haven't had contact with mentors of a certain caliber, perhaps because they live in remote places or haven't had a chance to build the right connections, I always tell them my theory about three kinds of mentor: the *ideal metamentor*, the *mentor by osmosis*, and the *virtual mentor*.

Focus on a unique and extraordinary feature of an individual who is near to you; do the same with another person, then another, still another, until you manage to form your ideal metamentor. Ask these people questions, establish a dialogue, make them inspire you.

Sometimes in your life, you'll come across someone particularly special; statistically there's a high chance that sooner or later this will happen. When it does, however, you need to be ready, with all of your receptors open, antennae raised, prepared to embrace teachings and inspiration that otherwise might be invisible. You have to be a student for life! Look for your Claudio Cecchetto, and absorb that person's energy. Make the person your mentor by osmosis.

And finally, today more than ever before, through the internet, we have access to an infinite stock of potential virtual mentors, often with a direct daily connection to them through their social media platforms. We can observe them in their professional lives and often in their private ones, too. We can study them, and sometimes we can even ask them questions. It's up to us to choose who are the right people to select as our sources of inspiration. It's up to us to find a Stefano Marzano. If that person then interacts with us, even if only sporadically, then the person begins to become a mentor, with a more or less active role in our existence.

But even if that person has no way of interacting with us, if we pose a whole set of questions and try to respond, inspired by the contents of the person's mind and experience as shared in books and interviews, articles and talks, then we at least have the opportunity to transform this individual into a role model, benefiting indirectly from the person's wisdom. Over the past three decades, I have chosen role models among a range of figures: Plato, Aristotle, Seneca, Leonardo da Vinci, Blaise Pascal, Nietzsche, Andy Warhol, Steve Jobs. And sometimes I have *almost* transformed them into metamentors—a little fantasy doesn't hurt! With a pinch of imagination, I ask them questions and receive answers. What would Andy do in this moment? How would Steve reply to this email? How would Blaise react to this problem? The replies that I give myself are based on their principles, their philosophies, their approaches to life.

Whatever you want to call them, identifying figures who can inspire us, even when they can't give us replies or meet with us, is a precious art. Over the years I've tried to transform some of these individuals into sources of inspiration for my team. I did so with Steve Jobs, for example. Walter Isaacson's biography of Jobs is one of the most stimulating books that I've ever read. I bought a hundred copies a few years ago and gave one to every designer on my team at PepsiCo, hoping that in reading it, they would find the same drive, energy, and excitement that I had felt when I finished the hundreds of pages in that tome. I felt a mix of emotions that is difficult to describe: I closed the book, got up from the couch, and was ready to change the world!

If, instead, you are a successful leader and coming into contact with people inspired by you or simply interested in learning from your experience, don't be miserly: share with generosity, listen, offer something in return, give back a little of that inspiration that you've received, a little of the luck that was given to you. A book dedication changed my life. That's enough. And today, in the world of social media, this is all simpler than ever before. A well-considered reply to a question received over social media can have a deep impact on the existence of another human being if that person is open to receiving it and appreciates both the act and the message. It doesn't cost you anything, but it can mean everything to another person. This is what happened to me twenty years ago, and since then I've always borne it in mind, every day of my life.

CONCLUSION
DESIGNING HAPPINESS

In all these years of work and study, in universities, start-ups, and corporations, I've always had the same dream: making something that touches people's lives, generating a positive impact on the world. It's a goal that I had as a child. I wanted to create something that human beings need, that people want, that in some way would provide them with some form of value. It could be an idea, a product, an experience. I didn't know it back then, and I didn't realize it for a long time, but what I was looking for was actually that sort of immortality that the production of meaningful value for people surrounding you, and for society as a whole, can give you. It's a desire, a necessity, an instinct that in and of itself is placed at the very peak of Maslow's pyramid, in the realm of dreams, self-realization, and transcendental aspirations.

Through these ideas, products, and experiences, we can live forever, even when we're no longer physical guests of this world. This is why I've always believed in the generation of real, tangible value that is sustainable over time. In English, we have a powerful and concise word for this concept that we don't have in Italian: *legacy*, a cultural inheritance that is more abstract than concrete in its substance.

When I left 3M to join PepsiCo, my heart was full of enthusiasm for the new challenge that was in front of me, but it was also heavy with sadness. I felt that I was leaving behind something unfinished. The project that I had begun ten years earlier in Milan, in a small office of a US corporation, to build a new culture of design-driven innovation, was not completed yet. But I wanted design to survive my departure; I wanted design to keep on growing under a new leadership. That was my legacy there.

Over the course of the years, I had tried to build an organization that could keep on going after me, but its journey to maturity simply wasn't complete. It needed more time, other resources, further projects, new unicorns. When I told the company that I was leaving, I also said that I was ready to help them identify the best leader to take the reins of a capability that we had formed over the span of ten years. We had built a design center in Saint Paul, Minnesota, a physical space with colored walls, pink carpets, and eye-catching furniture. It was a space that we filled with brilliant, creative, and kind people who were pursuing their ideas, visions, and projects to generate material and creative wealth for 3M and for the whole world. Once I was already at PepsiCo, I spent time with 3M's HR team to remind them about my theory of the unicorn so that they could apply it to their search. When Eric Quint—whom I didn't know directly—contacted me through LinkedIn, telling me that he was interested in my previous position as chief design officer and asking me if I could put him in touch with 3M, I was more than happy to do so. He had also come out of the "Philips School" of Stefano Marzano. And when Eric was then chosen for the role, I wrote to him right away, congratulating him and making myself available to pass some time together in New York, to share with him everything I knew about the company, in the hope that I could give him the tools necessary to work successfully in that organization right from the start.

It's been a number of years now since I left the Twin Cities, and today—looking at 3M from afar—I'm genuinely happy about how design has continued to develop and prosper in the service of the company; it's precisely what I had worked toward. Eric has guided design at 3M into its new phase, continuing from the foundation that I had laid, and when he left in 2020, he passed it into the hands of a new leader, Brian Rice, who is bringing it into new territory and reaching for new goals.

And at PepsiCo then, from the very beginning, my aim yet again was to form an organization that can continue to create value for decades to come, whether I myself am there or not. This is the most important metaproject that I have been driving forward for years. It might seem like a noble act of generosity, but in truth it is the most direct consequence of another journey in which I have always been immersed: the intimate, constant, perennial journey that all of us undertake in looking for our own personal happiness.

Inspired by theories that have their roots in the world of the human sciences, over the years I have identified three dimensions in my life where I want to invest time, energy, and resources with a particular focus.

Me

The first dimension is that of personal realization, which manifests itself through *defining our own identity* in relation to others. This dimension is often reified in our own profession or in the results of our work—but it is not only developed in this way. It can also be reached in our private life through hobbies, commitments, and engagements of every kind. Are you happy with what you do, and does it represent you in the right way? If not, then the time has come to make a change.

Me and You

The second dimension is about our *connection with others*, especially with family, friends, and loved ones. This is a two-way exchange in which happiness is realized through the satisfaction derived from offering love, kindness, respect, passion, and inspiration and at the same time through the intense pleasure that one feels in receiving these from others.

Us and Everybody Else

The third dimension *transcends ourselves*: it is the search for something greater than us, something that moves on an exponentially greater scale than our own personal interest, creating value for a specific community or for society as a whole. This dimension is based on the gift of the self to the universe, without expecting anything in return. The range of application is vast, spanning from the generous sharing of know-how to acts of charity, from religious missions to political ones, to every form of generating progress and prosperity in the world through one's own professional, social, and private platforms.

Translated into my professional context, these three dimensions have always driven me in three directions.

Who I Am

First, they have inspired me to define my professional identity in a precise, distinct, unique, and innovative way, suspended between design and business, between the United States and Italy, between rationality and creativity, between praxis and theory, between execution and strategy, immersed in the largest organizations in the world but always managing agile, flexible, streamlined groups, almost as if they were start-ups, at perfect ease in the discomfort of continuous change and constant evolution. My passion, my projects, my experiments, my successes, and my failures are the important pillars of my identity and my personal satisfaction.

Personal Relations

The second dimension, the one of personal relations and love, might seem to be a clearly private sphere, disconnected from the professional world. And for many people this is the case: they put on their jacket and tie in the morning, they get their keys and their badge from their nightstand, and they leave their love and their smile at home. And just like that, they go to work devoid of empathy, grinning and bearing it—"with a knife between their teeth," as we say in Italy. They recover their positive emotions only in the evening, when they come home exhausted from battle, drained by their own internal solitude. My world has never been

Never say never:
It's never too late!

like that. I have built a team in which personal connections, deep respect, reciprocal kindness, and platonic friendships are foundational virtues. And they are also indispensable for generating value for the company, for the user, and for society as a whole. We spend the majority of our lives at work: voiding that world of personal emotions makes no sense—it's the best recipe for unhappiness.

Personal Purpose

The third dimension is that of my dream, my cause, my purpose, which transcends me and gives me meaning. In my professional life I have always had two great missions.

The first is to create value for the world, generating design solutions that somehow respond to people's needs and dreams, producing a tangible, perceived benefit. The second is to help reposition the design community within the business world, explaining it, giving it a new role, and growing its credibility, authority, presence, and impact. If you believe in the idea that design is a discipline based entirely on the production of value for people (or human-centricity), then you will understand how this second goal is entirely an enabler of the first one.

Over the years I have tried in every way to support the design tribe in this journey and in this battle for recognition of a role that has often been misunderstood. From the global stages of 3M and PepsiCo, I have cried out to the world that this professional community can offer much more than it has been allowed to do up until now. I have allied myself with the business world; I have dreamed, worked, and created with the people in that world, always thinking about how to offer new opportunities to the world of design, in every enterprise around the globe.

I have accepted the invitation to sit on boards such as those of the Design Management Institute, the International Child Art Foundation, and the Foundation of the university Politecnico of Milan. And I have taken part in TV shows such as *America by Design*, to reach the general public with our purposeful design message, and in initiatives such as the Design Vanguard, a pledge for creative leaders to leverage our resources and influence in service of creating a more just, safe, and beautiful world, promoted by my friends Joe Gebbia, cofounder of Airbnb, and Tim Brown, executive chair at IDEO. I have been generous with my time dedicated to conferences, schools, and the media. I have put myself at the service of other chief design officers when they have taken on their roles, always with the aim of elevating the role of design on this planet.

But, once more, the final goal has always been that of creating value for the society we live in. I wanted to identify the needs and aspirations of the people I design for and to respond with relevant solutions made up of meaningful products, brands, spaces, services, and experiences. I understood very early on that the journey of searching for my own happiness aligned perfectly with the great metaproject of creating happiness for others through my projects—because satisfying those needs and desires is, in the end, the ideal gateway to collective happiness, individual and social.

Everything That Surrounds Us Has Been Designed by Someone

Everything that surrounds us, and that hasn't been created by Mother Nature, has been imagined, thought up, designed, and built by a human being, by a designer, an innovator, an entrepreneur. Every single thing. The computer that I'm using to write these words, the clothes I'm wearing, the chair I'm sitting on, the apartment I live in, the airplane passing by the window, the cup of coffee (now cold) that looks at me with curiosity from across the kitchen table—even the packaging of the products that just arrived at my house and the ad campaign that they're part of. Everything is designed by someone.

And thus collectively, through the products, brands, services, and experiences that we design, we touch the lives of billions of human beings across the world every single day. If our solutions are conceived in the best possible way, then we will end up adding value to these people's lives, generating moments of positivity made up of security, comfort, utility, convenience, pleasure, style, beauty, enjoyment, meaning, and poetry. When our solutions are not designed well, we make people's lives more complex, more difficult, less pleasurable, less enjoyable. If all the companies in the world, great and small, collectively followed the principles of meaningful design in their innovation processes—if they imagined solutions that would be sustainable from an aesthetic, functional, ecological, social, emotional, intellectual, and financial point of view—then those solutions would consequently become a myriad of precious fragments of a vast, universal, virtual metaproject, the most beautiful and important project that exists, the project for global, social, and planetary happiness.

As designers, innovators, and entrepreneurs, we thus have a unique opportunity in our hands and also an immense responsibility: to design products that favor a better future, that push our society in the right direction, that imagine and produce the well-being of an entire planet.

That doesn't mean that every product we create will be perfect, that every company we work for will have this mission. It would be naive to think this—an unrealizable dream. The dream that I have, instead, is real, concrete, and feasible. We must insert this tension toward perfection into every product we create; we must try to create the most meaningful solution within the limits of the historical, social, technological, and business contexts imposed upon us, always redefining these limits, reimagining the boundaries of the possible and the credible.

Let's Design a Better World

This means that in every company we work for, whether as employees, owners, clients, or consultants, we must push the principles of meaningful design to the extreme, in an unbiased way, interested only in producing a positive impact on the world. This effort, consequently, will generate immense value for those companies, too. What makes the times in which we live extraordinary is that this positive scenario is in many ways ineluctable. New technologies, globalization, and digitalization are breaking down many of the barriers to entry that have historically protected the mediocrity of so many products, brands, experiences, and services that surround us. But today, either you create excellent and meaningful solutions for people, or someone else will do it in your place. Sooner or later, it will happen. We are entering the age of excellence, a new world in which every company will always have a greater need for design-driven innovation—an entirely humanist type of innovation with a sincere, obsessive, unavoidable attention to the needs and wants of every human being.

We will innovate by bringing that human being with us, taking the user by the hand—that same person whom the business world loves to call the consumer. We will do so by thinking and acting as unicorns, because design-driven innovation without unicorns is a paintbrush without a Picasso, a pen without a Dante, a ball without a Ronaldo. It's useless—beautiful, but useless.

We will do so by embracing the people around us. This journey will define us. We will find our identity in this journey; we will make friends, allies, mentors, and coconspirators. We will convert hostile persons into extraordinary sponsors with the strength of good ideas and a good heart, with empathy, generosity, intelligence, optimism, resilience, curiosity, passion, respect, and love. We will be people in love with people.

Let's Design Our Happiness

The magical aspect of all this is that if we do it in an honest, spontaneous, coherent, and transparent way, if we do it without expecting anything in return, solely for the pleasure of generating progress for the world, then we will always nevertheless get something in exchange, a kind of positive collateral effect: our projects, thoughts, and actions will always represent a further step toward the accomplishment of our greatest dream and will bring us ever closer to the realization of our personal happiness. In a cycle that closes in a perfect way, the search for the happiness of others will be the key for reaching our own individual happiness. If we all thought and acted in this way, the interest of every individual, every company, every government, and every community would be perfectly synchronized with the interests of the entire planet. This is my dream, my life project—this is my life itself.

The Human Side of Innovation Discussion Guide

This is a series of questions that you can ask yourself, use to assess your teams, or leverage to appraise the culture of an entire organization. Are you *people in love with people?*

Am I Driving Innovation with a Human-Centered Approach?

- In my innovation projects, am I putting the creation of value for people as my ultimate goal? Or I am compromising too much, creating average solutions that I will then try to protect with barriers to entry?
- Am I trying to commercialize a technology just because it's in my pipeline and it's unique, or affordable, or defendable—but the technology doesn't deliver authentic value for people?
- Am I trying to commercialize a brand even if it doesn't resonate with people—just because I own it?
- Do I know how to use the mix of empathy, strategy, and prototyping to drive innovation? Let's share an example of how I do this.
- Do I prototype often—through sketches, quick mock-ups, and real prototypes?
- Do I frequently use prototypes to validate ideas with end users, to align the team members, to excite others, to unlock sponsorship?
- In my innovation project, does my company have the right culture to embrace the change I am proposing? If not, what's my plan to change the culture?
- In my innovation project, does my company have the right business model to support the solution (product, brand, service) that I am proposing? If not, what's my plan to change the current model or build a new one in parallel?
- In my innovation project, does my company have the right processes and technologies to support the change I am proposing? If not, what's my plan to build or acquire those processes or technologies?
- Am I using the three lenses of innovation—desirability, feasibility, viability—during my innovation project, from start to end?
- Am I using the right criteria to assess the innovation mindset of the people assigned to my innovation project?

Am I a Unicorn? Am I Doing Everything I Can to Become One?

Entrepreneurial Gifts

- Am I able to balance vision, experimentation, and execution?
- Do I have an original and unique perspective on things (briefs, issues, opportunities)?
- Do I trust my intuition?
- Am I able to combine intuition and analysis in everything I do?
- Starting from intuition, am I able to use a more analytical approach to build my plans?
- Am I proactive in identifying opportunities, no matter what my supervisor asks me to do? Or do I just wait to be assigned a task or a project?
- Am I always looking for the root cause, challenging the brief, questioning the question?
- Do I always go the extra mile, each and every time? When was the last time I went above and beyond what I was asked to do?
- Am I on top of the latest trends? Do I keep myself informed on what's going on out there, daily? How? What do I do exactly to stay informed?
- Did I ever try to set a trend? Why not? Why shouldn't I try?
- Do I genuinely care for the people I am innovating for? Do I really want to create something valuable for them? Am I *in love* with them? Or do I just want them to buy my product and make money for my company?
- Do I ever take a risk? When was the last time that I took a risk?
- What stops me from taking risks, and what am I doing to overcome that?
- When I take risks, am I able to protect myself and my team with the proper actions and protocols (the safety net)?
- Do I have good taste? Am I sure I do, or do I just think so? How can I be that sure? Am I really sure?
- Is your taste today the same or better than ten years ago? It should be better.

- If my taste is better than ten years ago, am I aware that my taste could be less refined today than ten years from now? And maybe less refined compared to others' taste today?
- What do I do to improve my taste level? Did I ever ask others to help assess my taste level and to help me improve it?
- If I am a design leader, how familiar am I with other design disciplines that are not mine?
- If I am not a designer, am I hiring design leaders for my innovation projects who have a holistic approach to the discipline—who are not hyperspecialized?
- Do I understand both the business variables and the technology variables of my innovation projects? What did I do to increase my knowledge of business and technology in the past year? What am I planning to do in the future?

Social Gifts

- Am I kind to other people on my team or in my community?
- Am I always sincere with other people, even when it's difficult? Especially when it's difficult?
- Do people trust me? Am I sure?
- Do I embrace people who think differently from me? Am I scared by people who think differently from me? Think carefully; don't be biased.
- Am I able to read the emotions of people in a room?
- Am I able to inspire people with my words? With my body language?
- Am I able to fine-tune my story and my words so they are more understandable by communities different from mine? For instance, if I am a designer, am I able to talk the language of finance, HR, or science? If I am a business leader, am I able to use the vernacular of an engineer, a psychologist, or an artist?

- Do I respect other professional communities, with backgrounds different from mine? For instance, if I am a designer, do I think that business leaders rarely understand my ideas? If I am a business leader, do I ever think that designers are not equipped to understand my strategies?
- Have I ever considered that I may be wrong about other communities? Talking to them with an open mind may be revealing and life-changing.
- Am I a storyteller? Am I able to share stories in a compelling way, inspiring others to follow my ideas?
- Do I mentor others? If not, why not?
- If I have never mentored anybody, what can I do to make this happen?
- Am I able to have fun? Do I find time to have fun at work as well?
- Do my colleagues like to have fun with me? Do I like to have fun with them? If not, why not?

Enabling Gifts
- Am I curious?
- Do I ask questions?
- Am I afraid of or embarrassed by asking question? If I am, then why?
- Do I ever pause to look at people in the street? At details of nature? Of buildings? Of objects?
- When's the last time I paused to look at a stranger, and what did I see that was interesting?
- If I don't remember the last time I paused to look, should I do it today, maybe for the first time in years?
- Am I humble? Do people think that I am humble?
- Did my arrogance ever stop me from achieving my goals? Am I sure?
- Am I self-confident? If not, what am I doing to increase my self-confidence?
- Am I aware of my strengths and my opportunities? Am I sure? Did I ever ask others what they thought my strengths and opportunities were?

- Do I listen to people, or do I always need to be the one talking? Am I able to stay silent in a meeting?
- Am I able to decide and act, without being paralyzed by (only) listening?
- Do I decide and act quickly enough? Do I ever slow others down?
- Do I see the glass as half full or half empty?
- Am I able to rely on my optimism to manage difficult situations?
- Am I resilient? If I am not, what am I doing to change that?
- What can I learn from others?
- Am I OK in uncomfortable situations, in transitions, in change?
- Do I like change, or does it scare me? If it scares me, what am I doing to find the positive in change?

Who Are My Mentors? Am I a Mentor to Others?

Let's build my ideal metamentor. Let's list a series of people who inspire me because of a specific skill that they manifest in an extraordinary way, writing each name and the skill next to it. That list defines my metamentor.

- Who could be my mentor by osmosis? Let's think of all the people close to me and identify somebody I consciously want to learn from.
- Who could be my virtual mentor? Let's follow the person; read the person's books, articles, interviews; watch the person's speeches. Let's try to reach the person on social media.
- Can I be a mentor for others? Am I making the extra effort to give back as a mentor, for instance by answering people who contact me through my social media or by acting as an example for a friend or a colleague?

Am I Designing My Happiness?

- What defines me and makes me unique?
- Am I doing everything I can to share my love and care for others? In my private life and at work?
- What's my purpose? What's the cause that transcends my personal interest, my way to build a legacy, to be remembered for the value I add to others?

Notes

1   Malcolm Gladwell, *The Tipping Point: How Little Things Can Make a Big Difference* (New York: Little, Brown, 2000).

2   Walter Isaacson, *Steve Jobs: The Exclusive Biography* (New York: Simon & Schuster, 2011).

3   Mauro Porcini, "Your Design Process Is Not Enough, Hire Design Thinkers," *dmi:Review* 20, no. 3 (September 2009); Mauro Porcini, "Love Letter to Design," *dmi:Review* 24, no. 1 (April 2013).

4   Bob Samples, *The Metaphoric Mind* (Boston: Addison Wesley Longman, 1976).

5   Gillo Dorfles, *Kitsch: The World of Bad Taste* (New York: Bell 1969).

6   David Hume, *Of the Standard of Taste* (1760).

7   Plato, *Phaedrus*, trans. H. N. Fowler, 265d–e.

8   Translated into English by Rosamaria Lavala in *The Eternal Child* (Chapel Hill, NC: Annali d'Italianistica, 1999).

9   Giacomo Leopardi, *Zibaldone* (New York: Farrar, Straus and Giroux, 2013), 204.

10 Giancarlo Dimaggio, "Miguel Benasayag: 'Noi, marionette in mano ai coach e agli smartphone,'" *Sette* 28 (February 28, 2020).

11 Miguel Benasayag and Angélique del Rey, *Elogio del conflicto* (Madrid: Tierradenadie Ediciones, 2012).

12 Dimaggio, "Miguel Benasayag."

13 Summarized by Umberto Eco in *Storia della bellezza* (Milan: Bompiani, 2018), 72.

14 See Luigi Pirandello, *Six Characters in Search of an Author* (1921), trans. John Listrum (London: Bloomsbury, 2016).

15 Carol S. Dweck, *Mindset: The New Psychology of Success* (New York: Random House, 2006).

16 A reference to the poem *"Il sabato del villaggio"* (1829), in Giacomo Leopardi, *The Canti*, trans. J. G. Nichols (Manchester: Carcanet, 1994).

Acknowledgments

The first people I want to acknowledge are all those I have met in my life who have inspired me with their presence, with their words, with their thoughts. You are too many to mention one by one, but I can't help mentioning you all, at least collectively. Each of you is in this book. All of you, in different roles and with different intensities, contributed to shape my way of thinking and feeling today. A fragment of each of you is cherished in my heart and in my mind, forever.

I then want to thank my design group at PepsiCo and the one I built at 3M. I want to thank the hundreds of designers scattered in every region of the world that make up those groups and, especially, the members of my PepsiCo leadership team. In strict alphabetical order, Matthieu Aquino, René Atchinson, Richard Bates, Martin Broen, Christianne Brooks, Marie-Thérèse Cassidy, Chanerica Evuen, Lisa Francella, Dennis Furniss, Leon Imas, Vasily Kassab, Leighsa King, Christian Saclier, Gianmauro Vella: thank you. As advisers, partners, and mentors, you have enlightened my path every day. Much of the content of this book was born from passionate exchanges, debates, and conversations with each one of you. And with you, I want to thank Ramon Laguarta, Jane Wakely, Ram Krishnan, Jon Banner, David Flavell, Carlo Massaro, and Jacob Lieberman, at PepsiCo, who in different ways have supported me in writing and publishing this book. I also thank Indra Nooyi, Laxman Narasimhan, and Brad Jakeman, who are no longer at PepsiCo, but who played an important role in my life as a designer and innovator. Finally, I am grateful to the myriad of agencies and creatives who have worked with me and my team in creating the projects described in this book. There is no way to mention them all individually, but each of them played a pivotal role in helping me to give tangible substance to my ambitious dreams.

A special thanks goes then to Steve Piersanti, who has believed in me and my ideas from the very beginning; to Michael Crowley, for his precious advices to position this book in the world; to Debbie Berne and Valerie Caldwell, for their special touch in the cover and book design; to the entire team at Berrett-Koehler—they are too many to mention one by one—who with passion and kindness have helped me in bringing this book to life. To Richard Braude and Cathy Cambron, who helped me make sure that the thoughts of an Italian wouldn't sound too weird when translated into English. To Dave Puente, for doing his magic with the cover photo.

Last, but not least, I want to thank the most important people in my life. First, my newborn daughter, Beatrice, for the inspiration she gave me to write this book, even before she was conceived. I hope my words can help her somehow in her journey, and I can't wait to start learning from her new truths about the infinite meaning of life. And then my wife, Carlotta, for her unconditional patience during the long months of intense writing and for her endless love, a constant beacon throughout my existence; my parents, Luisa and Eugenio, for exposing me from the time I was born to the true values of life, to the cult of culture, to the celebration of creativity, to the practice of kindness, to the love of love; my brother, Stefano, for being one of my mentors by osmosis with his imagination, resilience, humility, and goodness. Thank you. You are my continuous inspiration—inspiration of life, for all my life, in this life, and for eternity. This book is for you, and for Nicolò, Sebastian, Alessandra, Ombretta, Roberto, Francesco, and for those who will come, to radiate our existence and our family with even more brightness and love.

Index

technology
    advancements, 13–14, 20, 21, 91, 228
    "bag-in-box" technology, 44, 48, 52, 53
    business and design innovators'
        competency in, 102, 137–39
    incremental vs radical, 22–24
    Philips publications on future of, 212–13
television advertising, 59–60, 61, 76
Tendulkar, Sachin, 192, 196
Tesla, 23
3D modeling, 31, 71, 130, 134, 136, 201, 206
3M
    culture of, 114–15, 122–23, 138, 155, 222
    hires from, 45, 80–81, 83, 85
    innovation of, 44, 86, 107
    mentorship at, 138
    Porcini's employment with, 85, 86, 89,
        96–97, 105–6, 114–15, 118–19, 134
    Porcini's legacy at, 106–7, 221–22
    respectful collaboration at, 152–55
Tiësto, 198
Timberlake, Justin, 78
timing, 95, 169–71, 194, 206
The Tipping Point (Gladwell), 64
Tiscali, 201
Tokyo, 3M in, 96, 106
Tor San Lorenzo, Italy, 183
Toys "R" Us, 24
trends / trendsetters, 65, 102, 117–18
Triennale Design Museum, Milan, 137
Trudell, Cynthia, 51
trustworthiness, 102, 141–46
Twitter, 72
typography, 130, 133, 198

Uber, 14
UEFA Champions League, 75, 78, 196
unicorns / innovators
    abnormality of, 182–91
    designers as, 31, 37, 50
    education's role in, 191–96
    human-centered, 28, 29, 92
    innovator-owners, 116
    natural talent of, 192, 195
    qualities and skills of, 2, 3, 4, 9, 11, 65, 94,
        95–102, 232 (*see also* enabling gifts;
        entrepreneurial gifts; social gifts)
uniqueness, 39, 102, 107–9, 146, 185–91
Universal Pictures, 72
unknown, attraction of the, 6–8, 13
Urquiola, Patricia, 80
users
    licensing and, 83
    term usage, 28, 32
    user experience (UX) of soda fountains,
      53

user-generated content, 59–67
user journey mapping, 76–78
utility, 38, 39, 40
Utzon, Jørn, 124

Valentina (friend), 207, 208, 210
value
    aesthetic, 128–29
    creating, 22, 24–25, 221–29, 235
    designers' creation of, 10–11
    focus on, 24–25, 106, 226–27
    user-generated content and, 63–64
Varese, Italy, 162, 180, 182, 189, 190, 207,
    213
Vella, Gianmauro (Gimmy), 83, 85
Veuve Clicquot, 74
VIA 57 West, New York (Ingels), 105
Viñoli, Rafael, 105
virtual reality (VR), 17–18
visionaries, 2, 102, 103–7
Vision of the Future (Philips Design), 212
Vogue Italia, 79
Volo, Fabio, 196

Wakely, Jane, 90
Wallpaper, 63
Walmart, 71, 131
Warhol, Andy, 73, 218
wearable technologies, 133, 206
The Weekend, 78
West, Kanye, 198
Westinghouse Nuclear, 138
Wilde, Oscar, 107
Williams, Serena, 192, 196
Wisemad, 203–4
World Business Forum, 138
World Innovation Forum, 138

Yves Saint Laurent, 133

About the Author

 Mauro grew up in Varese, in the north of Italy, in a simple family that valued culture and kindness above everything else. Fame and wealth weren't seen by Mauro's parents as an aspiration for their son, but as a potential threat to one's moral compass. The family's passions were art and literature, and Mauro was raised surrounded by paintings and poems, playing with brushes and notebooks. Fast forward to forty-seven years later: Mauro, with his wife, Carlotta, and their daughter, Beatrice, now divides his time between his apartment in Manhattan and his house in the Hamptons. He is the first-ever chief design officer of PepsiCo, the food and beverage multinational corporation, and prior to that he was the first-ever chief design officer of 3M, another multinational company, this time in the world of science and technology. In the past two decades he built from scratch the entire design capability of both enterprises. Today he leads hundreds of people, based in more than fifteen locations around the world, and with them he drives a new and unique approach to innovation and branding—human-centered and design-driven.

Over the years, he has received a long list of honors and recognitions. Among them, the president of the Italian Republic recognized him with knighthood (Cavaliere dell'Ordine della Stella d'Italia); *Fortune* magazine listed him as one of the "40 under 40," the magazine's list of "the business's hottest rising stars"—the only designer included that year; *Ad Age* named him in its "Creativity 50," its list of the "world's most influential creative personalities"; *Fast Company* recognized him as one of the "50 Most Influential Designers in America," "Master of Design," and one of the "Most Creative People in Business"; Innovation Leader in Boston named him as one of the "Top 25 Most Influential Innovators"; Thomas Jefferson University of Philadelphia named him "Innovator of the Year"; and Pentawards in London recognized him with its Visionary Award. The World HR Forum in Mumbai presented him with its Award for Leadership and Innovation; the newspaper *Il Giornale* named him as "one of the ten Italians who will change the world"; and the *Wall Street*

Journal called him "the man putting 3M on the design map." In his professional career, he has been granted forty-seven patents in his name.

In the past twenty years, Mauro has taken his message about human-centered and design-driven innovation to the stages of hundreds of conferences in every region of the world. On many of these occasions, the hosts enjoyed introducing him with a touch of color, reminding the audience that on top of his business and design achievements, Mauro was also listed as one of the "30 Best Dressed Men" of his country by *GQ Italy*.

Regardless of this incredible journey, though, Mauro still cherishes in his heart, today, those values of culture and kindness that his parents taught him a long time ago, in a remote town in the north of Italy. And those values permeate this book, which he started writing more than thirty years ago, noting thoughts and ideas, theories and emotions, during his journey along the winding paths of life. He always knew that he wanted to write a book: writing, storytelling and sharing have always been passions of his, along with drawing and photography. And so, he started taking notes, composed of words, pictures, and sketches.

His obsession with the creation of value for humanity, *from people to people*, is at the core of everything he does. From his podcast *In Your Shoes—with Mauro Porcini*, to his role as a host of *America by Design*, airing on CBS and Amazon Prime Video, he doesn't miss an opportunity to deliver this message.

His professional journey has taken different and exciting turns. Before landing in 3M in Minnesota, and then at PepsiCo in New York, he earned a master's degree in design at the unveristy Politecnico of Milan with a thesis on wearable technologies that was selected to be showcased at the Louvre Museum in France and at the Seoul Art Center in South Korea. That project brought him to Philips Design, where he stayed for about a year. He left only to follow a bigger dream, that of creating his own agency with the celebrity producer and music star Claudio Cecchetto, working on innovation at the crossroads of digital media and entertainment.

This diversity of experiences and industries has given Mauro the holistic and humanistic approach to design, innovation, and business that he celebrates in every page of this book.

Berrett–Koehler
Publishers

Berrett-Koehler is an independent publisher dedicated to an ambitious mission: *Connecting people and ideas to create a world that works for all.*

Our publications span many formats, including print, digital, audio, and video. We also offer online resources, training, and gatherings. And we will continue expanding our products and services to advance our mission.

We believe that the solutions to the world's problems will come from all of us, working at all levels: in our society, in our organizations, and in our own lives. Our publications and resources offer pathways to creating a more just, equitable, and sustainable society. They help people make their organizations more humane, democratic, diverse, and effective (and we don't think there's any contradiction there). And they guide people in creating positive change in their own lives and aligning their personal practices with their aspirations for a better world.

And we strive to practice what we preach through what we call "The BK Way." At the core of this approach is *stewardship,* a deep sense of responsibility to administer the company for the benefit of all of our stakeholder groups, including authors, customers, employees, investors, service providers, sales partners, and the communities and environment around us. Everything we do is built around stewardship and our other core values of *quality, partnership, inclusion,* and *sustainability.*

This is why Berrett-Koehler is the first book publishing company to be both a B Corporation (a rigorous certification) and a benefit corporation (a for-profit legal status), which together require us to adhere to the highest standards for corporate, social, and environmental performance. And it is why we have instituted many pioneering practices (which you can learn about at www.bkconnection.com), including the Berrett-Koehler Constitution, the Bill of Rights and Responsibilities for BK Authors, and our unique Author Days.

We are grateful to our readers, authors, and other friends who are supporting our mission. We ask you to share with us examples of how BK publications and resources are making a difference in your lives, organizations, and communities at www.bkconnection.com/impact.

Dear reader,

Thank you for picking up this book and welcome to the worldwide BK community! You're joining a special group of people who have come together to create positive change in their lives, organizations, and communities.

What's BK all about?

Our mission is to connect people and ideas to create a world that works for all.

Why? Our communities, organizations, and lives get bogged down by old paradigms of self-interest, exclusion, hierarchy, and privilege. But we believe that can change. That's why we seek the leading experts on these challenges—and share their actionable ideas with you.

A welcome gift

To help you get started, we'd like to offer you a **free copy** of one of our bestselling ebooks:

www.bkconnection.com/welcome

When you claim your **free ebook**, you'll also be subscribed to our blog.

Our freshest insights

Access the best new tools and ideas for leaders at all levels on our blog at ideas.bkconnection.com.

Sincerely,

Your friends at Berrett-Koehler